Jepson Studies in Leadership

Series Editors
George R. Goethals
Jepson School of Leadership Studies
University of Richmond
Richmond, Virginia
USA

J. Thomas Wren
Jepson School of Leadership Studies
University of Richmond
Richmond, Virginia
USA

Thad Williamson
Jepson School of Leadership Studies
University of Richmond
Richmond, Virginia
USA

Managing Editor
Elizabeth DeBusk-Maslanka

Jepson Studies in Leadership is dedicated to the interdisciplinary pursuit of important questions related to leadership. In its approach, the series reflects the broad-based commitment to the liberal arts of the University of Richmond's Jepson School of Leadership Studies. The series thus aims to publish the best work on leadership from such fields as economics, English, history, philosophy, political science, psychology, and religion, and also contributions from management and organizational studies. In addition to monographs and edited collections on leadership, included in the series are volumes from the Jepson Colloquium, which bring together influential scholars from multiple disciplines to think collectively about distinctive leadership themes in politics, science, civil society, and corporate life. The books in the series should be of interest to humanists and social scientists, as well as to organizational theorists and instructors teaching in business, leadership, and professional programs.

More information about this series at
http://www.springer.com/series/14834

Jessica Flanigan • Terry L. Price
Editors

The Ethics of Ability and Enhancement

palgrave
macmillan

Editors
Jessica Flanigan
Jepson School of Leadership Studies
University of Richmond
Richmond, Virginia
USA

Terry L. Price
Jepson School of Leadership Studies
University of Richmond
Richmond, Virginia
USA

Jepson Studies in Leadership
ISBN 978-1-349-95302-8   ISBN 978-1-349-95303-5   (eBook)
DOI 10.1057/978-1-349-95303-5

Library of Congress Control Number: 2017954436

Cover illustration: © stock_colors / Getty Images

Printed on acid-free paper

This Palgrave Macmillan imprint is published by Springer Nature
The registered company is Nature America Inc.
The registered company address is: 1 New York Plaza, New York, NY 10004, U.S.A.

Acknowledgments

Many of the chapters in this volume came out of an academic colloquium on "Ability and Enhancement," held at the Jepson School of Leadership Studies at the University of Richmond on April 7–8, 2016. The Jepson Colloquium was associated with a year-long Jepson Leadership Forum series called "The Fix: Health, Science, and the Future." The lecture series investigated overarching questions about human health and well-being, such as the challenges of global health and poverty, genetics and individual decision-making, and the media's role in public health. The editors are grateful to all the speakers in the Forum series, notably Dr. Wendy Chung, whose lecture, "Is the Future of Medicine in our DNA," set the stage for two days of paper presentations and discussion. We are also grateful to all participants in the Colloquium, especially to those who submitted final papers for publication in this volume. To round out the coverage of the volume, we solicited papers from several scholars addressing problems of ability and enhancement. We thank them, too, for allowing us to include their work.

Large lectures series and academic colloquia require a great deal of support. Sandra J. Peart, dean of the Jepson School, was behind us from the start to the end, always making sure we had what we needed to include the very best people working in healthcare ethics. We greatly appreciate her intellectual and institutional support. The editors are indebted, as well, to two Jepson School staff members. Shannon Best not only handled all logistics for the Jepson Leadership Forum but also carefully managed every detail of the Colloquium. Moreover, she did so in a way that made two complicated events work together seamlessly. Elizabeth DeBusk-Maslanka, managing editor for this book series, collected the results of our labors and enabled us to get the ideas into print. Faculty members, including the editors, often need help hitting deadlines, and Elizabeth kept right us on track with direction that was always calm and kind. We are very lucky to have such accomplished individuals working with us at the Jepson School.

Palgrave's Marcus Ballenger served as our editor from proposal to publication. We thank him and all members of the Palgrave team who have supported this series over the years.

Finally, our family members: Esme, Harper, Hartley, Javier, Lori, and Sofia. To us, you are perfect as you are.

Contents

LIST OF FIGURES

CHAPTER 1

Ability and Enhancement

Jessica Flanigan

1 INTRODUCTION

Political philosophers, disability scholars, and bioethicists often refer to the concept of "normal species functioning" when they define concepts like disability or human enhancement. Disability rights advocates question whether the idea of normal species functioning is exclusionary or stigmatizing of people who are differently abled. In contrast, people who oppose human enhancement sometimes cite normal species functioning as an ideal that we should not try to improve upon by radically changing people's physical or cognitive abilities. Scholars who address questions of distributive justice sometimes cite normal species functioning as a normative baseline that informs people's entitlements with respect to the allocation of scarce medical resources. In all these conversations, normal species functioning is not a biological concept. Human lifespans and levels of physical and cognitive ability may change as a result of better nutrition, vaccines, science, and evolution. And people's perceptions of normal species functioning are constantly evolving as well. So, philosophers' tendency to imbue a particular level of ability and well-being with moral significance by calling it "normal species functioning" requires further justification.

J. Flanigan (✉)
Jepson School of Leadership Studies, University of Richmond, Richmond, VA, USA

© The Author(s) 2018
J. Flanigan, T.L. Price (eds.), *The Ethics of Ability and Enhancement*,
Jepson Studies in Leadership, DOI 10.1057/978-1-349-95303-5_1

For these reasons, we conceived of this volume as addressing ethical questions about disability and human enhancement without reference to a baseline of "normal species functioning." Instead, we conceive of questions about disability and enhancement as versions of the same question—what is the significance of differences in human ability?

2   WELL-BEING, RIGHTS, AND JUSTICE

The concepts of disability and human enhancement are evolving and contested. More generally, conceptions of human ability continue to change, as Sandra Peart and David Levy show in their contribution to this volume. And as David Wasserman and Stephen Campbell demonstrate in their contribution, recent medical and scientific advancements call into question our popular conceptions of ability. First, they argue that seemingly normatively significant distinctions between enhancements that modify a person's body and beneficial environmental modifications do not capture complex relationship between people and the assistive technologies, bodily modifications, and brain-machine interfaces. Second, competing conceptions of disability, namely the "medical model" and "social model" of disability also rely on a sharp distinction between environmental and bodily modifications, which is also challenged by emerging technologies that blur the lines between the body and the environment. Campbell and Wasserman's conviction that normative questions about ability extend beyond the limits of the body is echoed throughout the volume, which proceeds in three parts.

First, Christopher Riddle, Dana Howard, and Jessica Flanigan address disability. Riddle considers the relationship between various theories of distributive justice and concerns about disability stigma. Howard addresses the relationship between disability and theories of well-being and people's emotional responses to people with disabilities. And Flanigan considers how a broadly Kantian moral theory may inform ethical debates about disability rights and creating disabled people. Following this discussion of disability, the volume then turns to the morally distinctive questions raised by the ways that people's abilities change as they age. Ryan Davis discusses the reasons that people should consider as they plan (or fail to plan) for cognitive changes, such as age-related dementia. Aging raises other ethical questions as well, which Christine Overall discusses in her rich analysis of the political and ethical implications of changing conceptions of old age.

The last two papers in this volume address replies to the questions, initially raised by Wasserman and Campbell, about the social and environmental dimensions of ability and enhancement, focusing on the past, present, and future of human enhancement. Despite the complicated history of defining disability and promoting enhancement, people may still have reason to support and encourage certain enhancement going forward, either as a parent or as a public official. Christopher Freiman argues, "there is no principled difference between failing to enhance your children's environment and failing to enhance your children's (e.g.) genetic makeup," so just as parents ought to provide the best environment they can for their children, they should use biotechnological enhancements for their children as well. Javier Hidalgo's essay concludes the volume by returning to questions of justice. Hidalgo argues that people should support cosmopolitan moral enhancements, which may include either environmental or technological interventions that mitigate people's tendencies to act unjustly.

The three parts of this volume complement and enrich each other. After all, just as the boundaries of the human body seem to develop and expand with new technology, moral and technological progress should also prompt us to reconsider concepts like "normal species functioning," and human nature. The nature of human ability is not fixed, nor is our moral imagination, our understanding of well-being, or the scope of moral consideration that we extend to each other.

3   THE PLAN OF THE BOOK

In the remainder of this introduction, I will briefly summarize the argument and the broader significance of each paper for debates about the ethics of ability and enhancement. Part 1 places questions of ability and enhancement in perspective. In Chap. 2, Sandra Peart and David Levy provide a historical overview of nineteenth-century debates about human ability and social policy. Peart and Levy first describe the Millian assumption that "there are no racial or other distinctions to be made about our capabilities for labor market, family formation, or other decisions." Against this assumption, eugenicists argued that capabilities varied between groups and advocated for policies that limited "inferior" people's choices either for their own sake or for the "general good." The rejection of nineteenth-century eugenics illustrates that moral progress is possible. This historical moment also reminds us of the moral imperative to consider the harm of stigmatization, the risks of paternalism, and the epistemic limits of scientific experts in debates about human ability and public policy going forward.

In Chap. 3, David Wasserman and Stephen Campbell call for a reconsideration of our understanding of ability and enhancement in light of the increasingly blurry line between bodies and environments. They advocate for a way of seeing human enhancement in light of technologies that do not modify a person's body. Specifically, they favor a broader conception of enhancement that acknowledges that a person's abilities cannot be evaluated in isolation from a person's environment. This approach challenges the social model of disability by demonstrating that the distinction between a bodily modification and an environmental modification isn't always justified. Wasserman and Campbell's broader focus also demonstrates why it is a mistake for bioethicists and commentators to evaluate individual bodily changes in ability, without considering how those changes would also change human environments.

Part 2 addresses normative questions about disability. In Chap. 4, Christopher Riddle considers some difficulties associated with attempts to make disabled people's lives better or do justice with them. Specifically, doing justice often risks stigmatizing people by making them the targets of a justice-based intervention. Even if one has the correct theory of justice, implementing changes that aim to make the world more just, for example for disabled people, could implicitly or explicitly express harmful attitudes. To illustrate this general point, Riddle considers how efforts to implement various theories of justice can be demeaning to disabled people. He concludes that "our attempts to articulate a conception of justice that promotes he well-being of people with disabilities and other marginalized individuals are aimed to do good. But ... we need to be more cognizant of the process of 'doing justice.'"

In Chap. 5, Dana Howard also addresses whether some emotional responses toward disabled people are stigmatizing or unwarranted. In contrast to Riddle who is concerned that theories of justice prompt these responses, Howard considers whether these responses assume a controversial understanding of disability. Certain conceptions of disability express or reinforce harmful stereotypes of disabled people, cause mistreatment, and make people with disabilities feel isolated or misunderstood. Howard then considers that these considerations are the wrong kinds of reasons to inform a conception of disability. Howard replies that these considerations should inform our conceptions of disability, not because certain attitudes toward disability have bad consequences but because they represent disabled people's experiences.

In Chap. 6, Jessica Flanigan defends a broadly Kantian approach to disability and disability rights that also emphasizes the importance of considering disabled people's experiences. Flanigan begins with the claim that it is a mistake to define disabilities with reference to a theory of well-being because whether a person has the physical conditions associated with disability is a separate question from whether it is bad to have those conditions. She then makes the case whatever the relationship between physical disability and well-being, physical ability status *as such* should rarely influence how people treat each other or the kinds of people that are created. Throughout, Flanigan emphasizes the importance of deferring to people's testimony about how they experience physical disability rather than settling questions about disability rights and procreative ethics based on theoretical assumptions about the relationship between physical disability and well-being.

Part 3 raises questions related to the way people's abilities change over time. In Chap. 7, Ryan Davis addresses questions related to the prospect of becoming disabled in the future. Davis discusses both cognitive disabilities such as dementia and physical disabilities. Regarding dementia, Davis argues that the reasons which inform how people with dementia are treated resemble other cases where people's plans for their lives are informed by conflicting, seemingly irreconcilable considerations. In these cases, it is a mistake, Davis argues, to value one's current interests or values over the values she will have in the future. Instead, Davis suggests that people should allow more flexibility for their future selves to decide based on their values. Davis writes, "it is easy to demand too much consistency from one's own values," but instead people who are considering their future selves should be open to a range value shifts and plot twists as the stories of their lives unfold.

In Chap. 8, Christine Overall continues the conversation about people's changing abilities through time. Overall's aim is to show that conceptions of oldness are generally indeterminate, and potentially in need of revision in light of normative concerns about age discrimination and justice and in light of relatively recent advances in life expectancy. To be old is not to have lived to a particular age, but to have a social and political status or possess other normatively significant properties associated with old age. Overall describes various forms of discrimination against old people, such as ageism and ableism, and advocates for solidarity between the old and the not-yet-old in an effort to address the unjust marginalization of old people.

Part 4 is about human enhancement. In Chap. 9, Christopher Freiman argues that parents have a defeasible moral obligation to use biotechnological enhancements to improve their children's health and well-being. Like Wasserman and Campbell, Freiman is skeptical that the distinction between an environmental enhancement and a biological enhancement is morally significant in its own right. Freiman also rejects the claims that parents must only pursue treatment but not enhancement, as well as the claims that parents should avoid enhancement on the grounds that they are likely to do more harm than good by attempting to actively control their children. Freiman concludes by considering the social costs and benefits of allowing parents to enhance their children, and ultimately maintains that even if there are some social costs and if enhancement strikes some people as repugnant, concerns about costs and feelings of repugnance do not undermine the case in favor of enhancing one's children.

In Chap. 10, Javier Hidalgo considers the social benefits of enhancement in more detail. Hidalgo begins with a defense of cosmopolitanism—the view that people's ethnic or national identities do not have fundamental moral significance but rather that people have universal human rights. Critics allege that cosmopolitanism is infeasible given human nature. But the prospect of moral enhancements for humans illustrates that it may be possible to change human nature in ways that make cosmopolitanism possible. If so, then human enhancement may not only improve individuals' well-being, but enhancement can also make the world more just.

4   CONCLUSION

Together, the essays contained in this volume provide a broad overview of contemporary debates about the politics and ethics of disability and human enhancement. The authors also advance these debates in interesting and innovative ways, developing novel frameworks for understanding the environmental and social aspects of human ability and combating the stigma that is often associated with disability or changes in ability related to aging. And as the authors note, reflecting on the ethics of ability and enhancement can inform more general debates about well-being, human rights, and justice.

PART I

Ability in Perspective

CHAPTER 2

Theorizing About Human Capacity: A View from the Nineteenth Century

Sandra J. Peart and David M. Levy

1   Introduction

Discussions of eugenic policy of the nineteenth century are too often isolated from the larger debates in political economy over human capacity. These debates centered on two questions. First, do all people have roughly the same capabilities, or do some groups have a lower capacity than others? Second, capacity for what? In the nineteenth century, political economists in the tradition of Adam Smith through John Stuart Mill argued that, as Gordon Tullock would later put it, "people are people" and there are no racial or other distinctions to be made about our capabilities for labor market, family formation, or other decisions.[1] Late in the century, however, a coalition formed between progressives led by Thomas Carlyle and John Ruskin, and anthropologists and other so-called "scientists" who "demonstrated" the "inferior" capabilities of groups such as the Irish in Great Britain and former West African slaves, in Jamaica. This was the first, necessary "scientific" step towards the rise of eugenic policy-making.

S.J. Peart (✉)
University of Richmond, Richmond, VA, USA

D.M. Levy
George Mason University, Fairfax, VA, USA

© The Author(s) 2018
J. Flanigan, T.L. Price (eds.), *The Ethics of Ability and Enhancement*,
Jepson Studies in Leadership, DOI 10.1057/978-1-349-95303-5_2

9

The second required step was the transition from theorizing about capacity for happiness to capacity for something physical and additive, the "general good." For the political economists in the tradition of Smith through Mill, the desideratum was capacity for happiness. For the political economists, anthropologists, and biologists, in the eugenic tradition, the answer was capacity in some physical or intellectual sense. Of course, if the metric of capacity is happiness, then it is straightforward, though not entirely uncontroversial, to argue that individuals are the best judge of this.[2] By contrast, Carlyle and his followers argued that, left to their own devices, some inferior people would make poor choices, reducing the general good. Individuals, in this argument, ought not to be trusted to make the best choices for society at large (or, some also argued, for themselves).[3] Of course, the final step in the rise of eugenic policy-making was that they therefore needed the strong hand of the state to intervene in order to obtain the "general good."

Thus, in our view, the distinction between a metric of happiness, "general happiness," and physical capacity, "general good," is terribly important.[4] Charles Darwin used the "general good" metric in his 1871 *Descent of Man*. But Darwin was not the first to make this argument. Indeed, in *Descent of Man*, Darwin cited a political economist (W. R. Greg) who carried the burden of the argument in opposition to Mill's happiness metric and in favor of a physical measure of capacity.[5]

2   AGAINST ABSTRACT ECONOMIC PEOPLE

As is well known to those who have read our work, we attribute the notion of abstract economic persons to Adam Smith. Formulated most strongly in his 1776 *Wealth of Nations*, Smith there theorized that all observed differences in outcomes were the result of the division of labor. Thus, all people are equally capable and for Smith, specialization, luck, and history explain different outcomes. Racial[6] group differences are then simply the result of differential specializations.[7] From Smith's time, through the mid-nineteenth century, this position by and large characterized much of political economy. At mid-century, however, it was attacked on all sides, by anthropologists who claimed to have discovered racial differences between the Irish and the English, by biologists who sought the "general good," and by progressives who believed that the English were more capable than West Africans, Jews, and the Irish.

We have referred to the doctrine that people are essentially equally capable, as analytical egalitarianism. In what follows, we examine how the political economist and co-founder of eugenics W. R. Greg attacked this doctrine in the course of his forceful opposition to Mill's political economy. The context of the debate between Mill and Greg was whether the Irish were as capable as the English, in which case they possessed the capacity to govern themselves, as Mill argued, or whether they ought to be ruled by their superiors, as Greg maintained.[8] Underlying all of Greg's many essays was the claim that there is no abstract human. Instead, there are humans of different sorts or, to use an older phrase, people with different "national characters."

The most straightforward of Greg's exposition is his response to Mill's reform proposal to encourage peasant proprietorship in Ireland. Mill argued that Ireland's economic woes were the result of institutions and incentives, rather than the fault of some inherent flaw in the Irish character. He abstracted from race and focused instead on property rights, arguing that if well-established property rights were reinstated in Ireland, the Irish would respond accordingly and the Irish "problem" would be resolved. This position, outlined in Mill's 1848 *Principles of Political Economy* and elsewhere, was sharply disputed in the decades that followed. Greg objected specifically to the abstract accounts of human beings put forward by Classical economists on the grounds that Mill had neglected that the Irish were incapable. In Greg's view, by contrast, if the institutions were changed the Irish would remain impoverished because they simply were less capable—of saving, of producing, of planning—than the English. Mill's account failed because it abstracted from the racial difference:

'Make them peasant-proprietors,' says Mr. Mill. But Mr. Mill forgets that, till you change the character of the Irish cottier, peasant-proprietorship would work no miracles. He would fall behind the instalments of his purchase-money, and would be called upon to surrender his farm. He would often neglect it in idleness, ignorance, jollity and drink, get into debt, and have to sell his property to the newest owner of a great estate. ... Mr. Mill never deigns to consider that an Irishman is an Irishman, and not an average human being–an idiomatic and idiosyncractic [sic], not an abstract, man. (Greg 1869b, p. 78).

Greg published this essay in 1869. Although he was perhaps the most persistent theorist who presupposed that the Irish were inferior, he was by no means the only so-called scientist who made this case. Anthropologists of the time were busy constructing an "index of negrescence" by which to measure the inferiority of the Irish.[9] That home rule was at stake is clear from the below cartoon showing John Bright selling quackery medicine to the Irish whose eyes are bulging and whose jaws protrude. According to artist John (later Sir John) Tenniel, the principal cartoonist for *Punch* in the latter half of the nineteenth century, the Irish men depicted below are incapable of ruling themselves. Since the women are directed by their fathers or husbands, they have not devolved (Fig. 2.1).

What was the basis for his view that the Irish were inherently inferior, idle, ignorant, and drunk? Greg expounded that view in an earlier essay that attracted a good deal of contemporary attention.

3   THE SURVIVAL OF THE UNFIT

In 1868, Greg published his influential essay "On the Failure of 'Natural Selection' in the Case of Man" in *Fraser's Magazine*. It was here that he argued that those with inferior capabilities, without intervention, would multiply rapidly and thereby interfere with the attainment of the "general good." To testify to the significance of this essay, consider how Darwin described it in *Descent of Man*:

> I have hitherto only considered the advancement of men from a semi-human condition to that of the modern savage. But some remarks on the action of Natural Selection in civilized nations may be worth adding. This subject has been ably discussed by Mr W. R. Greg, and previously by Mr Wallace and Mr Galton. Most of my remarks are taken from these three authors. (Darwin 1871, p. 161)

The context of Greg's essay is the 1864 paper presented at the Anthropological Society by Alfred Wallace. Wallace (1864) described the law of natural selection, and then he argued that human sympathy for one another and the human division of labor both attenuate natural selection.[10] People

CARTOON.—NOVEMBER 10, 1866.

DR. DULCAMARA IN DUBLIN.

Fig. 2.1 Dr. Dulcamara in Dublin

care about people and they consequently assist the frail and less capable to survive. Further, with the division of labor, human strength, intellectual or physical, is no longer required for survival: the strong will take on tasks that require strength while those who are less strong are able to contribute to human happiness in other ways. For Wallace, this attenuation of the law of natural selection provided an interesting example of how humans differ from other species. For Greg, however, this interference with natural selection serves also to interfere with human progress: "The great wise, righteous, and beneficent principle which in all other animals, and in man himself, up to a certain stage of his progress, tends to the improvement and perfection of the race, would appear to be forcibly interfered with and nearly set aside; nay, to be set aside pretty much in direct proportion to the complication, completeness, and culmination of our civilisation." Greg continued to lament the interference with the survival of the fittest:

> Our thesis is this: that the indisputable effect of the state of social progress and culture we have reached, of our high civilisation, in a word, is to counteract and suspend the operation of that righteous and salutary law of "natural selection" in virtue of which the best specimens of the race—the strongest, the finest, the worthiest—are those which survive, surmount, become paramount, and take precedence; succeed and triumph in the struggle for existence, become the especial progenitors of future generations, continue the species, and propagate an ever improving and perfecting type of humanity. (Greg 1868, p. 356)

In his *Principles of Political Economy*, Mill had advocated for a self-directed Malthusian population restraint as a means to reduce human misery and attain happiness. For Greg, such Malthusian prudential restraint on population growth placed human happiness ahead of the new goal of human "progress" and, as such, Greg eschewed such self-directed choices. More than this, Greg argued that Malthus's population operated differently on those with different capacities. The "lower classes" multiply relatively quickly, because they are inherently "reckless," while those in the "improving classes" are more capable of abstention. In the 1868 essay, Greg wrote:

> Thus the imprudent, the desperate,—those whose standard is low, those who have no hope, no ambition, no self-denial,—on the one side, and the pampered favourites of fortune on the other, take precedence in the race of

fatherhood, to the disadvantage or the exclusion of the prudent, the resolute, the striving and the self-restrained. The very men whom a philosophic statesman, or a guide of some superior race would select as most qualified and deserving to continue the race, are precisely those who do so in the scantiest measure. Those who have no need for exertion, and those who have no opportunities for culture, those whose frames are damaged by indulgence, and those whose frames are weakened by privation, breed ad libitum; while those whose minds and bodies have been hardened, strengthened and purified by temperance and toil, are elbowed quietly aside in the unequal press. Surely the 'selection' is no longer 'natural'. (1868, p. 123)

Greg then provides a description for how the inferior Celts eventually out-populate the superior Saxon race:

The careless, squalid, unaspiring Irishman, fed on potatoes, living in a pig-stye, doting on a superstition, multiplies like rabbits or ephemera:—the frugal, foreseeing, self-respecting, ambitious Scot, stern in his morality, spiritual in his faith, sagacious and disciplined in his intelligence, passes his best years in struggle and in celibacy, marries late, and leaves few behind him. Given a land originally peopled by a thousand Saxons and a thousand Celts,—and in a dozen generations, five sixths of the population would be Celts, but five sixths of the property, of the power, of the intellect, would belong to the one sixth of Saxons that remained. In the eternal 'struggle for existence,' it would be the inferior and less favoured race that had prevailed,—and prevailed by virtue not of its qualities but of its faults, by reason not of its stronger vitality but of its weaker reticence and its narrower brain. (1868, pp. 123–24)

It is worthy of note that Darwin quoted, inexactly, this view of the Irish in *Descent of Man* (Darwin 1871, p. 167). For Greg, and those who endorsed this view, there was no point in suggesting, as Mill had, that the Irish would make different, more prudential choices, in the wake of new institutions. Nothing short of direction by their betters or a negative eugenic policy would improve the situation.[11]

The debate over the effects of Malthus's prudential restraint culminated in the 1877 Trial of Charles Bradlaugh and Annie Besant for the crime of distributing contraceptive information at a cost that poor people might afford.[12] Contemporary reports in *The Times* described the case as a conflict between the views of Mill and Darwin. It was, indeed, in this context that

Darwin clarified his views on contraception, in a direction that surprised some, including Bradlaugh himself. Before the trial Bradlaugh wrote to Darwin to ask whether the biologist might testify on Bradlaugh's behalf. Darwin responded to say that his failing health made travel to a trial a hardship, but that in any event if he were to testify he would oppose the widespread availability of such information because it would be used in such a way as to interfere with the attainment of the general good. At the trial, Annie Besant read widely from Mill's *Principles of Political Economy* in her defense, arguing that a law of selection entailing human misery and premature death is anything but "natural."

4   AGAINST HAPPINESS AS NORM

A fundamental issue that separated Millian-style political economists from racists such as Carlyle and Greg was whether individuals were to be allowed to select their own goals or whether their goals were to be determined exogenously in service of the "general good." In the former case, individuals are trusted to make choices that on balance lead to their individual satisfaction, or happiness. In the latter, a goal of human good is set and then experts determine the means by which the goal is attained. The means may entail individual sacrifice in service to the goal, the general good.

Perhaps the clearest illustration of this divide occurred in the context of colonial policy, in particular, the Governor Eyre Controversy (Semmel 1962; Peart and Levy 2005). The controversy surrounded the response by Governor Eyre to a minor uprising amongst former slaves in Jamaica, and whether the rule of law applied to former slaves, as to everyone else. For those who took the view that some are more capable than others, it would be appropriate to respond to the riots using piano wire as whips and murdering rebels without benefit of trial. For those, like Mill, who held to the analytical egalitarian view, Eyre's response was entirely unwarranted. Perhaps unsurprisingly, Mill was elected, in his absence, as the head of the group that sought to bring the Governor to trial for his crimes, while Carlyle's disciple, the artist John Ruskin, headed the movement to defend Governor Eyre.

Greg chose the occasion of the Eyre controversy to publish an essay in an 1866 issue of *Fraser's Magazine*—the periodical that in 1849 published Carlyle's "Occasional Discourse on the Negro Question"—on the issue of race and economic development (Greg 1866). The essay is particularly illuminating because Greg began with a statement of the orthodox race-blind account, that culture is endogenous to material incentives.

Greg begins by pointing out that it is too early to have an informed opinion on the events in Jamaica since the official inquiry had not been released. However, in his view it was not too early to ask whether emancipation has succeeded. He remarked, first, that emancipation had harmed the planters, who were "irretrievably ruined" and "leaving the island." Yet all that might be "little in our minds if the coloured population were growing prosperous, moral, educated, and contented." Greg next addressed this question. He first confronted the thesis of cultural endogeneity articulated in foundational form in the *Wealth of Nations*. Smith's central claim was that "all men" are predisposed to idleness:

> It will not, however, do to say, as some cynics and disappointed philanthropists are beginning to say, "Never mind if the negro is idle. All men, even Anglo-Saxons, will be idle under a tropical sun. Why should the negro work, if he can live without work? If the climate predisposes him to indolence and languor—if nature is so bountiful that she furnishes him gratuitously with all that is indispensable for comfortable existence—if his wants are few, and easily supplied, why seek to multiply them artificially, and thus to render life more difficult? If he prefers contentment with the bare necessaries of life, it may be that he is a truer philosopher than we who reprove him and would stimulate him. If he chooses to be lazy, he has a right to be so. It is sufficient that he is free, and that we have secured to him his rights." (1866, p. 279)

Against this Smithian thesis, Greg argues for an exogenously determined hierarchy of culture. Absent slavery, the Jamaicans have sunk into indolence. Greg is entirely clear that material output is critical:

> In our judgment it is *not* sufficient. It was not for this that we purchased his liberty and sacrificed his master. If this be the result, emancipation must be admitted to have failed. It may be assumed, and must be conceded, that content with the minimum that suffices for bare life, naked inaction, basking indolence, the animal enjoyment and dreary vacuity of barbaric ease, were not the purposes for which even Africans were created, or in which they were designed by Providence to remain; that savage existence—mere existence, vegetable life, life amid yams and plantains, with a cloth round their loins and a thatch over their heads—is not a condition into which England can or ought

to allow half a million of her subjects, whom she has taken in hand, to sink; that if this be the result of our work, we have done our work very ill, and must set to work at once to do it better. (1866, p. 279)

Unsurprisingly, Greg does not stop with this conclusion. He continues to argue that, lacking capacity and inclination, the former slaves must be forced to civilize, to work, to prevent a "relapse into savagery":

The negro must be civilised—brought up, that is, to such a stage of civilisation as he is capable of reaching, and to a higher and higher stage as years roll on and generation succeeds to generation. We cannot acquiesce without great guilt in his relapse into savagery. He has no right to be a savage; God made him and all men for advance; he must improve, or die out; . . . If the negro can rise and civilise, however slowly, by himself and under his own guidance, by all means leave him to himself, and give him time; if he cannot, then help him, guide him, control him, compel him; but never dream of sitting down helplessly content with a failure of hopes and prophecies and duties so signal—so fatal to him, so discreditable to ourselves. (1866, p. 279)

Since self-direction apparently failed to yield the largest physical output, Greg favors the path expounded by Carlyle, removing self-direction, placing Jamaicans under supervision:

under supervision and direction, and perhaps under contract, and thus developed in them the habits of industry, subordination, regularity, and discipline, which belong to what Mr. Carlyle calls 'regimented labour' and the moral virtues which directly or indirectly spring from the relation between employers and employed. (1866, p. 299)

Thus, for Greg, stationarity of output presents a justification for the direction of others (see also Greg 1869a). J. S. Mill had earlier taken up the issue of stationarity, and came to a very different conclusion. Indeed, in his *Principles of Political Economy* Mill examined, and defended, stationarity. For Mill, growth of material output is not an end in itself; rather as people's choices evolve over time they may well substitute into non-material output and enjoy more leisure with stable levels of material goods:

I cannot, therefore, regard the stationary state of capital and wealth with the unaffected aversion so generally manifested towards it by political economists of the old school. I am inclined to believe that it would be, on the whole, a very considerable improvement on our present condition. I confess I am not charmed with the with the ideal of life held out by those who think that the normal state of human beings is that of struggling to get on; that the trampling, crushing, elbowing, and treading on each other's heels, which form the existing type of social life, are the most desirable lot of human kind, or anything but the disagreeable symptoms of one of the phases of industrial progress. It may be a necessary stage in the progress of civilization, and those European nations which have hitherto been so fortunate as to be preserved from it, may have it yet to undergo. (Mill 1965, pp. 753–74)

At the end of the day, for Mill work is instrumental and people of all races (though, as noted above, perhaps not all cultures) are best able to make decisions about how much to work. The key for Mill is that those in what he thought of as "backward" cultures will acquire habits of decision making as education and experience enables them to do so.

5   A Concluding Image

The danger of focusing on the writings of one forgotten political economist is that it is all too easy to believe that Greg did not have much influence. Indeed, it may be well be that Greg was simply articulating the commonplace of one ideological faction. We close not by defending Greg's importance but by reproducing an image by Charles Bennett ("Slavey"), which depicts the theme that without direction, those who pursue happiness are doomed to devolve.[13] In the below image, a woman makes a self-directed choice to enter the labor market and earn wages. In so doing, she, like the former slaves in Jamaica, devolves into an inferior creature. To cement the comparison between Slavey and the former slaves, the caption to the image, contained in a book entitled *Shadow and Substance* Bennett and Brough (1860), refers to Carlyle's (1849) article about the former slaves in Jamaica (Fig. 2.2).

"SLAVEY."

Fig. 2.2 Slavey

NOTES

1. Tullock extended the range of analytical egalitarianism to include economists, explaining why differences in institutions make economics more of a racket than a science (Tullock 1966; Levy and Peart 2017).
2. Here we set aside consideration of F. Y. Edgeworth's views. Edgeworth's eugenic argument rested on the supposition of a differential capacity for happiness. To get around the difficulty noted in the text, he supposed the existence of a hedometer that would enable the expert to measure the time integral of happiness (Edgeworth 1881; Peart and Levy 2005). As far as we can determine, Edgeworth's argument was simply too difficult for a popular audience.
3. Thomas Carlyle's "Negro question" (Carlyle 1849) opened the debate between Victorian literary figures and adherents of the "dismal science" (his coinage) over the use of the "beneficent whip" to improve people.
4. "The term, general good, may be defined as the means by which the greatest possible number of individuals can be reared in full vigour and health, with all their faculties perfect, under the conditions to which they are exposed. As the social instincts both of man and the lower animals have no doubt been developed by the same steps, it would be advisable, if found practicable, to use the same definition in both cases, and to like as the test of morality, the general good or welfare of the community, rather than the general happiness; but this definition would perhaps require some limitation on account of political ethics" (Darwin 1871, p. 94). We have elsewhere stressed the importance of this distinction (Peart and Levy 2004).
5. Donald Winch's studies of the period do not notice the significance of Greg (Winch 1965, 2001). As we shall see, Darwin quoted Greg with approbation. Greg was elected a member of the Political Economy Club in 1867 (Political Economy Club 1872).
6. It will soon become clear that notions of "race" are rather ill-defined at this time but in essence the word is a way to describe a group with so-called lower ability than others. As such, Irish, Jews, Africans, and even women are sometimes included in the analysis. For more on the shifting of the argument, see Peart and Levy (2005).
7. "The difference of natural talents in different men is, in reality, much less than we are aware of; and the very different genius which appears to distinguish men of different professions, when grown up to maturity, is not upon many occasions so much the cause, as the effect of the division of labour. The difference between the most dissimilar characters, between a philosopher and a common street porter, for example, seems to arise not so much from nature, as from habit, custom, and education. When they came into the world, and for the first six or eight years of their existence, they were perhaps, very much alike, and

neither their parents nor playfellows could perceive any remarkable difference. About that age, or soon after, they come to be employed in very different occupations. The difference of talents comes then to be taken notice of, and widens by degrees, till at last the vanity of the philosopher is willing to acknowledge scarce any resemblance. But without the disposition to truck, barter, and exchange, every man must have procured to himself every necessary and conveniency of life which he wanted. All must have had the same duties to perform, and the same work to do, and there could have been no such difference of employment as could alone give occasion to any great difference of talents" (Smith 1904, Book I, chapter 2).

8. We have discussed analytical egalitarianism in several places, for example, Peart and Levy (2005). In Levy and Peart (2016), we take up Smith's attack on the doctrine of natural character. There we document how Smith uses "race" as a term to describe occupation. The link between his usage and that which would be common in our language community is the caste system in which an occupation is inherited. John Rawls questioned the assumption of roughly natural equality of capacity in the case of caste systems, a consideration that precedes his brief consideration of eugenics (Rawls 1971, p. 107).

9. For a detailed review of the contemporary literature on this topic, see Peart and Levy (2005).

10. We discuss the role of sympathy in nineteenth-century evolutionary thinking in Levy and Peart (2009, 2015).

11. In terms that the eugenicists employed, "positive" eugenics encouraged births from the desired part of the distribution of the population whereas "negative" eugenics discouraged births from the undesired part. In Levy and Peart (2015) we trace negative eugenics to an 1874 essay by George Darwin in which he criticized Francis Galton's "positive" proposals as insufficient to attain the "general good." Darwin criticized Greg's unwillingness to put his concerns into legislation.

12. In Peart and Levy (2005) we discuss the secondary accounts of Darwin's letter; we publish the letter in Peart and Levy (2008).

13. The theme of without direction, devolution, is systematically laid out by Charles Kingsley (Levy and Peart 2006). Kingsley, as far as we know, never attacked Mill's positions. Kingsley, however, did offer a theological interpretation of natural selection that Darwin was very quick to seize upon in the second (and in all later) editions.

References

Bennett, Charles H., and Robert B. Brough. 1860. *Shadow and substance*. London: W. Kent.

Carlyle, Thomas. 1849. Occasional discourse on the negro question. *Fraser's Magazine for Town and Country* 40: 670–679.

Darwin, Charles. 1871. *The descent of man, and selection in relation to sex.* New York: Appleton and Company.

Edgeworth, F.Y. 1881. *Mathematical psychics.* London: C. Kegan Paul & Co.

Greg, W.R. 1866. The Jamaica problem. *Fraser's Magazine for Town and Country* 73: 277–305.

———. 1868. On the failure of "natural selection" in the case of man. *Fraser's Magazine for Town and Country* 78: 353–362.

———. 1869a. The doom of the negro race. In *Literary and social judgments,* 339–389. London: N. Trubner.

———. 1869b. Realities of Irish life. *Quarterly Review* 126: 61–80.

Levy, David M., and Sandra J. Peart. 2005. From ordinal to cardinal utility: Darwin and differential capacity for happiness. *American Journal of Economics and Sociology* 64: 851–880.

———. 2006. Charles Kingsley and the theological interpretation of natural selection. *Journal of Bioeconomics* 8: 197–218.

———. 2009. Sympathy, evolution and the economist. *Journal of Economic Behavior and Organization* 71: 29–36.

———. 2015. Sympathy caught between Darwin and eugenics. In *Sympathy: A history,* ed. Eric Schliesser, 323–358. Oxford: Oxford University Press.

———. 2016. Group analytics in Adam Smith's work. *Eastern Economic Journal* 42: 514–527.

———. 2017. Gordon Tullock's ill-fated appendix: "Flatland revisited". *Constitutional Political Economy.* 28 (1): 18–34. doi:10.1007/s10602-016-9232-8

Mill, J.S. 1965. The principles of political economy with some of their applications to social philosophy. In *Collected works of John Stuart Mill,* ed. John Robson. Toronto: University of Toronto Press.

Peart, Sandra J., and David M. Levy. 2004. Sympathy and its discontents: "Greatest happiness" versus the 'general good'. *European Journal of the History of Economic Thought* 11: 453–478.

———. 2005. *The "vanity of the philosopher": From equality to hierarchy in post-classical economics.* Ann Arbor: University of Michigan Press.

———. 2008. Darwin's unpublished letter at the Bradlaugh–Besant trial: A question of divided expert judgment. *European Journal of Political Economy* 24: 343–353.

Political Economy Club of London. 1872. *Names of members, 1821–1872, rules of the club, and list of questions discussed, 1860–1872.* London: Political Economy Club of London.

Rawls, John. 1971. *A theory of justice.* Cambridge: Harvard University Press.

Semmel, Bernard. 1962. *The Governor Eyre controversy.* London: McGibbon & Kee.

Smith, Adam. 1904. In *An inquiry into the nature and causes of the wealth of nations,* ed. Edwin Cannan. London: Methuen & Co., Ltd.

Tullock, Gordon. 1966. *The organization of inquiry.* Durham: Duke University Press.

Wallace, Alfred R. 1864. The origin of human races and the antiquity of man deduced from the theory of 'natural selection'. *Journal of the Anthropological Society of London* 2: clviii–clxxxvii.

Winch, Donald. 1965. *Classical political economy and colonies.* Cambridge, MA: Harvard University Press.

———. 2001. Darwin fallen among political economists. *Proceedings of the American Philosophical Society* 145: 415–437.

CHAPTER 3

A More "Inclusive" Approach to Enhancement and Disability

David Wasserman and Stephen M. Campbell

1   INTRODUCTION

Discussions of enhancement and disability tend to draw a sharp line between modifications to the individual and modifications to her environment. According to one popular conception, an enhancement is an improvement to or within one's body or mind that enables one to exceed species-typical functioning in some respect. The narrow focus on such "internal improvements" is shared by most proponents and critics of various forms of enhancement (Juengst 2000).

An equally sharp line between the individual and her environment is drawn in disability scholarship. Thus, the so-called "medical" model of disability identifies disability with a physical or cognitive impairment that

We thank Tina Rulli, Sven Nyholm, and the participants at the Jepson Colloquium 2015–2016, "Ability and Enhancement," University of Richmond, for their comments on a draft of this paper.

D. Wasserman (✉)
Department of Bioethics, National Institutes of Health, Bethesda, MD, USA

S.M. Campbell
Bentley University, Waltham, MA, USA

© The Author(s) 2018
J. Flanigan, T.L. Price (eds.), *The Ethics of Ability and Enhancement*,
Jepson Studies in Leadership, DOI 10.1057/978-1-349-95303-5_3

25

places one below species-typical functioning in some respect. It therefore treats disability as a feature of the individual, not of her environment. The social model of disability, which arose as a critical response to the medical model, sees disability as emerging from the interaction between the individual's condition and her environment (Wasserman et al. 2016). However, this view is standardly enlisted in support of modifications to the environment rather than modifications to the bodies or minds of disabled people. Thus, like the medical model, it embraces the strong distinction between environmental modifications and bodily modifications. But, unlike the medical model, it is sharply opposed to the push for human enhancement, narrowly conceived.

We seek to complicate this picture by highlighting three types of enhancement that defy the narrow conception insofar as they go beyond mere bodily modification. They call for a broader, more inclusive understanding of enhancement. In arguing for this broader understanding, we also raise questions about the social model of disability. Without entirely rejecting a presumption in favor of environmental modifications, we contend that a sharp dichotomy between changes to the individual and the environment obscures significant conceptual complexities and moral tradeoffs, and ignores the extent to which technology itself may blur the boundaries between the individual and her environment.

Our discussion will focus on physical impairments and enhancements related to mobility. This is an area where recent technology is bringing about dramatic improvements, all along the spectrum from prosthetic limbs to driverless cars. Focusing on these technologies will allow us to challenge narrow understandings of enhancement and disability without entering into the controversies over certain kinds of enhancement, especially intellectual and moral enhancement (Farah et al. 2004; Douglas 2008).

2   Questioning a Narrow Conception of Human Enhancement

It is certainly understandable that the enhancement debate has focused on "internal improvements." The focal point of that debate is the actual or anticipated applications of biotechnology to individual bodies and minds. Such developments are quite recent. Most of the technological advances in human history, from agricultural cultivation to electronic communication, did not appear to modify their human beneficiaries, or did so only indirectly.

Fritz Allhoff et al. defend a conception of enhancement as improvement to or within the body, including implanted devices such as brain chips. The internal/external distinction they favor is not based on the notion of a natural or organic body, since it includes (some) wearable tools as well:

> [w]e might reasonably understand the distinction between human enhance-
> ment and mere tools by looking for an always-on (i.e., on-demand or perma-
> nent) feature, as opposed to the temporary or contingent access of our daily
> gadgets and tools (e.g., a mobile phone that can be easily lost, stolen or left
> behind). (Allhoff et al. 2009, p. 10)

They argue for a narrow conception on the grounds that treating enhance-ment as "the mere use of tools would render the concept impotent, turning nearly everything we do into cases of human enhancement" (Allhoff et al. 2009, p. 9).

In contrast, we will argue that a narrowly focused conception of human enhancement, however understandable, is misguided. The position of Alhoff et al. strikes us as mistaken for several reasons. First, it ignores the fact that, in many cases, a feature can be "always on," "permanent," or "on demand" *only* in a congenial environment. This is not to deny that the range of congenial environments may be wider or narrower for a given feature. But dependence may also vary across environments: some features may be more permanent, accessible, and reliable in certain environments; other features in others. Electronic implants may depend on the vagaries of transmission as much as mobile phones do.

In general, the functioning of specific "internal" devices may be as environmentally contingent as the functioning of "external" ones. Accessi-bility and reliability do not track an ordinary external/internal distinction. Internal equipment can be controlled or influenced by external agents or forces, and external equipment can be reliably accessible to and controllable by the individual. An individual with the latest Google translation app may have a more enhanced ability to converse in a foreign language than an individual with an implanted chip containing an outdated version. And a breakdown in an internal chip may be more disruptive and costly than a breakdown in an app. Moreover, we may sensibly regard *both* the app and implant users as having the capacity to converse in the foreign language. We could see the translation app as extending the mind of one, the translation chip as enriching the mind of the other.

Finally, it is a commonplace in the philosophy of action that conduct and capacity can be described at varying levels of generality (Wilson and Shpall 2012). For example, we can describe the act of walking either more narrowly, in terms of various combinations of its component voluntary actions, or more broadly, in terms of "locomoting," or even more broadly, as getting from place to place. The broader the description of the conduct or capacity, the more likely it is to encompass the use of what Allhoff et al. regard as mere tools. While walking can be done unaided or with a cane or walker, "locomoting" can also be done with a wheelchair; and a vast array of vehicles can get us from place to place. The narrow conception of enhancement tends to rely on narrower levels of description. But we have yet to see a good argument for limiting the discussion of enhancement this way.[1]

Enhancement at a narrow level of description need not result in enhancement at a broader level of description. Some athletic and gymnastic abilities, for example, require a balance between the strength or flexibility of the component body parts that might be impaired by the enhancement of only one of them. In part for this reason, training for one kind of athletic or gymnastic event may interfere with training for another. There need not be such a direct conflict between efforts to enhance more narrowly described functions, like walking, and efforts to increase more broadly described functions, like getting from place to place—efforts that can involve the use of external devices such as bicycles, segways, and express buses. But such efforts may compete for individual commitment, institutional priority, and public funding.

Broader levels of description have the advantage of being more "inclusive." As recent work in the philosophy of disability has argued, the broader the level of description, the less likely the activity is to be precluded by more narrowly defined impairments (Wasserman 2001). Thus, someone paralyzed below the hip cannot walk, but can get from place to place in a wheelchair, car, or other vehicle.

We are not claiming that there is a *correct* level of description for all purposes, or that broader levels of description are more apt regardless of context. Indeed, the broadest levels of description such as "achieving goals" or "engaging in purposeful activity" would be far too general to be helpful in almost any practical context. Our claim is merely that broader levels are appropriate and useful in assessing the various means by which humans can now, or will soon be able to, do things with technology.[2]

3   THREE TYPES OF BROAD ENHANCEMENT

Without providing a precise definition of broad enhancement, we will limit our discussion to modifications which require both "internal" and "external" changes.[3] The internal changes may be as minimal as learning to operate a complicated device, by hand or by thought; the external changes may be as minimal as creating public repositories of detachable prosthetics or extenders accessible at different times to a variety of users (like bikeshare stands). In requiring some change in the individual as well as the environment, our notion of enhancement is narrower than Allen Buchanan's (see n. 8), which includes scientific advances from which an individual may benefit in an entirely passive way.

There are three ways of improving function that call for the broader understanding of enhancement we are proposing. The first, most familiar, is the use of "assistive technology"— technology designed for individual use and targeted for people with disabilities. Such technology does not modify the body but does enhance its functioning, broadly construed. Assistive devices are operated using typical functions—pushing a walker, rolling a simple wheelchair, or using an electronic chair by moving a stick, pressing a button, or even blinking one's eyes. Assistive technology involves no modification of the individual, except to the extent that it is seen as extending her body.

In contrast, the second type of enhancement involves such bodily modifications as attaching a prosthetic, extender, or exoskeleton. These parts need not resemble, or function the same way as, typical parts; indeed, they may serve the individual better if they do not. More than assistive devices, they may be seen as extensions, or even parts, of the user's body. At the same time, they often have features that make them seem less like body parts and more like tools: they may, for example, be detachable and adjustable.

These two types of broad enhancement come together in a third: brain-machine interfaces (BCIs). BCIs enable an individual to manipulate objects at a distance from his body by using a computer that "reads his thoughts," or more accurately, responds to patterns of neural activity he has been trained to generate. Although BCIs currently use implants or electrodes, in the near future they will be able to operate without any physical connection.

In what follows, we suggest that all three types of modification raise questions about the boundary between the body and the environment. In the case of the first and third, this is in part because they often can work only with complementary modifications to a previously uncongenial environ-ment. In the case of the second, this is because the prosthetics, extender, or exoskeleton, even if temporarily attached and integrated with the bio-logical body, usually can be separated from its user and often made available to others.

Employing Assistive Technology to Improve Activity Performance

Often, there is a choice between training that improves an impaired species-typical function and training that circumvents it by the use of unimpaired functions and assistive devices. The latter may be more effective at improv-ing activity broadly conceived, and may often enable the individual to do better in that activity than she could using species-typical functions. Dis-ability critics challenge the traditional presumption in physical rehabilitation for restoring species-typical function like leg motion when only slight gains in mobility are likely to be achieved that way, and significantly greater gains are likely from mastering other means of locomotion, using assistive devices like walkers or wheelchairs (Gibson and Teachman 2012).

To enable people with mobility impairments to get around, though, it is not enough to provide individuals with assistive devices and training in their use. Those devices have limited value in making their users mobile without complementary environmental modifications, such as ramps, elevators, curb-cuts, and wide doors that open electronically. Conversely, such envi-ronmental features can be useless in the absence of the corresponding technologies they were designed to accommodate. So, even though we can distinguish the individual and environmental components of an inclu-sive environment, the enhancement should be seen as encompassing both.

Broadening the Type of Bodily Modifications

A second type of broad enhancement modifies the body, at least in the limited sense that it is temporarily attached to it and moves in coordination with it. This category includes standard prosthetics, which attempt, with growing success, to mimic the appearance and performance of natural body parts. But this type of modification also includes attachable parts that do not look or function like biological parts, like the running "blades" of Oscar Pistorius. Some of these attachments, like Hugh Herr's bionics, are modeled after biological limbs and joints, although they do not look like them (Herr and Grabowski 2012). They function similarly, but in some cases, more efficiently, than those body parts, and they can be designed not only as prosthetics for individuals with impaired or missing parts, but as supplements for individuals with the standard complement of parts (Mooney et al. 2014; Smith 2014).

Without addressing the complex and contested issue of what it means to regard an object as an incorporated body part rather than a mere tool, it is clear that these inorganic additions will have features that biological body parts lack. Most will be detachable, many by the user herself. Some will have adjustable dimensions, color, and texture. Some will be available for nondisabled as well as disabled users, with different attachment features. And some may be flexibly designed for a variety of temporary users, to be borrowed or rented rather than owned. All of these features would make the attachments seem less "internal" to the current user.

Moving Distant Objects: Brain-Machine Interfaces

Emerging technologies for the computer-mediated control of objects out-side the corporeal body require only normal psychological functioning. They can be employed by any human being, however physically impaired, who has the cognitive capacity to reliably produce specific thoughts or images that a computer can translate into signals to a detached movable device. The paralyzed user of a BCI will not be enhanced in a narrow sense, but her ability to manipulate objects at a distance will vastly exceed the species-typical ability to reach, grasp, and move objects.

BCIs defy easy classification. On the one hand, they may look like assistive devices, even if they gain widespread use. They are customized to individual users, and do not necessarily require any modification of the user's body. On the other hand, the mental control their trained users can exercise, as well as the "internal" feedback they provide, may make them appear more like such bodily extensions as physical prosthetics and exo-skeletons (Aas and Wasserman 2016; Wasserman and Aas 2016).

To the extent that they enable users to manipulate distant objects by their thoughts, and receive detailed feedback from those objects, BCIs may tend to be seen as extensions or parts of their bodies (Clark 2007). In the near future, though, the possibilities for their full "incorporation" are limited—less by their distance from the body or their inorganic composition than by their shared use and control. It is difficult to see how a computer network with multiple users could be partitioned or otherwise incorporated into their discrete bodies. Although BCI hardware may become individual property as the devices move from the lab to the market, the networks that operate them may have to be coordinated in ways that limit or preclude personal ownership. But even if they are seen as individual possessions, BCI devices may make physical impairments less of an impediment for a wide variety of activities. Moreover, unlike current prosthetics, BCIs are likely to be sought by people without physical impairments.[4] Their widespread use and efficacy in an increasing number of tasks is likely to further diminish the salience and practical importance of impairments—at least those that do not limit the capacity to engage in computer-mediated communication.

4   BALANCING THE COSTS AND BENEFITS OF BROAD ENHANCEMENT

Many proponents of the social model of disability question the societal preference for modifying the individuals disadvantaged by their environments rather than modifying those disadvantaging environments (Imrie 1997; Wasserman et al. 2016). But the emergence of broad enhancements suggests that we cannot adhere to a simple policy of modifying environments rather than bodies and minds. Instead, we must examine—usually on a case-by-case basis—the benefits and costs of specific enhancements.

For illustrative purposes, we will focus on BCIs. Whether they primarily modify the individual or the environment, their widespread adoption may have significant costs as well as benefits. There might be difficult tradeoffs between reducing the practical disadvantages and stigmatization of physical impairment, on the one hand, and preserving an important role for the human body, on the other. These tradeoffs are described by Stella Palikarova, who argues that the human capacity to communicate, as employed and extended by BCIs, may

eventually render bodies largely superfluous. Perhaps the most indicative representation of this phenomenon was seen in the assimilation of [BCI] technology in both rats and primates, who learned to communicate with, and control, an actuator without needing to use their own limbs. Astonishingly, once the animals had learned to communicate with the actuator using only brain activity, they ceased using their own limbs to attain what they desire (i.e. food or an object). The potential consequences of using similar technology on humans are not far from the imagination....largely disembodied human beings that have become reliant upon the technological instruments that have replaced bodily functioning, resulting in obesity, muscle atrophy, and an absence of physical human contact. A society so reliant upon technology would be unable to function in the case of technological breakdown. Yet, one could say that the body itself is a kind of "machine", in constant need of maintenance and repair. In repairing one kind of impairment (disability), are we effectually creating another? Would we be better or worse off for relying on machines and computers, instead of on our own physiology? (Palikarova 2009, p. 6)

Notably, these complaints resemble those now being made about the increasing reliance on the Internet and social media by millennials. While this reliance does not make physical functioning hostage to the performance of machinery in the same way as it does for BCI users, the growing dependence of social and institutional functioning on electronic communication creates similar vulnerabilities—from the diminishing role of face-to-face interaction to the dangers of being hacked. It is, of course, easy to exaggerate the costs of decreasing reliance on the body. Few people in developed countries now earn their living "by the sweat of their brows" and the exercise of our bodies has been increasingly consigned to a recreational role. But we need not be the worse for that. We may be able to perform many of our professional tasks with electronic mediation and still enjoy an intimate face-to-face conversation or a vigorous game of touch football or wheelchair basketball. We should keep in mind that while the demands of physical labor can strengthen human bodies, they can also injure, sicken, and exhaust them.

Moreover, BCIs may expand the range of physical interaction at the same time that they attenuate it. People unable to move their limbs may be able to deliver BCI-mediated caresses, as will people with standard limb function who are separated by long distances. The old Bell Telephone slogan— "Reach Out and Touch Someone"—may acquire more literal meaning. At the same time, clumsy mechanical caresses might be superseded by sensations delivered directly to the tactile regions of the recipient's brains, affording a more intimate, if less physical, form of long-distance connection.

Less speculatively, there are clear benefits to people with disabilities in having nondisabled people rely on the same or similar technologies for an increasing range of activities. As stressed in the literature on assistive technology and universal design, widely-used technologies are more likely than disability-specific ones to be well-manufactured, carefully maintained, and gently handled by third parties (Center for Universal Design 2001; Tobias 2003; Foley and Ferri 2012; Phillips and Zhao 1993; Doe and Noakes

2008). Perhaps the most salient example is the development of the "driverless" car, which is seen as an epoch-making technological breakthrough, not a disability-specific project. When mechanical failures occur, as they inevitably will (indeed, they already have), they will be less stigmatizing and better accommodated than those for disability-specific devices like wheelchairs, even though—and in part because—their breakdown will cause massive inconvenience. (Wheelchair users could only envy the allowances made for Washington, DC subway users recently when the system was suddenly closed for a weekday to permit emergency repairs. Workers who did not normally telecommute were permitted or encouraged to do so, and employers were urged to offer unscheduled leave (Thorton 2016)).

Yet we should not discount the possibility that "ableism" will prove resilient in the face of broad enhancements that make nondisabled people dependent on the same technology as disabled ones. Perhaps a socially recognized distinction will emerge between "us"—BCI users— and "them"—"the BCI bound." The need to rely on BCIs for many routine activities may be regarded as harsh bondage by those who enjoy unimpaired limb movement, even if they are well aware of how much more one can do with a BCI. The persistence of stigma is not a foregone conclusion, however. Much will depend on the way the markets develop for disabled and nondisabled users, and on the extent to which the products designed for their use are clearly differentiated. The more differentiated they are, the more likely disability-specific products are to be subject to a kind of "courtesy stigma"—Erving Goffman's term for stigma by association (Goffman 2009; Aas and Wasserman 2016). We certainly do not claim that stigmatization will remain as virulent as ever, merely that technology, however widely embraced and universally enhancing, may not ensure its disappearance.[5]

5   CONCLUSION

In this essay, we have tried to illustrate the value of seeing the enhancement of individuals in the context of an array of technological modifications, many of which involve no changes to bodily form or function. In challenging the dichotomy of individual and environment, our account also challenges the social model of disability. To the extent that the model gives strict or very strong priority to changing the environment rather than the individual, it either discourages or fails to address the existence of broad "interactive" enhancements, which require changes to both. Such resistance or neglect would be unfortunate, because some of these enhancements might weaken oppressive biological norms, reduce the functional significance of many impairments, and have powerful appeal for nondisabled as well as disabled users. We are confident, however, that the social model can be amended to take account of the liberating potential of these interactive enhancements without losing its emphasis on exclusionary environments and stigmatization.

One final advantage to a broader focus is that it serves as a brake against rampant speculation. The deliberate modification of individual bodies and minds advocated by "bio-progressives" and decried by "bio-conservatives" will occur, to the extent it does, in interaction with intended and unintended modifications to human environments, and with a variety of modifications that defy classification as either individual or environmental. It is misguided to attempt to evaluate individual changes in isolation, and it is highly speculative to assess the outcome of the complex interactions that will take place in the future. This does not mean that we can or should refrain from speculation altogether—we have done our share—but that in debating as well as in implementing human enhancement, we should proceed cautiously.

Disclaimer The views expressed in this essay are the authors' own. They do not represent the positions or policies of the National Institutes of Health, U.S. Public Health Service, or Department of Health and Human Services.

NOTES

1. Admittedly, an internal feature may make the individual *appear* more enhanced. This point is well made in an example from Keith Abney:

   [C]ompare a person who uses Google Translate on their mobile device to communicate with the local population on their trip to a foreign land, versus a person with a Google translation chip implanted in their head. The first would be recognized by the natives merely as someone who knows how to use a computer; the latter, meanwhile, might well be taken as fluent in the foreign language, with whatever social advantages that would entail. In other words, when it comes to proximity of a technological aid to the user, the less visible the tool is to outsiders, the better. (Abney 2013, p. 35)

   But it is hard to see why the appearance of enhancement should matter in assessing the extent to which a person is in fact enhanced. The practical advantages of this appearance do not by themselves lead to greater ability or function in the second tourist.

2. We are hardly the first to suggest a broad view of human enhancement. In Buchanan (2011), Allen Buchanan embraces the very broad conception of "enhancement" that Allhoff et al. (2009) reject, e.g., classifying literacy and science as enhancements. He utilizes this broad understanding to argue that enhancement is nothing new and nothing objectionable, so we shouldn't be so fearful of the enhancements on the horizon.

3. We will also bracket the question of whether the term "enhancement" should be limited to improvements that raise a function above the normal range, or should include improvements that raise a function to, or within, the normal range. We will use the term in the latter sense.

4. To indulge in a bit of speculation, if BCI technology becomes widespread, people may eventually get "wired" to their home environment so that they can effect all sorts of changes (turn on/off lights; open blinds; alter the structural layout) by mental effort alone. This would represent an even more dramatic challenge to the distinction between modifying the individual and the environment, and a further reduction in the functional significance of impairments.

5. We say "may not" rather than "cannot" because we cannot rule out futures in which technology really does make variations in human bodies almost irrelevant and undetectable. For example, the film *Surrogates* depicts a society in which almost everyone lays at home in their "experience machines" and remotely controls a robot surrogate that does all of their living for them. If nondisabled people stop using their bodies (as it happens in that society), perhaps some kinds of disability, particularly motor and sensory disabilities, would cease to matter. In such a society, it might not even be known who had these disabilities, since people will only interact with others' surrogates and never encounter their actual bodies. It's not clear that many disability categories would still be relevant in a world where this surrogate lifestyle was universal.

REFERENCES

Aas, Sean, and David Wasserman. 2016. Brain–computer interfaces and disability: Extending embodiment, reducing stigma? *Journal of Medical Ethics* 42: 37–40.

Abney, Keith. 2013. Problematizing the "natural": The internal/external distinction and technology. *Synesis: A Journal of Science, Technology, Ethics, and Policy* 4: T29–T36.

Allhoff, Fritz, Patrick Lin, James Moor, and John Weckert. 2009. The ethics of human enhancement: 25 questions & answers. *Studies in Ethics, Law, and Society* 3 (3): 1–41.

Betsy, Phillips, and Hongxin Zhao. 1993. Predictors of assistive technology aban-
donment. *Assistive Technology* 5 (1): 36–45.

Buchanan, Allen E. 2011. *Beyond humanity? The ethics of biomedical enhancement.*
Oxford: Oxford University Press.

Center for Universal Design. 2001. *Principles of universal design.* Raleigh: North
Carolina State University.

Clark, Andy. 2007. Re-inventing ourselves: The plasticity of embodiment, sense,
and mind. *Journal of Medicine and Philosophy* 32: 263–282.

Doe, Tanis, and Amy Noakes. 2008. The effectiveness of assistive technology in
enabling community integration and independent living: What we know now.
In *Is it working? A review of AT successes and barriers*, ed. Tanis M. Doe.
Sacramento: California Foundation for Independent Living Centers.

Douglas, Thomas. 2008. Moral enhancement. *Journal of Applied Philosophy* 25 (3):
228–245.

Farah, Martha J., Judy Illes, Robert Cook-Deegan, Howard Gardner, Eric Kandel,
Patricia King, Eric Parens, Barbara Sahakian, and Paul Root Wolpe. 2004.
Neurocognitive enhancement: What can we do and what should we do? *Nature
Reviews Neuroscience* 5 (5): 421–425.

Foley, Alan, and Beth A. Ferri. 2012. Technology for people, not disabilities:
Ensuring access and inclusion. *Journal of Research in Special Education Needs*
4: 192–200.

Gibson, Barbara E., and Gail Teachman. 2012. Critical approaches in physical
therapy research: Investigating the symbolic value of walking. *Physiotherapy
Theory and Practice* 28 (6): 474–484.

Goffman, Erving. 2009. *Stigma: Notes on the management of spoiled identity.*
Engelwood Cliffs: Prentice Hall.

Herr, Hugh M., and Alena M. Grabowski. 2012. Bionic ankle–foot prosthesis
normalizes walking gait for persons with leg amputation. *Proceedings of the
Royal Society B* 279 (1728): 457–464.

Imrie, Rob. 1997. Rethinking the relationships between disability, rehabilitation,
and society. *Disability and Rehabilitation* 19 (7): 263–271.

Juengst, Eric T. 2000. What does enhancement mean? In *Enhancing human traits:
Ethical and social implications*, ed. Erik Parens, 29–47. Washington, DC:
Georgetown University Press.

Mooney, Luke M., Elliott J. Rouse, and Hugh M. Herr. 2014. Autonomous
exoskeleton reduces metabolic cost of human walking during load carriage.
Journal of Neuroengineering and Rehabilitation 11 (1): 80–90.

Palikarova, Stella. 2009. The ethical integration of brain machine interfaces:Toward
the cyborgization of the disabled. *Faculty of Information Quarterly* 2 (1): 1–18.

Smith, David W. 2014. Merging man and machine. *Salt*. http://www.wearesalt.org/
merging-man-and-machine. Accessed 29 Nov 2016.

Thorton, David. 2016. OPM encourages unscheduled leave, telework for D.C. feds on March 16. *Federal News Radio*. http://federalnewsradio.com/opm/2016/03/metro-close-march-16. Accessed 29 Nov 2016.

Tobias, James. 2003. Universal design: Is it really about design? *Information Technology and Disabilities* 9 (2): 2003. http://square.umin.ac.jp/DMIESemi/y2004/20040531/20040531_3.pdf

Wasserman, David. 2001. Philosophical issues in the definition and social response to disability. In *Handbook of disability studies*, ed. Gary L. Albrecht, Kathrine Seelman, and Michael Bury, 219–251. Thousand Oaks: Sage.

Wasserman, David, and Sean Aas. 2016. BCIs and disability: Enhancement, environmental modification, and embodiment. *Brain-Computer Interfaces* 3 (3): 126–132.

Wasserman, David, Adrienne Asch, Jeffrey Blustein, and Daniel Putnam. 2016. Disability: Definitions, models, experience. In *The Stanford encyclopedia of philosophy, summer 2016*, ed. Edward N. Zalta. http://plato.stanford.edu/archives/sum2016/entries/disability/

Wilson, George, and Samuel Shpall. 2012. Action. In *The Stanford encyclopedia of philosophy, summer 2012*, ed. Edward N. Zalta. (Summer 2012 edition). http://plato.stanford.edu/archives/sum2012/entries/action/

PART II

Disability

CHAPTER 4

Disability and Doing Justice

Christopher A. Riddle

The Joneses were shown into the dentist's office and Mr. Jones was clearly in a big hurry. "No fancy stuff, Doctor," he ordered. "No gas or needles or any such things. Just pull the tooth and get it over with." "I wish more of my patients were as brave as you," said the dentist admiringly. "Now, which tooth is it?" Turning to his wife, Mr. Jones said, "Open your mouth and show the dentist which tooth, honey" (Adapted from Cathcart and Klein 2007, p. 80). There are always better or worse ways to do things on behalf of other people. As such, we should take into account not only the desired outcome when taking action on behalf of other people, but how we bring about that outcome as well. After all, the *process* of doing a good deed for another may very well minimize or diminish the desirable effects of that deed (or perhaps even introduce a new harm altogether).

All philosophical discussions concerning justice involve the process of "doing justice." We aim to engage in a causal process of implementing change and making material lives better, or more just.

I would like to thank Sophie-Grace Chappell, Jessica Flanigan, David Gordon, Terry Price, Thomas Sturm, Jonathan Wolff, and audiences from McGill University, Concordia University, Université de Montréal, and Université du Québec à Montréal for helpful suggestions and comments.

C.A. Riddle (✉)
Department of Philosophy, Utica College, Utica, NY, USA

© The Author(s) 2018
J. Flanigan, T.L. Price (eds.), *The Ethics of Ability and Enhancement*, Jepson Studies in Leadership, DOI 10.1057/978-1-349-95303-5_4

In "doing justice," there is a risk of potentially harming people by stigmatizing or demeaning them through the identification and rectification of inequality.[1] This process requires us to be careful of not only what our principles of justice have to say about ideals of equality, fairness, and impartiality (to name a few), but we also have to be cognizant and careful of what the process of "doing justice"—articulating and operationalizing these principles—does to the subjects of justice.

Elizabeth Anderson has given us an example of what a luck egalitarian might say to those he or she deems to be worthy of additional resources or other compensation due to the suffering of bad brute luck in the receiving of natural endowments. She asks us to imagine that alongside the compensation check received in the mail from the State Equality Board, there is a letter that states:

> To the disabled: Your defective native endowments or current disabilities, alas, make your life less worth living than the lives of normal people. To compensate for this misfortune, we, the able ones, will give you extra resources, enough to make the worth of living your life good enough that at least one person out there thinks it is comparable to someone else's life.
>
> To the stupid and untalented: Unfortunately, other people don't value what little you have to offer in the system of production. Your talents are too meager to command much market value. Because of the misfortune that you were born so poorly endowed with talents, we productive ones will make it up to you: we'll let you share in the bounty of what we have produced with our vastly superior and highly valued abilities.
>
> To the ugly and socially awkward: How sad that you are so repulsive to people around you that no one wants to be your friend or lifetime companion. We won't make it up to you by being your friend or your marriage partner— we have our own freedom of association to exercise—but you can console yourself in your miserable loneliness by consuming these material goods that we, the beautiful and charming ones, will provide. And who knows? Maybe you won't be such a loser in love once potential dates see how rich you are. (Anderson 1999, p. 305)

Anderson's example is meant to highlight not only how the provision of compensation might explicitly or implicitly lead one to draw conclusions about the recipients of aid, but additionally, how the principles endorsed as a matter of justice may very well be the culprit and lead to harm.

In what follows, I highlight how our attempts to "do justice," as a matter of principle, tend to be more inclusive of people with disabilities and other marginalized groups. Nonetheless, these attempts, as a matter of practice, continued to stigmatize and do harm. I proceed by dividing this chapter into four large sections that each contain a subsection.

Section 1 explores the distributive principles of Robert Nozick and libertarianism. I ask what it means to suggest that some citizens are worthy of charity or acts of benevolence. I explore the potential harm associated with distributing resources and addressing need in this manner.

Section 2 marks a significant shift to liberal egalitarian theories of justice and explores the egalitarian principles of Ronald Dworkin and what I refer to as *weak equality of resources*. I explore how the suggestion that we ought to insure against possessing particular traits or disabilities might demean those possessing those attributes. Furthermore, I explore the absence of an acknowledgement of social constructivism and disability and suggest that this too further marginalizes and damages subjects of justice.

The third portion of this chapter examines what I call the *strong equality of resources* theory of John Rawls. I ask what it might mean to suggest that social contractors are limited to "normal" members of society.

The fourth and final section explores the capabilities approach and, in particular, Martha Nussbaum's conception of justice. Here I examine what it might imply for the value of lives to situate difference vertically, rather than horizontally.

1   Nozick and Charity

Nozick's famous play on Marx's words, "from each as they choose, to each as they are chosen" (Nozick 1974, p. 160), summarizes his entitlement theory. His Lockean and Kantian emphasis on viewing individuals as ends in themselves leads to a prioritization of self-ownership—individuals ought only to part with what they wish to, and others ought to only receive what others wish them to (or what they otherwise earn on their own) because people are the sole owners of their labor.

Nozick's tale of the slave and discussion of taxation as a form of forced labor and thus, partial slavery, results in the exclusion of many rights commonly thought to be assured under most conceptions of justice. Nozick denies appeals to a social good in the context of distributive justice however. He suggests

...there is no social entity with a good that undergoes some sacrifice for its own good. There are only individual people, different individual people, with their own individual lives. Using one of these people for the benefit of others, uses him and benefits the others. Nothing more. What happens is that something is done to him for the sake of others. Talk of an overall social good covers this up. (Nozick 1974, pp. 32–33)

But far from viewing this denial of rights as problematic, Nozick's parting remarks in *Anarchy, State, and Utopia* seem to suggest that any form of mandatory redistributive welfare could be seen as an affront to the dignity of those forced to part with their own wealth on behalf of others (Kymlicka 2001, p. 125):

The minimal state treats us as inviolate individuals, who may not be used in certain ways by others as means or tools or instruments or resources; it treats us as persons having individual rights with the dignity this constitutes. (Nozick 1974, pp. 333–334)

For the liberal egalitarian, this is a bizarre line of reasoning. Surely a denial of dignity must emerge from Nozickian principles, but does the damage not occur to those who are refused forms of redistributive welfare? Brian Barry agrees with my conclusion and finds Nozick's remarks repugnant. Barry claims that Nozick is:

proposing to starve or humiliate ten percent or so of his fellow citizens (if he recognizes the word) by eliminating all transfer payments through the state, leaving the sick, the old, the disabled, the mothers with young children and no breadwinner, and so on, to the tender mercies of private charity, given at the whim and pleasure of the donors and on any terms that they choose to impose. (Barry 1975, p. 332)

Having said this, I suspect we often move too quickly to dismiss Nozick and the entitlement theory. While Nozick's principles do not provide for people such as those living with disabilities, he does not feel that natural disadvantage such as disability should go unaddressed. He devotes a section of his work to philanthropy and to a discussion of why those who currently value giving aid would not cease to provide assistance to those in need if compulsory giving should stop.[2]

Furthermore, Nozick feels we have a moral obligation to help those in need. Wolff claims that:

[Nozick] may even go so far as to say that it is immoral for the rich to let the poor starve if they are in a position to do anything about it: the rich ought to engage in private redistribution schemes. But it is essential to make the distinction between what is morally right and what it is right to enforce by the law. (Wolff 1991, p. 12)

While a discussion of this sort is notably absent from *Anarchy, State, and Utopia*, it appears in Nozick's later work when he discusses ethics and suggests that there are multiple layers and

[t]he second layer is the *ethics of responsiveness*, which is based upon an underlying notion of the inherent value of (all) individuals. It mandates acting in a way that is responsive to people's value, enhancing and supporting it, and enabling it to flourish. (Nozick 2001, p. 280)

Nozick clearly does not want those who express serious need to do without aid. He simply thinks that a conception of justice ought not to be the mechanism to redistribute wealth to those in need. Instead of forced redistribution, Nozick believes we should rely upon charity and acts of benevolence. We should give, and it would be wrong not to give, but we are under no formal obligations as a matter of justice to provide aid to those in need.

English Poor Laws

What does it mean to say that one's disadvantage is not a matter of injustice, but that instead, one should rely on charity to provide what is necessary to live a life worthy of human dignity?[3] Whether philanthropic activity does provide all that is needed to satisfy the basic needs of all members of society or not, there appears to be residual harm left from forcing some to be the recipients of charity and to be subject to the whims and desires of those they are forced to beg from.

The stigmatization that occurs as a result of this form of voluntary transfer risks demeaning the recipients of aid in similar ways to the Elizabethan Poor Laws of 1594 and 1601 that American colonies and state governments would emulate. These laws classified people according to perceived level and cause of need. In effect, these laws divided the poor into two classifications: the worthy, and the unworthy. The worthy poor were those who could demonstrate an adequate level of need and, most often, also demonstrate that this need did not arise as a result of one's own actions or inaction. The unworthy poor were those suffering from disadvantage that was perceived to be due to laziness or drunkenness.

Not only do those with unmet basic needs through no fault of their own find themselves at the whims of those who are advantaged through instances of good brute luck, but they must also demonstrate that their need is in fact worthy of compensation. Thus, one finds themself not only disadvantaged because of impairment and disabling barriers, but also because of the attitude and stigma associated with being the recipient of charity, and having to demonstrate that one is disadvantaged enough to warrant aid.[4]

While Nozick surely does not intend for those in need to suffer, whether his principles of justice or morality achieve that end is a distinct question from what those principles do in practice to disadvantaged individuals. Forcing the disabled and other marginalized and disadvantaged individuals to rely upon charity or acts of benevolence seems to, as a matter of process, do further harm to those we aim to aid. Nozick's process of "doing justice" seems to cause significant negative impacts and to perhaps undermine justice in so doing.

2   DWORKIN AND HYPOTHETICAL INSURANCE

Dworkin, on the other hand, does think that natural disadvantages such as disability ought to be viewed as a matter of justice. Dworkin's basic distributive principle is that "resources, suitably defined, should be distributed equally" (Stein 2006, p. 120). Dworkin hypothesizes about what principles ought to be established for a group of immigrants that find themselves newly stranded on a desert island (Dworkin 1981, pp. 284–285). According to Dworkin, the best manner to distribute resources would be to distribute a resource that exists with no inherent value to use as currency in an auction (Dworkin 1981, p. 285). Bidding would commence, and would end when all of the island's resources were distributed.

It is important to note that Dworkin does not think it suitable to consider natural endowments as being part of one's initial bundle of resources.[5]

But surely natural endowments will impact equality in our society. Equalizing resources at the outset is problematic because some people have different, more expensive needs, through no fault of their own. Dworkin acknowledges this and suggests that a hypothetical insurance scheme be implemented to address the disadvantage associated with disability:

We are to imagine that people do not know whether they are or will be disabled. We then ask how much insurance people would buy, from an initially equal stock of resources, against the risk of being disabled. The average level of coverage and its corresponding premium amount would form the basis of a system of redistribution to the disabled. The premium amount would be collected from each person as a tax, and the revenue raised would be used to pay each disabled person, as compensation, the average level of coverage that hypothetically would have been purchased. (Dworkin 1981, p. 285)

This method is only a second-best solution however. If it were possible to discover how much insurance each individual person with a disability would have purchased in the hypothetical insurance market, we could award individualized payouts of the precise sum they specified. This individualized approach would be preferable to Dworkin were it possible (Dworkin 2000, p. 478).

The Medical Model and Tragedies

But what might it say about those living with impairments if we view these and other states of being as things we ought to insure against? In my mind, this conclusion leads to at least two concerns.

First, Dworkin seems to suggest that individuals with disabilities are disadvantaged because of their impairment, and as such, the method to address this impairment is an individualized one. This smacks of an individual pathological model of disability.

I have highlighted elsewhere how "the medical model. . .treats any functional limitations that arise from the experience of disability as a medical phenomenon, treatable by medical or technological means and perhaps even preventable through biological engineering or screening" (Riddle 2014, p. 14).[6]

Under this individualized manner of conceptualizing disability, disability resides in the individual, and is a feature of that individual that needs to be corrected. The World Health Organization (2001) suggests that thinking about disability in this manner results in viewing disability "as a feature of the person, directly caused by disease, trauma or health conditions, which requires medical care provided in the form of individual treatment by professionals [. . .] to 'correct' the problem with the individual."

Viewing disability in such a manner undermines disability rights initiatives and involves viewing disability as a state to be insured against.

While not without problems of its own, the social model of disability views disability as residing in society, and allowed people with disabilities to become empowered. In other words, social model proponents suggest that impairment is not the problem; it is disabling barriers that disable. Because of this shift in attention, significant social change was brought about by reformulating how disability was viewed:

> [N]o longer did [people with disabilities] have to feel sorry for themselves for being defective—they did not have to change: society had to. Instead of feeling at fault, people with disabilities could feel angry. They could feel angry that society was structured in such a manner that they were limited in ways others were not. (Riddle 2014, p. 16)

Second, by organizing compensatory schemes around the hypothetical auction, Dworkin asks us to imagine just how *tragic* it would be should we become disabled in manner *x*, *y*, or *z*. We are led to view disability as a personal tragedy. People with disabilities become pitiable because of the terrible bad luck they have suffered.

Whether the resources Dworkin provides through his hypothetical auction are adequate to integrate people with disabilities into society or not (and I strongly suspect "not"), his process of providing additional resources to the disadvantaged introduces a level of harm that was not previously present.

3   RAWLS AND SOCIAL CONTRACTORS

Perhaps Rawls's *strong* resource egalitarianism can help us avoid this pitfall.[7] Rawls calls the hypothetical situation that arrives at an agreement among free and rational persons about principles of equality, the original position. The original position consists of rational, mutually disinterested individuals (Rawls 1971, p. 12).

As Cureton summarizes:

> [t]hey are presumed to know basic facts about social life, but none of them knows anything about her particular natural or social endowments. The so-called veil of ignorance, which excludes information of this sort, is a feature of the original position that reflects the basic Rawlsian theme that no one should be advantaged or disadvantaged in the choice of principles of justice by natural or social contingencies. (Cureton 2008, pp. 3–4)

Rawls postpones questions concerning disability however. He limits those in the original position to those who are normal and fully cooperating members of society over a complete life (Rawls 1971, p. 10; 1993, p. 18). In other words, he excludes people with disabilities from the original position as they are not "normal" members of society, requiring or wanting "normal" distributional principles. He states:

> [W]e do not mean to say, of course, that no one ever suffers from illness and accident; such misfortunes are to be expected in the ordinary course of life, and provision for these contingencies must be made. But given our aim, I put aside for the time being these temporary disabilities and also permanent disabilities or mental disorders so sever as to prevent people from being cooperating members of society in the usual sense. (Rawls 1993, p. 20)

I suspect a good deal of people have been too hard on Rawls however. The Rawlsian circumstances of justice are not meant to delineate who is deemed worthy of compensation as a matter of justice (Cureton 2008, p. 3). Instead, Rawls excludes people with disabilities from the design of justice, but not from its redistributive scope.[8]

Exclusion and Normalcy

But does Rawls's postponing the discussion of how to address disadvantage associated with disability harm people with disabilities? Rawls's notion of "normal" individuals, perhaps obviously, affirms an able-bodied conception of normalcy. Need and difference amongst non-disabled contractors is seen as desirable diversity, capable of both enriching a conception of justice and of being addressed as a matter of justice. The difference associated with disability stands in stark contrast to this however. Disability is not normal, despite the fact that most of us will become, at one point in our lives, disabled (Bickenbach 2012, p. 14).

While it may very well be true that promoting justice for people with disabilities is a difficult task, it has always struck me as odd to not start with the most difficult cases and to work one's way backward—if our principles promote justice for people with disabilities, surely mostly everyone else will fall in line as well (Riddle 2010, p. 527). Nonetheless, to view disability as a problem to be dealt with later sends a strong message regarding the urgency and import of justice for people with disabilities.

I am not alone in expressing such a concern however. In Nussbaum's critique of primary goods and Rawls, she suggests

> the postponement is not innocent, clearly. The parties are being asked to imagine themselves as if they represent citizens who really are 'fully cooperating...over a complete life,' and thus as if citizens have no needs for care in times of extreme dependency. This fiction obliterates much that characterizes human life, and obliterates, as well, the continuity between the so-called normal and people with lifelong impairments. (Nussbaum 2006, p. 121)

Kittay's concerns echo both my own and Nussbaum's. She is concerned with the process of normalization and the defining of difference that occurs. In making this observation, she arrives at a similar conclusion:

> [Rawls'] idealization is seriously misleading...[Rawls puts] too much distance between the "normal functioning individual" and the person with special needs and disabilities. Not a single citizen approaches the ideal of full functioning throughout a lifetime. The idealization, in contrast, suggests that those who are not fully functioning are relatively few, and that consequences of special needs is brokered only in monetary terms. (Kittay 1999, p. 88)

Whether we can extend Rawls's limited conception of justice to include people with disabilities or not, the postponement of this issue puts disability-related issues on the backburner and makes an implicit statement about the value of a life lived with a disability.

4   NUSSBAUM AND VERTICAL INEQUALITY

Perhaps a shift away from resources might help us. Sen states, "the conversion of goods to capabilities varies from person to person substantially, and the equality of the former may still be far from the equality of the latter" (Sen 1995, p. 329). As such, our conception of justice must shift our focus to what people are capable of doing with goods or resources (Sen 1995, p. 329).

Martha Nussbaum has suggested that "one way of thinking about the capabilities list is to think of it as embodied in a list of constitutional guarantees" (Nussbaum 2006, p. 155).

Thinking of capabilities in this manner is helpful. What matters when assuring rights is not the resources individuals possess, but instead if they have the opportunity to realize the important rights we set out to provide. The capabilities approach does not deny the importance of resources, but as Sen has powerfully stated,

> Primary goods suffer from a fetishistic handicap in being concerned with goods, and even though the list of goods is specified in a broad and inclusive way, encompassing rights, liberties, opportunities, income, wealth, and the social basis of self-respect, it is still concerned with good things rather than with what these good things do to human beings. (Sen 1995, p. 328)

The value of resources is impacted by conversion factors that take at least three forms: the personal, the social, and the environmental (Robeyns 2005, p. 99). Personal matters such as physical condition and intelligence impacts one's ability to utilize resources. Public policies and social norms create social conversion factors that can diminish the value associated with particular resources. Finally, the physical or built environment creates environmental factors that influence precisely what it is people are capable of doing with the resources that are allocated to them.

It is only with both adequate resources, as well as fair and just conversion factors, that individuals are capable of deriving the true value of resources; it is only when this combination is adequately structured that people are capable of doing valuable things. When resources and conversion factors meet, individuals can be said to have the capability to function—to realize a valuable end state. Individuals then exercise choice to materialize a particular capability.

Horizontal Assessments

Pogge has suggested that the shift from resources to capabilities has resulted in the capabilities approach suffering from what he calls the vertical-inequality problem. I have argued elsewhere that Pogge suggests the capabilities approach is less "stigma-sensitive" than resource-based theories.[9] In other words, Pogge suggests that the capabilities approach risks stigmatizing individuals when assessing need, thus generating greater inequality.[10]

He suggests that by compensating individuals for natural inequalities in endowments, capabilities theorists are forced to make interpersonal comparisons and to judge people as being better or worse than others

(Pogge 2002, pp. 204–205). He suggests that capabilities theorists are committed to regarding human diversity in vertical terms—as better or worse.

Put another way still, irrespective of whether adequate change is implemented to address a lack of endowments, by classifying individuals as better or worse than others, we stigmatize and place a value on the quality of lives that some live.

Perhaps obviously, the process of "doing justice" for the capabilities theorist involves assessing how much of a capability an individual has access to and whether they are living a life worthy of human dignity. We need to evaluate the substantive opportunities available for individuals to pursue and only then can we classify some individuals as residing below our fundamental threshold—we create a hierarchy with some inequalities being permissible (those occurring above our threshold), while others still are impermissible (those resulting in individuals not having genuine opportunities for secure functionings[11] and falling below our threshold).

This problem emerges because the capabilities theorist acknowledges that people ought to be compensated for how natural inequalities manifest themselves in our social environment (Pogge 2002, pp. 204–205).

He suggests that the capabilities theorist is unable to view differences in horizontal terms. If we celebrate diversity and acknowledge how our lives are enriched by variety, we do not thereby commit ourselves to viewing differences as better or worse—we do not have to hold a conclusion about whether having brown eyes is better or worse than having blue ones.

Furthermore, Pogge suggests that not only is the capabilities theorist committed to the view that one is worse in respect to a particular capability, but that this deficit makes that individual worse overall (Pogge 2002, p. 206). Pogge makes the further claim that the judgment being made about individuals is not simply one of personal preference, but that it is instead, a judgment made from a position of overlapping consensus—from a shared public criterion (Pogge 2002, p. 206).

In an important way, we can relate this to discussions about the proper allocation of blame for disability or inability that occurred when discussing Dworkin. Pogge suggests that under the capabilities approach, the blame associated with an inability to secure a capability because of one's disability will be placed on the individual, and not necessarily the social barriers that disable (Pogge 2002, p. 206).

5   CONCLUSION

Carl Knight has suggested that "the social stigma of compensation would almost always be outweighed by the benefits of compensation" (Knight 2005, p. 64), and while I tend to be somewhat sympathetic to this claim,[12] I take my concern to stand: compensation remains to be only part of the equation of justice and providing effective assistance is no excuse, or grants no right, to demean or insult when providing aid or giving to others.

We have been so busy planting seeds and ensuring that our roots grow in a healthy manner that we have ignored the potential destruction being caused by the new branches growing unfettered above the ground. Just like Mr. Jones, in the opening story, attempted to have the end result of his actions—encouraging the dentist to remove his wife's tooth—result in a positive outcome, our attempts to articulate a conception of justice that promotes the well-being of people with disabilities and other marginalized individuals are aimed to do good. But just like Mr. Jones needs to realize that there are indeed better or worse ways to proceed to have another's tooth pulled, we need to be more cognizant of the process of "doing justice" as just principles are only part of the entire picture when it comes to equality and justice.

NOTES

1. This is similar to, but distinct from, the kind of harm one can risk doing to themselves by acknowledging difference that is discussed in Minow (1990, p. 3).
2. See Nozick (1974, pp. 265–268) for a discussion of this.
3. The idea of living a life worthy of human dignity and how it relates to justice stems from Nussbaum (2006, p. 74).
4. This instance of harm more closely resembles what is discussed in Minow (1990, p. 3).
5. Hence, I refer to Dworkin's version of equality of resources as *weak*.
6. See the following for more on this: Riddle (2013a, c).
7. I refer to Rawls's understanding of resources as *strong* because natural endowments can be viewed as resources under his conception of equality.
8. This, of course, may still be problematic for reasons specified by Nussbaum (2006, p. 16).
9. For more on this, see Riddle (2014, pp. 62–65) and Riddle (2013b).
10. Anderson responds to this criticism in great length and I discuss her response in greater detail in Riddle (2013b). In short, Anderson's view suggests that

capabilities, and more generally, justice, ought to concern relational equality
fundamentally, and thus, the process by which we do justice is part of the
central concern when establishing principles.
11. The phrasing of genuine opportunities for secure functionings comes from
Jonathan Wolff and Avner De-Shalit (2008, p. 80).
12. For more on this, see Riddle (2014, pp. 59–75).

References

Anderson, Elizabeth S. 1999. What is the point of equality? *Ethics* 109 (2): 287–337.
Barry, Brian. 1975. Review of "Anarchy, state and utopia", by Robert Nozick. *Political Theory* 3 (3): 331–336.
Bickenbach, Jerome. 2012. *Ethics, law, and policy*. London: Sage.
Cathcart, Thomas, and Daniel Klein. 2007. *Plato and a platypus walk into a bar: Understanding philosophy through jokes*. New York: Abrams Image.
Cureton, Adam. 2008. A Rawlsian perspective on justice for the disabled. *Essays in Philosophy* 9 (1): 3–4.
Dworkin, Ronald. 1981. What is equality? Part 2: Equality of resources. *Philosophy and Public Affairs* 10 (4): 283–345.
———. 2000. *Sovereign virtue*. Cambridge: Belknap Press of Harvard University Press.
Kittay, Eva Feder. 1999. *Love's labor: Essays on women, equality, and dependency*. New York: Routledge.
Knight, Carl. 2005. In defense of luck egalitarianism. *Res Publica* 11 (1): 55–73.
Kymlicka, Will. 2001. *Contemporary political philosophy: An introduction*. Oxford: Oxford University Press.
Minow, Martha. 1990. *Making all the difference: Inclusion, exclusion, and american law*. Ithaca: Cornell University Press.
Nozick, Robert. 1974. *Anarchy, state, and utopia*. New York: Basic Books.
———. 2001. *Invariances: The structure of the objective world*. Cambridge: Belknap Press of Harvard University Press.
Nussbaum, Martha. 2006. *Frontiers of justice: Disability, nationality, species membership*. Cambridge: Belknap Press of Harvard University Press.
Pogge, Thomas. 2002. Can the capability approach be justified? *Philosophical Topics* 30 (2): 167–228.
Rawls, John. 1971. *A theory of justice*. Cambridge, MA: Harvard University Press.
———. 1993. *Political liberalism*. New York: Columbia University Press.
Riddle, Christopher A. 2010. Indexing, capabilities, and disability. *The Journal of Social Philosophy* 41 (4): 527–537.
———. 2013a. Defining disability: Metaphysical not political. *Medicine, Health Care, & Philosophy* 16 (3): 377–384.

————. 2013b. Natural diversity and justice for people with disabilities. In *Disability and the good human life*, ed. B. Schmitz, J. Bickenbach, and F. Felder, 269–297. Cambridge: Cambridge University Press.

————. 2013c. The ontology of impairment: Rethinking how we define disability. In *Emerging perspectives on disability studies*, ed. Matthew Wappett and Katrina Arndt, 23–40. New York: Palgrave Macmillan.

————. 2014. *Disability and justice: The capabilities approach in practice*. Lanham: Lexington/Rowman & Littlefield.

Robeyns, Ingrid. 2005. The capability approach: A theoretical survey. *Journal of Human Development* 6 (1): 93–117.

Sen, Amartya. 1995. Equality of what? In *Equal freedom: Selected tanner lectures on human values*, ed. Stephen Darwall, 307–330. Ann Arbor: University of Michigan Press.

Stein, Mark. 2006. *Distributive justice and disability: Utilitarianism against egalitarianism*. New Haven: Yale University Press.

Wolff, Jonathan. 1991. *Robert Nozick: Property, justice, and the minimal state*. Stanford: Stanford University Press.

Wolff, Jonathan, and Avner De-Shalit. 2008. *Disadvantage*. Oxford: Oxford University Press.

World Health Organization. 2001. *International classification of functioning, disability and health*. Geneva: World Health Organization.

CHAPTER 5

Disability, Well-Being, and (In)Apt Emotions

Dana Howard

Consider the following three perspectives on what counts as an appropriate attitude toward someone with a disability:

> To think that a particular disability makes someone's life less good is not one of the ugly attitudes. It does not mean that the person who has it is of any less value, or is less deserving of respect, than anyone else. (Glover 2006, p. 35)

> In January, I was hospitalized with severe pneumonia in both lungs. On two separate occasions, doctors told me they assumed if I fell unconscious I wouldn't want to be given life saving treatment. I was so frightened of what might happen to me that I kept myself awake for 48 hours. My husband brought in a photo of me in my graduation gown and stuck it on the bed-head to remind the hospital staff that there was more to me than the shriveled form they saw lying in front of them. I was lucky: although I could barely breathe, I had an assertive husband insisting to the authorities that I had everything to live for. Imagine what it would like if you were too weak to communicate. Or your relatives less positive about the quality of your life. (Campbell 2003)

> I will always believe that blindness is a neutral trait, neither to be prized nor shunned. Very few people, including those dearest to me share that

D. Howard (✉)
Clinical Center Department of Bioethics, National Institutes of Health, Bethesda, MD, USA

© The Author(s) 2018   57
J. Flanigan, T.L. Price (eds.), *The Ethics of Ability and Enhancement*, Jepson Studies in Leadership, DOI 10.1057/978-1-349-95303-5_5

conviction. My husband, my parents, and so many others who are central to my life cannot fully relinquish their negative assumptions. I feel that I have failed when I run into jarring reminders that I have not changed their perspective. In those crushing moments I fear that I am not truly accepted after all. But in recent years a new insight has gradually come to me. Yes, my own loved ones hold the unshakeable belief that blindness is and always will be a problem. Nevertheless, these same people have made me welcome. Though they dread blindness as a fate to be avoided at almost any cost, they give me their trust and respect. I don't know how they live without discomfort amid such contradictions. But I recognize that people can and do reach out, past centuries of prejudice and fear, to forge bonds of love. (Kent 2000, p. 62)

Many people view disabilities as misfortunes. They think that disabilities such as deafness, blindness, paraplegia, or autism have a significant negative impact on one's overall quality of life. I will call this the Standard View (Amundson 2005). Jonathan Glover's position, as is evidenced by the above passage, is a clear articulation of such a view. As he points out, the Standard View does not entail that a life with a disability is not worth living or that it would be better to never have been born than to have been born with a disability. Rather the Standard View is a comparative, counterfactual claim: a life with a disability can certainly be a good and worthwhile life, it is just not as good as that life would have been without the disability. According to Glover and others who defend the Standard View, what is disvalued is the condition of disability and not the people who have the condition. The Standard View thus lends itself to certain practical commitments concerning procreative and medical ethics. If disability is a misfortune, then prospective parents seem to have a significant moral reason to do what they can to create children who are not disabled.[1] Moreover, if disability is a misfortune, then parents and society seem to have a significant moral reason to seek out cures to eliminate such conditions.

The Standard View has been challenged by a number of philosophers and disability rights advocates. Some have argued that we should think of (at least some) disabilities as prudentially neutral traits rather than unfortunate ones—as the sorts of features of a person that are neither good nor bad for that person, or good and bad for a person to roughly the same extent.[2] Call this the Prudential Neutrality View. Alternatively, some have argued that insofar as being disabled carries with it certain disadvantages, these disadvantages are the product of an unaccommodating social and physical environment (which includes social stigma and prejudice against disability), not of the specific condition itself. Thus having a disability should neither be celebrated nor shunned.[3] Call this the Evaluative Neutrality View.

Both neutrality views offer us a way to think about disability that directly contrasts with the Standard View. However it is questionable whether the Prudential Neutrality View is really a plausible view to hold given the world we live in and the high impact that having a disability has on the shape of one's life. It would be a great coincidence if having a disability turned out to be good and bad for a person to precisely the same degree. Moreover, it is questionable whether the Evaluative Neutrality View is the best way to understand the position held by many people in the disability community themselves who celebrate and value their condition. For example, the Evaluative Neutrality View does not seem to capture the motivation behind couples who wish to have children who are disabled like them. Take for example a deaf couple who solicited a sperm donor who himself was deaf in order to have the best chances of conceiving a deaf child (Mundy 2002). The couple insisted that they would love their child regardless of whether or not it was deaf. They claimed, "a hearing baby would be a blessing. A deaf baby would be a special blessing." The Evaluative Neutrality View cannot make sense of the excitement that these mothers would experience if they found out their child was also deaf.

In this chapter, I want to turn our attention to a different sort of challenge that has been launched against the Standard View—one that does not rely on the notion that having a disability is neutral in any way. Instead this line of argumentation claims that the Standard View is reflective of and brings about inappropriate emotional responses toward people with disabilities and their circumstances. Rather than determine in advance whether having a disability is good or bad for a person, we should look at what *viewing disability as a misfortune* disposes us to feel. If such a view disposes us to feel inappropriate emotional attitudes toward people with disabilities, this is itself a consideration against holding it. In a recent paper, Stephen Campbell and Joseph Stramondo warn us that once we start viewing disability as a misfortune, we become prone to a destructive kind of unwarranted pity (Campbell and Stramondo 2017). And as I will argue, Eva Kittay can be understood as recently defending the claim that viewing disability as a misfortune leads us to hold certain untenable or inappropriate hopes for our children and for our society (Kittay 2017). I want to ask, what makes these emotions unwarranted, untenable, or otherwise inappropriate? And how does the inaptness of these emotions bear on whether or not we should reject the Standard View?

As the second and third opening passages illustrate, our perception on the quality of disabled peoples' lives ends up influencing the actual quality of disabled people's life. For Jane Campbell, who has spinal muscular atrophy, her doctors' negative view of her overall quality of life is a source of deep and unnecessary anxiety that not only negatively affects her hospital experience but can have drastic implications for her health—requiring her to stay awake and vigilant at a time when she should be resting. On the other hand, her husband's positive view of her quality of life motivates him to act as a dogged advocate for her rights and interests. For Deborah Kent, the mismatch between her views and her loved ones' views on the effects that blindness can have on a life is a source of confusion and frustration. Perhaps her family sees Deborah as an exception to the general rule that blindness makes a person worse off. Or perhaps they think that Deborah herself would have been better off had she not been blind. Either way, her family's outlook causes for Deborah certain feelings of isolation and being misunderstood. Do Campbell, Stramondo, and Kittay's challenge to the Standard View offer any sort of clarification about what is going on in these interpersonal cases? Do they offer us a new way of thinking about the sorts of "ugly attitudes" that Jonathan Glover and other bioethicists worry about and want to avoid?

Here is the structure of the chapter: First, I will introduce the two arguments against unwarranted pity and against untenable hope. I will then take a step back and examine how these two arguments fit in the general debate concerning well-being and disability, and in particular how they are related to past Expressivity Arguments that have been launched against proponents of "procreative beneficence." I will suggest three ways we can interpret the force of Expressivity Arguments and consider whether an upshot of Campbell and Stramondo's and Kittay's arguments is that certain emotional responses to disability are unfitting because of what they express. I think their challenge to the Standard View has a lot of appeal, but I worry that if it is not properly articulated, the approach is vulnerable to what has been known as "The Wrong Kind of Reason" problem.[4]

I should note that for the purposes of this chapter, I remain agnostic about the correct model or definition of disability. Rather I will follow Campbell, Stramondo, and Elizabeth Barnes, in using disability as an umbrella term to pick out a class of conditions that are commonly labeled "disabilities" (and where there is a distinction between impairment and disability, the term picks out conditions of "impairment") (Campbell and Stramondo 2017; Barnes 2014). Down syndrome, deafness, paraplegia, autism, blindness, are all paradigmatic examples of disability. This inclusive terminological strategy allows us to examine the merits of the different arguments without first assuming there is some constitutive relationship between disability and well-being.

1   UNWARRANTED PITY AND UNTENABLE HOPE

Let me start by considering the argument against unwarranted pity. In their paper, *The Complicated Relationship of Disability and Well-Being*, Campbell and Stramondo examine the many ways in which disability might have an impact on well-being. Their analysis ends up undercutting the plausibility of both the Standard View and the Prudential Neutrality View. Ultimately, they argue, we cannot generalize about the impact that having a disability will have on an individual's life—not even that it will have an overall neutral impact. This is because of the highly individualized and context-sensitive nature of the experience of living with a disability: "One's response to the challenges that a disability can bring, the way in which one's disability factors into one's sense of identity and purpose, the opportunities that are created as a result of one's condition—these are all things that may render people better off than they would have been in the absence of disability" (Campbell and Stramondo 2017, p. 161). Moreover, as they note, these are all things that may render people worse off as well. Ultimately, disabilities are "high impact traits" according to Campbell and Stramondo; they significantly influence the character of a person's life and so we should not assume that they typically will make no difference to one's level of well-being.

There is, however, one relationship between disability and well-being that they do admit as likely to hold: while it is not the case that being disabled is generally bad for a person, it is the case that being disabled makes it more likely that one will have a lower level of well-being because of their condition. This is a "probabilistic claim" about an individual's susceptibility to facing certain hardships as a result of disability rather than a general claim about the prudential impact of having a disability in a vast majority of cases (Campbell and Stramondo 2017, p. 168). So Campbell and Stramondo maintain that for a majority of cases, we cannot say that having a disability has been or will be bad for that person; however, they do concede that given the unjust social conditions we live in and given the suffering and early death associated with specific disabilities [which "pull down" the average for all those with disabilities], having a disability raises the probability that a person will be worse off for it than a nondisabled person would have been worse off in light of possessing other high impact traits.

Campbell and Stramondo go on to argue that insofar as generalizations about disability and well-being are not well-founded, certain emotional reactions that nondisabled people have in regard to disabled people become questionable. More specifically, nondisabled people often pity disabled individuals without knowing much about how having that disability has affected their lives. According to Campbell and Stramondo, this is an unwarranted reaction. Here is their general argument.

Unwarranted Pity Argument

1. Pity is an emotional response to the perception that someone is doing poorly in some significant respect or on the whole.
2. The prevalence of pity directed at people with disabilities is an indication of the widespread acceptance of the Standard View.
3. The Standard View is false and should be rejected.
4. Therefore, pity toward people with disabilities is unwarranted.[5]

One immediate question we should have about this argument is what are we to do with the Standard View as it is interpreted in probabilistic terms. If we should accept the probabilistic interpretation of the Standard View, then isn't it the case that pity would be warranted in situations where the person feeling the pity recognizes that—while it is not set in stone—things *could* go much worse for the person pitied just in virtue of their disability? In such a situation the pity doesn't seem to rest on a mistaken generalization about the disabled person's condition, so why not think the pity is warranted?

Campbell and Stramondo don't accept that pity is warranted in such cases even if they are willing to accept that the probabilistic attitude underlying the pity is itself warranted. This leads to their second argument against pity, which we can call the *Anti-Proleptic Pity Argument*:

> If enough people believe that having a disability is likely to make an individual worse off and respond with pity, this will diminish disabled people's well-being and make it more likely that they are worse off. (Campbell and Stramondo 2017, pp. 171)

You treat someone as pitiable (whether it is warranted or not) and you make it more likely that they become an appropriate object of pity. This of course doesn't mean that pity is warranted after all. On the contrary, Stramondo has suggested elsewhere that a more appropriate and constructive response to the predicament of people with disabilities would be shared sense of moral outrage (Stramondo 2010, pp. 121–134).

I find the Anti-Proleptic Pity Argument to be quite compelling and want to further investigate how we should evaluate the aptness of certain emotions on Campbell and Stramondo's view. We should notice that on this second argument, the standard of correctness [or fit] for the emotion of pity is not determined by whether or not it rests on warranted beliefs; rather it is determined by whether the emotion itself is of practical use. Given that our perceptions of disability have an effect on the experience of living with disability, perhaps we should aim to view disability in a way that is most conducive to the lives of people who are disabled; and perhaps our emotional responses are only appropriate when they reflect these more conducive views.

We need to clarify what conditions are necessary for pity to be fitting in such cases. Is it the fact that people with disabilities are pitied regardless of whether or not they are actually worse off? Or is it the fact that being pitied (warranted or not) makes it more likely that people with disabilities are worse off? One way to address these questions is to argue that although pity is a warranted response to the situation, it isn't the most constructive way to emotionally respond to the facts on the ground. That is, shared outrage is also warranted in such situations and shared outrage doesn't itself contribute to the likelihood that someone's life will go less well for them just in virtue of their disability. While both pity and outrage may be warranted, only outrage leads to better consequences and is thus more fitting. However this is not what Campbell and Stramondo want to say; they want to criticize pity in such circumstances as unwarranted, not just less warranted than other emotions. I will return to why in the third section.

For now, let us move on to Kittay's argument against what I will call "Untenable Hope." I should note that hope isn't something that is mentioned in her article, but she does entertain the desirability and even the imaginability of certain future states of affairs. Moreover, she is responding to two sets of philosophers in particular who motivate their argument by presenting to their readers what they take to be a utopian vision of the future—that is, a future worth hoping for.

Allen Buchanan, Dan Brock, Norman Daniels, and Daniel Wikler: "[T]here can be a obligations of justice… to require genetic interventions. From this perspective, we are committed to the judgment that in the future the world should not include so many disabilities and hence so many people with disabilities. But it is not the people with disabilities that we disvalue; it is the disabilities themselves." (2000, p. 287)

Glover: "Great changes in what human beings are like are becoming possible [3]…I think that, other things being equal, it is good if the incidence of disabilities is reduced by parental choices to opt for potentially more flourishing children. To think that a particular disability makes someone's life less good is not one of the ugly attitudes. It does not mean that the person who has it is of any less value, or is less deserving of respect, than anyone else." (2006, p. 35)

Let me highlight a few features about Brock et al.'s and Glover's hopes. First, Brock et al. believe that the future world *should not* include as many people with disabilities, whereas Glover (at least when he is talking about the society at large) argues only that *it would be good* if fewer people with disabilities were born. Accordingly, both of these arguments defend a variation of the view often called "Procreative Beneficence," which holds that parents and society have moral reason to do what they can to produce children with the best chance at flourishing (Kahane and Savalescu 2009). While Brock et al.'s position is that these moral reasons constitute a duty on the part of parents and society, Glover seems to believe that such reasons can be overridden by other considerations. Regardless of the flavor of their procreative beneficence, both views see a future world with fewer disabled people as both desirable and feasible. It is a world for which it is reasonable to hold out hope.

Second, if we are to bracket the first sentence—i.e. "that justice requires genetic interventions"—there is a way for many people in the disability rights community to get on board with Brock et al.'s utopian future. To do this, of course, we would have to keep in view the distinction between impairment and disability. Hoping for a world with less disability and fewer disabled people can be understood more specifically as hoping for a world where more people with impairments are not disabled. Such a world would be achieved primarily through social and material accommodations rather than through genetic interventions. This indeed seems like a future that we can all hope for, regardless of whether we accept the Standard View. It is not the world that Brock et al. have in mind however. Their vision of a world is one in which fewer people are born with disabilities as a result of prenatal genetic selection and individual reproductive choices.

I think some important lessons can be drawn from how Kittay responds to these utopian visions. In reaction to Brock et al.'s hope for a future world in which disability is for the most part eradicated, Kittay asks, "Do I accept that the universe would be better without the disability my daughter has?" This is not merely a rhetorical question. She tries to the best of her abilities to imagine what that world would be like and whether it would be a better world than the one we live in:

> Although it is a difficult place to go, I will on occasion try to imagine my daughter, who is multiply disabled (she was born with significant intellectual disability, seizure disorders, and mild Cerebral Palsy), without her disabilities—but my imagination quickly falters. I have no way of knowing which aspects of her personality, appearance, emotional makeup, and so on, are ones that she would have without the disability....To imagine what a life like that would be otherwise would be a vain and futile exercise. (Kittay 2017, p. 196)

For Kittay, it seems that the kind of utopia for which Brock et al. are holding out hope (both for society and for individuals) is not one that is accessible to her as the mother of a daughter who is multiply disabled. If it is a world that doesn't include her daughter, Sesha, it is not a world she is interested in. And if it is a world that includes Sesha but without her disabilities, it is not a world Kittay can easily picture. It is a mere abstraction—a contentless possibility—that is not fully fleshed out. Such a world does not seem to warrant hope since there is nothing particularly good about that world to fix one's attention.

Glover, for his part, insists that his hopes for the future are not one of the ugly attitudes. This is because he argues that the following two propositions are not in conflict:

Claim 1: Having a disability makes someone's life less good.
Claim 2: Having a disability makes a person's life no less deserving of respect.

Glover is not specifically hoping for a world that is rid of people with disabilities; he is rather hoping for a world in which the children born are the ones who have the best possible chance to flourish—which may happen to mean fewer people with disabilities. So he maintains that he can hope for a world where disability is diminished, without expressing any disrespect to people with disabilities.

In response to this argument, Kittay's concern is not about the compatibility of the two propositions in theory, but rather the tenability of *holding* both positions in practice:

> ...if we equally respect that life, we also think that we should not settle for a lesser life.
>
> Thinking about what respecting a disabled life equally means reveals for us the tension [between claim 1 and claim 2]. That is, if we respect a life as being of equal worth, that impels us to do what we can to ensure that the disability not be a disadvantage, that her life not be less good. (Kittay 2016, p. 177)

In what way does Kittay take claims 1 and 2 to be in tension? It seems, at least in the abstract, there is no contradiction in believing both that people with disabilities are worthy of equal respect and that people with disabilities have lives less good. Kittay's point, however, is that things change when we pay closer attention to what these beliefs dispose us to do and to feel. Kittay argues that if one really appreciated the truth of the view that a person with a disability is worthy of equal respect, one would be motivated to do everything in one's power to ensure that that person has an equal chance at a flourishing life just like everyone else. So if one really believed claim 2, one would not be able to endorse claim 1. To hold both views at once is practically unsustainable.

Glover's vision of what the world full of flourishing children looks like also happens to be a vision where fewer of those children will be disabled. As it is the case with Campbell and Stramondo's rejection of proleptic pity, it seems that there is something untoward about hopes that accept as a given that a person's disability will ultimately lead to misfortune. Such hopes concede too much too soon. They are not the sorts of hopes that will appeal to many people who are disabled themselves or to those who care for and about people with disabilities; insofar as they are working hard to ensure that a life with a disability is not inherently a life that is less good or with less opportunity to flourish. To hope for Glover's world is to view as unnecessary one's present efforts at making this world more accommodating. We may thus understand Glover's and Brock's hopes, as exclusionary hopes. They are hopes for the future of society and for one's children that cannot be shared by many people with disabilities or many of their loved ones. One remaining question to consider is whether the fact that these hopes cannot be shared by all itself constitutes a reason to reject such hopes.

So here are my two general questions moving forward in the chapter. In regard to Campbell and Stramondo's argument, is pity ever warranted? If so, under what conditions? And what is it about pitying people with disabilities that makes it unfitting? Is it the consequences of the emotional response or is it something about what the emotional response is attaching to? Similarly, in regard to Kittay's argument, what is it about holding out hope for a world without disability that is unfitting? Is it the fact that such a world is undesirable in itself, that it is not accessible to many people within the disability rights community, or can the problem be found in what holding onto such hope does to a person (i.e. that it leads them to be complacent about certain features of society that can be changed)?

These two sets of questions can be put most broadly in terms of the fittingness relation between the world and our emotions. How are we to evaluate these emotional responses that we have in such situations and when can we say that certain emotional responses are unwarranted? These questions are important to ask for two reasons. First, examining our emotional responses to people with disabilities can lead to a fascinating contribution to the philosophy of emotions and to moral psychology. Second, there is reason to worry that these arguments put forward by Campbell, Stramondo, and Kittay are going to be disregarded or misunderstood by their interlocutors. In order to see this worry, I want to place this discussion in relation to the ongoing debate about the relationship between disability and well-being and the susceptibility of some views to the expressivity argument.

2   RESPONDING TO EXPRESSIVITY ARGUMENTS AND THE WRONG KIND OF REASON DEFENSE

There is often a sense in the debate surrounding disability and well-being that the positions are intractable. That is, for disability rights advocates, the Standard View is a non-starter for our ethical and political thinking. For many philosophers and bioethicists, on the other hand, such a view seems to be self-evident. And regardless of the evidence offered by disability rights advocates, which demonstrates that people with disabilities lead satisfying lives and thus calls into question both the truth and the practical implications of the Standard View, bioethicists and philosophers continue to assert it and offer up new arguments in the service of fortifying the Standard View against the provided evidence or in the service of disregarding the evidence in the first place as unreliable, confused, or biased. Reciprocally, when proponents of the Standard View offer evidence that people with disabilities are disadvantaged on numerous objective metrics of quality of life—poverty rate, morbidity, mortality, etc.—disability rights advocates point out that these metrics cannot disambiguate the effects resulting from the disability itself and those resulting from the unjust social marginalization and lack of accommodation for people with disabilities.

In light of the contentious nature of the debate and the seeming intractability of the positions on each side, there is a sense in which Kittay's as well as Campbell and Stramondo's challenges embody an important philosophical virtue of argumentative modesty. Early on in our philosophical training, we are taught that we should not start out an argument with assumptions that our opponents are sure to reject and that we should not overstate our case in the conclusions that we make. This strategy broadens the reach of our arguments to the widest possible audience, inviting people from deeply disparate perspectives to engage with our views—and hopefully to be persuaded.

These two challenges employ this strategy well. They do not start out their argument with the general assumption that a life with disability is no worse than a life without disability, nor is this an ultimate conclusion. Rather they approach the debate from an agnostic position, questioning whether it is possible to make such general assumptions about how living with a disability will affect an individual life. For example:

> **Kittay:** "Life is so strewn with contingencies that the presence or absence of a disability in an individual's life is still a poor predictor of what would be a better life for that person." (Kittay 2017, p. 197)

> **Campbell and Stramondo:** "The diverse contingencies of life lead to all kinds of variations in well-being—even among similar people living in similar environments. Given all of these variables, it is impossible to make any true generalization about the tendency of disabilities to generate intrinsic goods and bads." (Campbell and Stramondo 2017, p. 160)

Perhaps no stronger claims are forthcoming not because of any philosophical virtue on their part but merely in light of the fact that Kittay, Campbell, and Stramondo recognize that their position will seem counterintuitive to the majority of people (most of whom happen to be nondisabled). Nevertheless, their agnosticism seems warranted, especially given all the empirical data and testimony concerning the life satisfaction level of people with disabilities, along with the fact that those who do not live with a disability cannot fully understand what it is like to have a disability and those who do live with a disability cannot fully understand what it is like to live without one. Given the limited epistemic situation that everyone in the debate find themselves in, isn't the philosophically responsible posture here one of agnosticism about the possibility of making non-invidious comparisons?

Not according to those who hold the Standard View. Regardless of what one thinks about the validity of the view, we should recognize how strong of a thesis it is, especially in comparison to the relatively modest positions argued for in these two challenges. Those that hold the Standard View either presume at the outset that disability is a misfortune, or they make arguments in defense of that presumption, usually in the service of defending further ethical or political claims about parental reproductive obligations or the justice of certain distributive schemes.

The thing is, however, the Standard View is not even a necessary position to take up in order to defend these policies and practices that advocates of the Standard View want to defend. First, you don't need to presume that it is worse to be disabled than nondisabled in order to see what is wrong about causing someone to have the disability or even failing to prevent someone in your charge from becoming disabled. Blindness doesn't need to be worse than sightedness for us to see what is wrong with shining a blinding laser into someone's eyes, nor is the comparison necessary for us to see what is wrong about refusing to vaccinate one's child against the measles. Becoming blind can be bad for a person without it being comparatively bad for a person to have always been blind (Barnes 2014). Second, as Kittay convincingly argues, you don't need to presume that it is worse to be disabled than nondisabled in order to see why it is important to protect women's rights to make informed reproductive choices—especially when such choices have a significant impact on their lives and against the background of a history of taking these choices away from women. Genetic testing and accessible and safe abortion procedures can thus feature into the rights of women to make informed decisions about their health and well-being. As a final example, you don't need the Standard View to explain why governments may be justified in funding medical research on and offering treatments for certain impairments (Kamm 2009, p. 317). So philosophers and bioethicists can argue in defense of prenatal testing, the right to have abortions, the right to genetic testing, social programs that encourage vaccinations and research, etc. without holding onto the strong and contentious view that disability is a misfortune.

Why, then, the continued insistence on the Standard View? I think the answer to this question is not only that these philosophers think the Standard View is correct, but that they also judge it to be *the realistic* view to hold. By "realism" here I mean the opposite of the naïveté that is associated with idealism. I imagine that those who continue to defend the Standard View think that it contains a hard and inconvenient truth about people with disabilities—a truth that is understandable, perhaps even admirable, for people with disabilities and for their loved ones to reject.

There is evidence of this in the way that upholders of the Standard View tend to respond to the Expressivity Argument. The Expressivity Argument, as it is usually made, claims that certain practices such as genetic selection against disabilities *express views* that stigmatize and reinforce discrimination against disabled people. One way of understanding what is novel about the challenge that Kittay, Campbell, and Stramondo are putting forward is that they are extending the Expressivity Argument to matters concerning our attitudes rather than focusing on matters concerning social practices and policies. In light of this expansion, one can understand the Expressivity Argument as the following claim:

> **Expressivity Argument:** Certain practices and sentiments, such as genetic selection or pity, express views that stigmatize and reinforce discrimination against disabled people.

Expressivity Argument

Here is how Glover and Brock et al. each have responded to the possible charge that some of their views concerning disability fall prey to such stigmatizing expressions:

> **Glover:** "People should not be prevented from choosing children with more rather than less potential for flourishing. And sometimes it may be a good thing to make such choices. But there is a possible cost to the self-esteem of people already disadvantaged. I think that, other things being equal it is good if the incidence of disabilities is reduced by parental choices to opt for potentially more flourishing children. But we should not deny the potential cost to which the expressivist argument draws attention. And we should try to reduce the cost as far as possible." (2006, p. 35)

Brock et. al.: [After arguing against the Expressivity Argument,] "None of this is to deny that some members of the disabilities rights community are genuinely offended by what they take to be the misplaced zeal to harness the powers of science to prevent disabilities. Granted the shameful history of discrimination against and insensitivity toward persons with disabilities, their taking offence is perfectly understandable. However, it is one thing to say that a certain behavior is offensive to a particular group, and quite another to say that the fact that the group is offended constitutes a violation of anyone's rights." (2000, p. 281)

What do we notice about these two responses? First, that Glover and Brock et al. understand the Expressivity Argument to be one primarily concerned with the negative consequences of expressing an attitude or proposing a policy rather than the truth or fittingness of that attitude or the value of that policy. Second, they understand the negative consequences to be primarily its offense to people with disabilities or the lowering of their self-esteem. This understanding of the force of the Expressivity Argument allows Glover and Brock et al. to continue to think that their views accurately represent the world but also to concede that publicly expressing these views and acting on these views may upset certain populations. The solution then, as Glover makes clear, is not to change one's position, but to do what is in one's power to minimize hurt feelings.

There is reason to worry that similar responses may be made by advocates of the Standard View to the arguments concerning unwarranted pity and untenable hope. In response to Campbell and Stramondo, they may say: "Sure the fact that we think disability is a misfortune may lead us to pity people who have disabilities and this may lead to a loss of well-being. But the pity is fitting, living with a disability closes off opportunities that they otherwise would have. It is *this* feature of their condition that makes it appropriate to pity them, regardless of the consequences that the pity may bring about." In response to Kittay, they may say: "Sure that fact that we hope for a world with fewer disabled people may lead to some bad consequences in the present. It may make us more complacent about creating certain opportunities for existing people with disabilities. But we shouldn't get rid of our hope, we should instead counteract its negative effects. The hope is fitting; its target is a world that is both desirable and achievable. It is these two features that makes this future world worthy of our hope, regardless of the consequences the hope may bring about."

These two possible responses defend the Standard View by employing "Wrong Kind of Reason" (WKR) arguments. Justin D'arms and Daniel Jacobson (2000), among others, have argued that our emotional responses can be fitting despite it being bad (or vicious) to feel them (2000). This is because our emotions are tracking certain evaluative features of the world. According to D'arms and Jacobson, "we must be able not simply to distinguish good and bad reasons to feel an emotion...we must also be able to distinguish good but irrelevant reasons to feel from those that can properly brought to bear on a property ascription [of whether the emotion is fitting]. The fact that shame is an unpleasant feeling, for instance, or that it would be counterproductive to feel on some occasion, are perfectly good reasons not to be ashamed, which are nevertheless irrelevant to whether what one has done is shameful" (D'arms and Jacobson 2000, p. 69).

That the lion will smell our fear is not the right sort of consideration in determining whether fear is fitting. What determines whether fear is fitting is some attribute inherent in the lion (and its relationship to us and our interests). The lion poses a real danger to us; therefore fear is fitting even if feeling fear is injudicious. That it is petty to feel envy for someone else's good fortune does not yet prove that such envy is inapt. The envy may be fitting given that this other person has something valuable that one lacks. Therefore, moral and prudential considerations about whether to have an emotion are irrelevant to whether the emotion accurately represents the world. They offer us a wrong kind of reason in favor of the emotion. Ugly attitudes can nonetheless be fitting and virtuous attitudes can nonetheless be unfitting.

We should note that there is a difference between being responsive to bad reasons in favor of some attitude and being responsive to the wrong kind of reasons in favor of that attitude. The fact that your daughter took sixth place in her class spelling bee is conceivably a good (albeit perhaps minor) reason to be proud of her. The fact that being a proud parent improves your daughter's self-esteem and may result in greater achievements down the line is a potentially strong consideration in favor of being proud of her. However, this pragmatic consideration about the effects of your attitude on your daughter's behavior is at best a good but WKR to be proud of her. While the attitude of pride may be beneficial in such a case, such benefits do not weigh on whether your daughter's actions merit your pride.

If you don't find this distinction persuasive, contrast this scenario with the following: the fact that your daughter has kicked a puppy is clearly a bad reason to be proud of her. The fact that being a proud parent improves your daughter's self-esteem and may result in less animal cruelty in her future is a potentially strong consideration in favor of being proud of her. However strong the considerations about the benefits of your attitude, it seems clear that your daughter's actions in this case do not merit your pride. Up to some limit, being a good parent may entail being responsive to WKRs for being proud of one's children, even when their actions barely merit pride.[6] However, claiming that you should be responsive to WKRs in some situations does not change its direction of normative force. The right kinds of reasons for pride should track good-making features of the potential object of pride itself rather than the good-making features of holding the attitude of pride.

So the difference between bad reasons and wrong kinds of reasons is this: That she kicked a puppy is a *bad* Right Kind of Reason to be proud of your daughter. The potential improvement of your daughter's behavior as a result of your pride is a *good* Wrong Kind of Reason (WKR) to be proud of her. WKRs for pride are at best considerations in favor of attempting to get yourself to be proud of your daughter; however, they cannot offer any consideration in favor of evaluating her actions as worthy of your pride. Similar to the attitude of pride, one can ask whether the attitude of hope or the attitude of pity is merited in a specific case. We may want to distinguish between an argument offering reasons for why it would be better to be hopeful about some desired end and an argument offering reasons for why some desired end merits our hope. We may also want to distinguish between offering reasons for why it would be better to not pity a person and offering reasons for why some person does not merit our pity.

Do Campbell, Stramondo, and Kittay offer us arguments of the right kind? Campbell and Stramondo's Anti-Proleptic Pity Argument may be offering us a wrong kind of reason to refrain from feeling pity insofar as the inaptness of the pity is grounded solely in the negative consequences of holding the attitude of pity. Kittay's argument against untenable hope may be offering us a wrong kind of reason to reject certain hopes insofar as the inaptness of these hopes is grounded in the negative consequences of holding them or the viciousness of our character were we to hold them. However, I do not think that this is the best way to interpret the challenges that these authors present to the Standard View.

3   DETERMINING THE APTNESS OF EMOTIONS

Kittay, Campbell, and Stramondo have ways to handle the Wrong Kind of Reason Defense. Both challenges to the Standard View highlight the fact that there is no matter of fact at present about how people's lives will go. They suggest that given the contingencies of life and that certain things don't (yet) hold true, certain attitudes that proponents of the Standard View maintain are unfitting and not merely inconvenient or upsetting. To see this, let me offer the following distinction of how to interpret the Expressivity Argument.

When we say "certain practices and sentiments *express views* that stigmatize and reinforce discrimination against disabled people," we can mean a number of different things:

First Interpretation: We can mean that the views underlying the practice or sentiment are *informed* by harmful stereotypes of disabilities; therefore, the practice or sentiment is itself *unwarranted*. Views that result from stereotypes fail to be reliably truth dependent. Take for example, the practice of speaking louder to a person who has a foreign accent. Regardless of the intentions of the speaker, such a behavior expresses a view—that people with foreign accents cannot understand English when it is spoken at the normal register—that is informed by certain stereotypes about their fluency. This view and the subsequent behavior is unwarranted, not necessarily because it is annoying or harmful, but because the stereotype is not moored in reality.

Second Interpretation: We can mean that the views underlying the practice or sentiment *express* harmful stereotypes of disabilities; therefore, the practice or sentiment that is associated with such views is itself *vicious*. It is not the consequences of the expression, but the expression of the view itself that invites negative evaluation of the character of the person. For example, Virginia Woolf's description in her diary of walking past a group of people with cognitive disabilities: "It was perfectly horrible. They should certainly be killed" (Glover 2006, p. 29). Let's imagine that Woolf did not intend for her thoughts to reach any public audience. They were just thoughts she had and expressed to herself. No matter. Expressions of harmful stereotypes are vicious in themselves; they needn't contribute to furthering the stigma or discrimination against people with disabilities.

Third Interpretation: We can mean that the practice or sentiment itself *perpetuates* harmful stereotypes of disabilities; therefore, these behaviors are themselves *deleterious*. Here what invites the negative evaluation is the choice to express the sentiment or attitude given the consequences, not that there is anything wrong with the sentiment or attitude in the abstract. I take it that Brock et al. and Glover see the Expressivity Argument as mainly challenging their views on this third sort of interpretation. If not accurately understood, expressing their views and prescriptions *may* lead to harmful stereotypes of people with disabilities. The solution then is to ensure that in expressing these views, they are not giving credence to certain ugly attitudes of the past. However, nothing in their view is itself taken to be a misrepresentation of the world as it is or expressive of a vicious and biased character.

However, as Kittay, Stramondo, and Campbell suggest, under such uncertain conditions, some hopes and bouts of pity do not accurately reflect our current condition. These attitudes hold as fixed certain features of the world that are still malleable and they disvalue certain features of people's lives that should be taken into consideration. So it is not merely the consequences that make such attitudes inappropriate, it is the way they represent our world and the way they reflect on the character of our relationships to others. It follows that the first interpretation of the expressivity charge is open to Campbell and Stramondo as well as Kittay. They can argue that the Standard View and its attendant feelings of pity and hope are unwarranted, not necessarily because they are harmful, but because they are not properly moored in reality. Campbell and Stramondo explicitly employ this sort of strategy by arguing that pity is not a fitting response to the mere likelihood that one's disability is bad for a person; rather, the disability must actually be bad for that person. We often do not know a person's circumstances well enough to determine whether their situation has indeed been made worse off given their disabilities. Rather than immediately experiencing pity, it is appropriate to approach people with disabilities with "a degree of measured curiosity" about their life and the impact that having a disability has had on it (Campbell and Stramondo 2017, p. 174). Campbell and Stramondo can make this sort of argument without fear of offering any reason of the wrong kind against the Standard View.

There is a sense however that the first interpretation of the Expressivity Argument does not address all that is problematic about certain policies and attitudes. The consequences of our hopes and bouts of pity do seem to matter in these situations; it is not just that they do not fully reflect the contingent nature of disability. Our hopes and bouts of pity can close us off from being motivated to work alongside people with disabilities to ensure that the contingencies of life work out in their favor and to take it to be a matter of justice (and not just of fortune) that they do. It seems then that an important feature of the arguments that Kittay, Campbell, and Stramondo put forward is that they raise the stakes of us having certain emotional responses to people with disabilities. Often, we think about our emotional apparatus as a private and reflexive matter—as an internal echo of the world that can have no practical effect on it. However, the arguments against unwarranted pity and untenable hope highlight the relationship between our emotions and our sense of agency. While we may not succumb to the sort of viciousness expressed in Virginia Woolf's diary, hoping for the wrong sort of thing and pitying people who do not merit it makes it harder for us to view ourselves as agents of change. Our unwarranted emotions can thus expose something more significant about us than the people we are reacting to. This may not itself be the right kind of reason not to have the emotion, but it can be a good reason to reassess our understanding of the facts of the matter and our beliefs about whether things ought to remain that way.[7]

Notes

1. These moral reasons should be contrasted from prudential reasons. The idea is not that it is in the parents' best interest to create children without disabilities, but rather that there is something morally problematic, perhaps even blameworthy, when they refrain from doing what they can to create children who are not disabled.
2. For a discussion of the prudential neutrality view, see Stephen Campbell and Joseph Stramondo (2017).
3. Deborah Kent's view of her blindness exemplifies this position.
4. On the idea of Wrong Kinds of Reason Arguments more generally, see Wlodek Rabinowitz and Toni Ronnow-Rasmussen (2004).
5. It should be noted that holding the Standard View is taken here to be a necessary but not sufficient condition for someone to feel warranted pity toward people with disabilities. That is, one may have other views both about their own relationship to the pitied person (i.e. that they are superior) and about the extent of the misfortune that a disability brings about in order for pity to be triggered. One may see a friend's peanut allergy as a misfortune without feeling pity for that person either because they do not take the

misfortune to be so dire so as to warrant pity or because they cannot feel pity for a friend who they recognize as an equal. These considerations are orthogonal to the argument that Campbell and Stramondo present. For their argument to work, all they need to do is to presume that viewing disability as a misfortune is a constituent feature of warranted pity, and since the Standard View is false, pity toward people with disability is unwarranted regardless of whether or not the pity would be warranted (or unwarranted) given other factors.

6. This view could be based on aretaic ideals rather than pragmatic considerations that weigh in favor of pride. That is, one could hold this view, not only because being a proud parent has good consequences but just in virtue of what it means to be a good parent. D'Arms and Jacobson argue that moral and pragmatic considerations for holding certain attitudes are often best understood as WKRs.

7. The views expressed in this chapter are the author's own and do not reflect the view of the National Institutes of Health, the Department of Health and Human Services, or the United States government.

REFERENCES

Amundson, Ron. 2005. Disability, ideology, and quality of life: A bias in biomedical ethics. In *Quality of life and human difference*, ed. David Wasserman, Jerome Bickenbach, and Robert Wachbroit. Cambridge: Cambridge University Press.

Barnes, Elizabeth. 2014. Valuing disability, choosing disability. *Ethics* 125 (1): 88–113.

Buchanan, Allen, Dan Brock, Norman Daniels, and Daniel Wikler. 2000. *From chance to choice*. Cambridge: Cambridge University Press.

Campbell, Jane. 2003. Choosing life. *The Guardian*. https://www.theguardian.com/society/2003/aug/26/health.lifeandhealth. Accessed 29 Sept 2016.

Campbell, Stephen, and Joseph Stramondo. 2017. The complicated relationship of disability and well-being. *Kennedy Institute of Ethics Journal* 27 (2): 151–184.

D'Arms, Justin, and Daniel Jacobson. 2000. The moralistic fallacy: On the 'appropriateness of emotions.'. *Philosophy and Phenomenological Research* 61 (1): 65–90.

———. 2014. Wrong kinds of reason and the opacity of normative force. In *Oxford studies in metaethics*, ed. Russ Shafer-Landau, vol. 9. Oxford: Oxford University Press.

Glover, Jonathan. 2006. *Choosing children*. Oxford: Oxford University Press.

Kahane, Guy, and Julian Savalescu. 2009. The moral obligation to create children with the best chance of the best life. *Bioethics* 23 (5): 274–290.

Kamm, Francis M. 2009. Disability, discrimination and irrelevant goods. In *Disability and disadvantage*, ed. Kimberley Brownlee and Adam Cureton. Oxford: Oxford University Press.

Kent, Deborah. 2000. Somewhere a mocking bird. In *Prenatal testing and disability rights*, ed. Erik Parens and Adrienne Asch. Washington, DC: Georgetown University Press.

Kittay, Eva Feder. 2016. *Invited symposium: Disability*. Paper presented to the Central Meeting of the American Philosophical Association, Chicago, IL, March 5.

————. 2017. How not to argue for selective reproductive procedures. *Kennedy Institute of Ethics Journal* 27 (2): 185–215.

Mundy, Liza. 2002. A world of their own. *The Washington Post*. https://www.washingtonpost.com/archive/lifestyle/magazine/2002/03/31/a-world-of-their-own/abba2bbf-af01-4b55-912c-85aa46e98c6b/. Accessed 29 Sept 2016.

Rabinowitz, Wlodek, and Toni Ronnow-Rasmussen. 2004. The strike of the demon: On fitting pro-attitudes and value. *Ethics* 114 (3): 391–423.

Stramondo, Joseph. 2010. How an ideology of pity is a social harm to people with disabilities. *Social Philosophy Today* 26: 121–134.

CHAPTER 6

Kantian Ethics, Well-Being, and Disability

Jessica Flanigan

Is it bad to be disabled? Does it matter morally whether it's bad to be disabled? Many policies and private medical choices explicitly distinguish disabled persons from nondisabled people, and some thereby effectively place disabled people at a disadvantage. In some cases, these choices are motivated by the view that it is bad to be disabled, or that disabled people face hardships that nondisabled people do not. In this chapter, I argue that whether disability makes people worse off is irrelevant to practical questions about whether causing disability or non-disability is permissible, whether officials should extend rights or resources to disabled people that they do not extend to others, whether and when disability requires accommodation, and whether disabled people should be protected from discrimination. My goal is to outline a broadly Kantian framework for understanding disability rights and to show that this framework has several advantages over welfarist analyses of disability.

I begin by arguing in favor of defining disability as a set of physical differences in contrast to definitions of disability that make reference to a theory of well-being (1). With this definition of disability in hand, I describe a Kantian approach to disability rights (2). In my view, disability rights, like all rights, are grounded in the value of humanity. All persons have rights in

J. Flanigan (✉)
Jepson School of Leadership Studies, University of Richmond, Richmond, VA, USA

© The Author(s) 2018
J. Flanigan, T.L. Price (eds.), *The Ethics of Ability and Enhancement*,
Jepson Studies in Leadership, DOI 10.1057/978-1-349-95303-5_6

virtue of their capacity to make autonomous choices, not in virtue of their interests or considerations of well-being (3). Practical questions about disability should therefore be settled by an appeal to facts about autonomy and more general rights-based arguments, not by an appeal to facts about well-being. Specifically, arguments on behalf of disability rights should appeal to arguments on behalf of the more general rights that people have in virtue of their autonomy (4). Following feminist arguments against institutional gender dichotomies, I argue that in a just society, a person's ability status would be no more relevant to how she is treated than her eye color. This is not to say that disability would not merit differential treatment or accommodation, but that disability *as such* would not dictate public policy. I then discuss the applications of this argument within non-ideal contexts (5). This framework can also inform our answers to questions about disability, such as "how should people treat non-autonomous disabled beings?" and "should people create disabled beings?" I argue that if it is possible to facilitate a disabled being's autonomous development, it is morally good to do so, but people are not required to refrain from creating disabled or non-autonomous beings (6). To close, I argue that these arguments against welfarist approaches to disability bolster arguments in favor of deferring to the testimony of disabled people about how they experience disability (7).

1   DEFINING DISABILITY

The word "disability" refers to a set of physical conditions. It may also refer to other things. Julian Savulescu, Guy Kahane, and Greg Bognar, among others, argue that disability is not just a physical condition that makes a person's body different from most other peoples' bodies, it is also a difference that makes a person's life worse than it would otherwise be (Bognar 2015; Savulescu and Kahane 2011). Elizabeth Barnes calls this "the bad difference view" (Barnes 2014). Savulescu and Kahane call this view "a welfarist approach" to disability. In contrast, Barnes argues that disability is a mere difference, just another way that a person's body can be, and it is a further question whether disability is good or bad of a person's well-being (Barnes 2014). Whether disability is a mere difference or a bad difference would depend on one's theory of well-being, and according to some theories, the way people with disabilities experience their condition. When it comes to matters of ethics and public policy, whether it matters that disability is a mere difference or a bad difference would depend on one's view of if and how welfarist considerations inform principles of ethics and public policy.

Begin with theories of well-being. Does having a disability make a person's life worse? Savulescu and Kahane state that the concept of disability is inherently normative. Though they do not think that the inherent pro tanto badness of disability establishes that it is bad to be disabled all things considered, or that disability ought to be prevented, on their view, a disability is just a physical condition that reduces a person's well-being for reasons that are not attributable to social prejudice. They contrast this welfarist approach to disability with the social model, which says that the kinds of physical conditions that are marked as disabilities are socially contingent, and that having one of these conditions is only bad for a person because of social prejudice. They also contrast their approach to disability with the medical model, which states that disability is any physical condition that negatively departs from the set of physical abilities that most people have (which is sometimes called normal species functioning). According to Savulescu and Kahane, an advantage of the welfarist approach is that it can accommodate changing conceptions of what is normal, so even if a physical condition causes someone to function in the way that most people do, it could still be a disability if it impairs a person's well-being. Against the social model, Savulescu and Kahane point out that their view can make sense of the intuition that it would be bad to be disabled even in the absence of social prejudice or for reasons other than social prejudice.

Savulescu and Kahane intend their approach to function independently from a theory of well-being. Though their view has "in-built normativity" because it defines disability in terms of the normative concept of well-being, they note that it does not take a stand on which theory of well-being is correct. And in this way, they do not take a stand on which conditions count as a disability because that will depend on one's theory of well-being. They do discuss some broad extensions of their view that will hold for any theory of well-being. For example, in their view disability is not intrinsically worse than other conditions that lower welfare, such as material depravation or bad luck, so it does not characterize certain physical conditions as intrinsically bad apart from their effect on a person's well-being. They also argue that everyone is disabled to an extent because everyone has physical properties that reduce their well-being according to a given theory of well-being.

Savulescu and Kahane's approach represents one way to answer questions about how disability relates to well-being, but critics point out that there is no principled reason to define disability in terms of well-being or to build normativity into the concept of disability at all. Elizabeth Barnes and disability rights advocates suggest that the claim that it is intrinsically worse to have a disabled body is akin to the claim that it is intrinsically worse to have a female body or a dark-skinned body or a short body or a fat body (Barnes 2009b). Some people may think it is worse to have these sorts of bodies, but others may enjoy having these sorts of bodies. In some cases, having this sort of body could make a person's life worse because of social prejudice. However, social prejudice would be unjustified because having a body that is different from the bodies of members of socially dominant groups is not intrinsically worse. Barnes argues that Savulescu and Kahane's position devalues disability and discounts the experiences of people who have disabilities (Barnes 2014).

If disability is a mere difference, defined apart from any particular theory of well-being, then questions about the relationship between disability and well-being are partly empirical questions. To answer them, one must first identify a disability or bodily difference as well as a theory of well-being. One must then ask whether having that particular bodily difference makes a person's life worse according to that particular theory of well-being.[1] If a disability makes a person's life worse according to a given theory of well-being only because those who suffer from it are the victims of prejudice, then it is not the disability that is bad for well-being but patterns of discrimination and disadvantage that one suffers as a result of disability. On the other hand, a disability may make a person's life worse according to a theory of well-being if reduced well-being is attributable to the physical difference even in the absence of social prejudice or a lack of accommodation.

In sum, welfarist accounts of disability, such as those discussed by Savulescu and Kahane define disability as a negative characteristic. In contrast, a descriptive account of disability, which defines it as a mere difference, yields no all-things-considered judgments about whether being disabled is bad for a person. It depends on the nature of the disability, what one thinks is bad for persons in general, and how a person experiences disability.[2] When people talk about disability in everyday conversation they use descriptive and welfarist uses of the term. There is no reason that either side has a particular claim to the term or concept of disability.

But one advantage of the descriptive account is that by defining disability apart from theories of well-being, the descriptive account can accommodate cases where the effect of a person's physical condition on her well-being changes over time. For example, the disability paradox describes a range of circumstances where people have physical conditions that would conventionally be understood as disabilities, but nevertheless they seem to experience the same levels of well-being as nondisabled people on most measures of well-being. If we use the term disability to describe only a set of physical conditions and do not define it in relation to well-being, then we can still maintain that conditions such as deafness and mobility impairment are disabilities despite the disability paradox, which finds that these conditions do not hinder well-being (Moller 2011).

A related advantage of a descriptive definition of disability is that it does not pre-judge how people should respond to disability. One may respond to the disability paradox by claiming that it is an artifact of people's adaptive preferences. One may claim, for example, that disabilities such as mobility impairments and deafness do in fact hinder well-being even if people do not experience being disabled in that way. The descriptive account can accommodate this thought as well, since it may be the case according to some theories of well-being that physical differences hinder well-being even though people with those differences do not experience the hindrances. For example, if well-being consists in what a person's fully informed and rational self would desire for her, then a person who never knew what it was like to see may not know that blindness is bad for her even though it is intuitively worse to be blind. But unlike welfarist approaches, a descriptive approach can also explain instances where a person is disabled but it is genuinely not bad for her.

These considerations may explain why many disability rights advocates insist on a descriptive approach to disability, such as Barnes's mere difference view. Though the descriptive approach can accommodate cases that proponents of welfarist approaches may emphasize (e.g. cases where disability is bad for a person who does not realize that it is bad), the welfarist approach cannot accommodate cases that proponents of descriptive approaches may emphasize (e.g. cases where disability is not bad for a person, but she still has a physical condition that would cause her to identify as disabled). In this way, the descriptive approach can allow for the possibility that a disabled person may not be a reliable judge of her own well-being but does not automatically discount the testimony of those who claim that disability as such does not make one's life worse.

Another advantage of the descriptive approach is that it is more faithful to ordinary uses of the term "disability." Savulescu and Kahane's welfarist approach to disability generates a revisionary account of disability. On their view, everyone is disabled, yet conditions that we normally think of as disabilities (such as deafness) may not be disabilities (Savulescu and Kahane 2011). For this reason, we must still develop arguments to answer normative questions surrounding disability with the welfarist definition in hand, but the arguments would address whether a physical condition is a disability according to the welfarist definition rather than whether a physical condition that we think of as being a disability is bad for those who have it.

So it is better to stick with the conventional categories of disability and just ask whether it is bad to have it than to adopt a revisionary conception of disability and then ask which conditions are bad to have, such that they should be called disabilities. For these reasons, I will use the term disability in the descriptive way going forward because I am interested in whether it is good or bad to have a body that is physically different from other bodies, and whether it is permissible or impermissible to cause a body to be physically different from other bodies.

2   A Kantian Proposal

With the descriptive definition in hand, we can then ask normative questions about disability beyond the question of whether it is bad for a particular person to be disabled according to a certain theory of well-being. For example, we can ask questions about disability rights such as:

- Should officials extend rights to disabled people that they do not extend to nondisabled people?
- Should officials provide disabled people with resources that they do not provide nondisabled people?
- Should officials prohibit people from discriminating against disabled people?
- Should officials require that people accommodate disabled people?
- Is it permissible to cause a person to be disabled?
- Is it permissible to cause a person to be nondisabled?

It is perhaps unsurprising that proponents of welfarist approaches to disability are likely to answer these questions on the basis of a broadly consequentialist moral theory.[3] For these theorists of disability, it is a short walk from a conception of disability that is defined with reference to normative concepts to normative conclusions about how disabled people should be treated. But I have suggested that these normative associations with disability require further argument and cannot be established via definition.

And I am skeptical that these questions should be answered with reference to considerations related to well-being. Rather, I will argue that we should think of disabilities as mere differences and refrain from evaluating these questions about the ethics of disability with reference to consequentialist considerations.

Consequentialist considerations are often cited in philosophical discussions of disability. For example, ethicists have argued that disabled people should have the same rights as nondisabled people and deserve equal treatment, while explaining these claims by an appeal to disabled people's interests (Harris 2001). Similarly, arguments on behalf of providing disabled people with additional resources appeal to considerations, such as diminishing marginal utility or disabled people's interest in receiving additional resources (Arneson 2015). Consequence-minded philosophers are hesitant, however, when it comes questions about whether it is permissible to create a disabled person, on the grounds they predict that a disabled life will be worse in expectation than a nondisabled life (Savulescu 2001; McMahan 2005; Kahane 2009). For similar reasons, some consequentialist philosophers have even submitted that it can be permissible to euthanize a disabled infant and replace her with a nondisabled infant in circumstances where a disabled child's life would otherwise prevent parents from conceiving a nondisabled child (Singer 2011, p. 163).

In contrast, I propose that we can set aside questions of well-being while answering the aforementioned questions about disability rights because, like other questions of rights, disability rights do not depend on whether having a disability is good or bad for a person. Moreover, I also propose that questions about disability rights do not even depend on whether a person's physical conditions qualify as a disability because, more generally, the scope of a person's rights do not depend on physical features of her body.

My argument for this claim relies on a broadly Kantian framework. For this reason, a quick detour into Kantian ethics may be helpful in explaining my claim that we should not consider questions of well-being when settling questions about disability rights. Kant was interested in questions about how to treat people, such as the questions listed above.[4] Kant's goal was to discover principles of action that applied in all circumstances, simply by reflecting on the nature of action. So, for example, you might reflect on the fact that deciding to eat an apple gives you a reason to eat the apple, and infer from that that your ability to decide to act is a source of reasons. Those reasons have authority, Kant argued, because you confer value on your choices by making them. And from that you should infer that you are a source of value, and that your value issues from your ability to make choices. Based on an argument like this, Kant concluded that people should act in ways that treat humanity, or human autonomy, as a source of value in itself and not merely as a means to one's own ends. He called this the Formula of Humanity.[5]

People disagree about whether Kant's argument for the Formula of Humanity or some version of it can successfully explain the whole of the moral landscape. And people also disagree about which substantive choices this formal constraint requires. Christine Korsgaard offers one interpretation of the Formula of Humanity that shows how we can deduce substantive moral principles by reflecting on what it is to act (Korsgaard 1996, p. 107). She argues that we should think of moral reasons as the objective reasons we have whatever our inclinations or desires (in contrast to the subjective reasons we have only in virtue of our desires) (Korsgaard 1996, p. 121). She then argues that people have objective reasons to respect other people's choices because the only thing that each person has reason to value is the capacity to value, which is same capacity as the capacity to choose. Crucially, well-being is *not* unconditionally valuable for people in this universal way because the choices that promote one person's well-being will not promote another's. In contrast, each person does have an unconditional reason to respect other people's choices because once you recognize the value of your own ability to choose, "you must view anyone who has the power of rational choice as having, in virtue of that power, a value conferring status" (Korsgaard 1996, p. 123). In practice then, Kant's argument requires that each person refrain from interfering with other people's choices, but people are not required to attend to conditionally valuable features of others, such as features of their well-being.

David Velleman and Stephen Darwall develop Kant's argument in different ways but with similar conclusions for our purposes. Velleman argues that people have a kind of value, in virtue of their autonomy, that cannot be traded off for the sake of greater well-being, and that the value of a person does not depend on her properties, such as the color of her hair (Velleman 1999a, b). Morality, Velleman argues, is largely indifferent to whether a person's desires are satisfied or whether she is happy. Instead, morality requires protection of and respect for autonomy.

Darwall is skeptical that Kant's project of deriving moral principles simply by reflecting on the nature of action can succeed (Darwall 2009). Instead, he proposes that we can derive moral principles by reflecting on the nature of moral address within a moral community. On his view, people within a moral community must hold one another to the same standards. And while Darwall doesn't say much about the substantive content of those standards, he does clarify that members of the moral community are required to respect each person's equal standing to act as an independent agent within the moral community. About this duty to respect Darwall writes,

> What we attend to [by respecting someone] is not (at least not primarily) what is for someone's welfare or good, but, among other things, what she herself values and holds good from her point of view as an equal independent agent. (Darwall 2009)

For this reason, Darwall argues that it is disrespectful to paternalistically interfere with someone in order to promote her well-being.

This is just a sketch of an argument in favor of a moral theory that does not accord welfarist considerations much weight when answering practical questions about how to treat people. But I think something like this sketch is the right way to think about rights in general, and disability rights in particular. However, I am not committed to the particulars of Kant's or Korsgaard's specific derivations of rights. For example, one might reject the claim that moral reasons are the objective reasons that all people must recognize regardless of their desires. But even if one holds that moral reasons are ultimately subjective, it is not clear that people have rights in virtue of welfarist considerations. Michael Smith argues that a person has moral reason to do what she would desire that she do were she fully informed and rational (Smith 2011, p. 357). And Smith concludes that such a being would desire that no one interfere with the exercise of her rational capacities and that she does what she can to ensure that she has rational capacities to exercise in the future, but she would not necessarily desire the promotion of her well-being (Smith 2011).

Others arrive at similar conclusions via a different route.[6] The conclusion of all these arguments is that considerations of well-being do not bear on questions about people's rights and duties. Utilitarianism, the view that we ought to promote the well-being of the greatest number of people, is the clearest philosophical rival to the Kantian approach. Against utilitarianism, Kantians reply that this kind of reasoning permits people to be used as means for the promotion of overall well-being. In principle, utilitarianism permits killing the one to save the many. Kantian ethics prohibits this kind of conduct. Each person has moral status in virtue of her autonomy that places everyone else under a duty to respect her choices as long as she is complying with her own duty to respect the choices of others. In this way, the Kantian approach protects individuals from being treated as means for the promotion of others' (or their own) well-being.

Turning to disability rights, Kantians would therefore emphasize that it is a mistake to focus on whether it is good or bad for a person's well-being to be disabled. So Kantians would echo the familiar critiques of utilitarian approaches that are advanced within the disability rights community, such as objections to the use of Quality Adjusted Life Years in decisions about resource allocation and objections to policies that permit euthanasia for disabled infants but not for nondisabled infants. In contrast, Kantians answer questions about disability rights with reference to the claims that disabled and nondisabled people have with reference to the value that is intrinsic to all autonomous people.[7]

3   DISABILITY RIGHTS

How does the broadly Kantian perspective that I have described bear on the above questions of disability rights? In this section, I will present some answers to questions about disability rights for people with physical disabilities.[8] For each normative question concerning physical disabilities, the crucial distinction between Kantian approaches and welfarist approaches to disability is that the effect of disability on a person's well-being does not bear directly on the normative question at stake. Though considerations of well-being may bear indirectly on questions related to the ethics of disability insofar as people make choices based on how being disabled or nondisabled will affect their well-being, ultimately a person's choices should dictate her treatment.

For example, imagine someone who chooses to undergo surgery that would restore her sight. Gaining the ability to see may improve her well-being by expanding her employment opportunities, improving her safety, and enabling her to enjoy visual forms of entertainment. Or gaining sight could hinder her well-being by alienating her from the blind community and causing her to feel pressure to comply with aesthetic norms that she previously felt free to ignore. But whether becoming disabled or nondisabled is good for her well-being is irrelevant to questions about whether she should be permitted or forced to undergo surgery. From a Kantian perspective, her choice to undergo surgery ought to be respected, even if surgery would set back her interests and welfare. If she chose differently, her decision to refuse surgery ought to be respected, even if surgery would have promoted her well-being.

Similarly, as Barnes argues, the reason that it is wrong to cause a nondisabled person to become disabled is that it would violate his bodily rights. Even if a person paternalistically disabled another person in order to promote his well-being, and the decision to cause disability did successfully promote the welfare of his victim, it would still be impermissible to assault another person and cause disability to a person who did not consent. On the other hand, if a person chooses to become disabled, his choice ought to be respected, even if it makes his life worse. In these cases, moral questions about disability are settled not by an appeal to considerations related to welfare but rather with reference to people's more general entitlement that others respect their freedom to choose what happens to their bodies.

In these and other questions concerning the rights of disabled and nondisabled people, disability per se is not normatively significant. What matters is whether a person's status as a disabled or nondisabled person is a result of her exercising her rights or a result of a violation of her bodily rights. So the reason that public officials should extend the same rights to disabled people that they extend to nondisabled people is that disabled people are capable of making autonomous decisions, just as nondisabled people are capable of choosing. To say that disabled people deserve equal treatment because treating them like nondisabled people would promote their well-being or aggregate well-being would be to cite the wrong kind of reason in favor of equal treatment.

These insights can shed light on specific questions about whether disabled people should have rights that nondisabled people do not have, such as questions about the right to die. In some jurisdictions, only people with terminal or degenerative diseases or disabilities are permitted to choose assisted dying. In contrast, healthy, nondisabled people are not permitted to choose to die with assistance from a medical professional. Though proponents of the welfarist approach generally recognize the importance of autonomy, if only as a way of promoting well-being on balance, a welfarist might support this policy to the extent that disability and illness reduced a person's well-being and public policy aimed to promote well-being on balance. If so, then a disabled person's death would involve less of a total loss of lifetime well-being than a similarly situated nondisabled person's death. So differential treatment could be warranted in light of the discrepant experiences of each group.

Yet disability rights advocates argue that polices that single out disabled people as having rights to die implicitly suggest that disabled lives are less valuable because it is worse to be disabled, all else equal. This criticism is apt if nondisabled people are prevented from assisted dying for the sake of their future well-being. If so, then one might reasonably ask why paternalistic officials do not value disabled people's future well-being in the same way.

But on the Kantian approach, paternalistic prohibitions of assisted dying either should be permitted for all persons or prohibited. Some Kantians (including myself) argue that officials should respect people's autonomous choices to die because the right to die is a species of more general bodily rights and rights against paternalistic interference. But other Kantians, notably Velleman, argue that while moral requirement that people respect the value of autonomy generally calls for people to refrain from interference and to respect others' choices, it would be a contradiction to argue that the decision to destroy one's autonomous capacities ought to be respected in virtue of the value of those very same autonomous capacities. Either way, according to the Kantian approach, a person's ability status is irrelevant to her moral status. As above, if a person has the right to die or a more general right against interference, it is in virtue of her autonomy and not in virtue of whether she has a physical condition that sets back her welfare.

A feature of this Kantian approach to disability is that a person has the standing to demand that her choices be respected once her autonomous capacities exceed a particular threshold. So, it is not as if people whose autonomous capacities are more developed are worthier of respect.[9] This dichotomous approach to moral status reflects the kind of treatment that people have in virtue of their autonomy.[10] To respect a person is generally to refrain from interfering with her choices. It is not as if a person can interfere to a greater or lesser extent. Interference is disrespectful whenever it deprives a person of the ability to make her own choices, which she is entitled to do in virtue of her autonomy. For this reason, once a person is sufficiently autonomous, she has equal standing within the moral community to demand that others respect her choices.[11]

The Kantian approach can also explain why disabled people have rights against discrimination and rights to accommodation. Consider anti-discrimination requirements first. In some circumstances, people's rights against interference require that others respect their rights to act in ways that discriminate against certain groups (Zwolinski 2006). Though refusing to date people on the basis of physical characteristics, such as disability or race, may reflect poorly on a person's character, anti-discrimination law should not prohibit people from choosing romantic partners without reference to physical characteristics. This is because people may have legitimate reason to consider physical characteristics when choosing a romantic partner since one of the goods of a romantic relationship is mutual physical attraction.

But in other cases, physical characteristics shouldn't determine the range of choices that are available to a person. For example, in most cases landlords do not have good reason to consider whether their tenants are deaf, Latina, short, or attractive when they consider rental applications. Sophia Moreau argues that in these circumstances discrimination is wrong because it hinders people's interest in deliberative freedom, which is the freedom to make decisions in ways that are insulated from the influence of normatively extraneous traits (Moreau 2010). Though Moreau characterizes this argument in terms of interests and welfare, a Kantian may similarly cite cases where discrimination, especially by public officials, unduly limits people's entitlement to make decisions about how to live.

Another way that a Kantian may explain the wrongness of discrimination is that discrimination is often incompatible with the ideal of human dignity. Within the Kantian framework, a person's choices ought to be respected in virtue of the value of her autonomy. In this way, the value of autonomy sets limits on how people must treat each other. Paternalistic interference is therefore wrong because interference disrupts the exercise of an intrinsically valuable capacity (autonomy) for the sake of goods that are only conditionally valuable, such as welfare.[12] Kantians may advance a similar criticism of discrimination. As Deborah Hellman argues, discrimination can be demeaning insofar as it conveys ideas that a person's value is determined by features of her body (Hellman 2008, p. 172). In this way, discrimination implicitly denies the Kantian premise that all autonomous people have equal moral worth and merit equal respect.[13]

Turning to matters of public accommodation, the Kantian approach could also justify policies that support the public provision of accommodation for disabled people or it could justify policies that do not accommodate people's physical disabilities. The case against public accommodation would appeal to the view that public officials should avoid coercing people in order to advance perfectionist aims.[14] If we think of accommodation as valuing certain goods, such as mobility and accessible communication, over others, then accommodation might be seen as violating the ideal of equal treatment that justifies anti-discrimination policy.

On the other hand, proponents of a broadly Kantian approach might also argue that public services are provided by coercing citizens in order to advantage some and disadvantage others. Since all policies limit people's autonomy without their consent to some extent, we must ask whether the interference was justified to assess the permissibility of such a policy. And it is not justified that public officials design buildings and communications in ways that systematically disadvantage and exclude people with certain physical characteristics. So officials should be required to accommodate people with disabilities. Moreover, insofar as policies have historically encouraged or facilitated private patterns of exclusion and disadvantage within the public sphere, public officials today may require public accommodation for people with disabilities as a kind of compensation for previous acts of state-sponsored injustice.

These arguments show that the Kantian approach has the resources to answer normative questions about disability and disability rights. Though the Kantian arguments I presented do not settle many of these questions either way, they point to the ways that we can answer questions about the treatment of disabled and nondisabled people without first answering questions about the relationship between disability and well-being.

4   IDEAL AND NON-IDEAL QUESTIONS

According to the position that I have defended, there are no intrinsic differences between the rights that people with disabilities have and the rights that all persons have in virtue of their autonomy. This position complements analyses that characterize disability as a social construction or a mere difference, though my argument does not directly refute the claim that disabled people are intrinsically different. I only deny that the differences between disabled and nondisabled people are not themselves morally significant because, though it may be more difficult in some cases to respect disabled people's rights, having a disabled body does not undermine a person's moral status or claims to equal rights.

An analogy to gender may clarify this point. Some people argue that gender differences (which they sometimes conflate with sex differences) are intrinsic. Others claim that gender is a social construction. I am sympathetic to the latter view. But whatever one's views about whether gender is socially constructed, it remains true that disrespect or legal discrimination on the basis of gender is wrong and that people of both genders should have the same rights. This is not to suggest that people should always minimize the salience of gender. People may identify with a particular gender and take pride in that identity. But when the salience of gender becomes more than a personal identity and officials create gendered locker rooms or bathrooms in public buildings, people of both genders no longer have the same rights and such policies violate the principle of equal respect that is central to the Kantian ethos (Overall 2007).

For these reasons, Susan Okin argued that social policy should aim to reduce the social salience of gender identity in order to diminish the marginalization and stigmatization of women. She argued that ideally, "in social structures and practices, one's sex [and gender] is of no more social relevance than one's eye color or the length of one's toes" (Okin 1991, p. 171). Similarly, whether one is disabled or nondisabled should also be of no more social relevance than physical characteristics like eye color or toe length in social and political contexts, even if disabled people identify and take pride in being disabled within the private sphere.

Okin's argument describes an ideal. In non-ideal contexts, where people do treat people differently on the basis of gender or disability, acting as if gender and disability are irrelevant may be counterproductive. In some circumstances, when people fail to comply with principles of justice, it is appropriate to act in ways that would be incompatible with principles of justice in ideal circumstances (Valentini 2012). For example, invoking Kant's metaphor of the Kingdom of Ends, Rae Langton argues that even though people have a duty not lie or treat others strategically, when people fail to comply with their duties, "strategy for Kingdom's sake" is warranted (Langton 1992). Similarly, Tamar Schapiro argues that people may permissibly violate one's duty as a member of the moral community in order to bring people who are grossly immoral back into a moral relationship (Schapiro 2006). Thomas Hill even goes so far as to say that one may have a Kantian duty of self-respect to resist the unjust conduct of others (Hill 2010).

All of which is to say that even if it were wrong in principle to treat people in ways that emphasize gender identity or disability over their identities as people who have full moral status whatever their characteristics, when faced with unjust circumstances, it may be permissible to violate this principle in order to bring about a more just society for women and disabled people. The questions then turn to matters of strategy. If accounting for gender or ability status could rectify existing inequalities between men and women or nondisabled and disabled people, then it may be permissible to act on the basis of these distinctions in order to bring about a society where such distinctions are no longer entrenched in our social institutions. If providing disabled people with additional medical resources could compensate them for the harms caused by institutionalized discrimination against disabled people in the allocation of medical resources, then perhaps officials should provide disabled people with additional resources. Or perhaps such efforts would be counterproductive. But at least in principle, the Kantian approach allows that officials and citizens may in some circumstances treat people differently on the basis of their physical characteristics in order to bring about the ideal of equal respect.

5   CAPACITY AND DISABILITY

To this point I have focused on physical disabilities, such as deafness, blindness, and mobility impairments. I argue that it is wrong to cause a nondisabled person to become disabled or to cause a disabled person to become nondisabled without her consent, but that the wrongness of these actions derives from the moral significance of autonomy and bodily rights. Considerations related to well-being do not explain why it is wrong to cause disability or nondisability, because if a person consented to become disabled or nondisabled and even if her choice made her worse off on balance, it still wouldn't be wrong to change her ability status, and likewise without consent, it is always wrong to change a person's ability status.[15]

The Kantian approach is less clear in cases concerning disability and beings that are not autonomous. In this section, I will address the ethics of causing disability and nondisability for non-autonomous beings at the point of conception and during infancy. I will also offer some tentative remarks on the moral status of people with cognitive disabilities that permanently undermine their autonomy.

Let us begin with cases of conception. Savulescu and Kahane argue that while parents should have the procreative freedom to deliberately conceive children with disabilities like deafness or dwarfism, they ought not do it because they predict that disabled people are worse off simply because they are disabled. McMahan argues similarly that it would be wrong for a person to recklessly conceive in a way that caused her to conceive a disabled baby when she could have conceived a nondisabled baby instead.

In response, Elizabeth Barnes argues, "it is not wrong to cause a disabled rather than a nondisabled person to exist" because it is not intrinsically worse to be disabled (Barnes 2014). Similarly, Adrienne Asch and David Wasserman argue that prospective parents have duties, in virtue of their role as parents, to "unconditionally welcome" their children whatever their ability status (Asch and Wasserman 2014, p. 428). As long as a child has a life worth living, the hardship associated with being disabled is a "perfectly acceptable price to pay for a life he [or she] could not have without it" (Wasserman 2005). So, while there may be other reasons to discourage people to actively attempt to select their child's traits (Sandel 2004), parents do not have a duty to refrain from conceiving disabled children as such.

Proponents of a Kantian approach to disability should side with the latter camp. Even if disability were a hardship, it would not be wrong to conceive a disabled child because a person's life is valuable in virtue of the value of the autonomous person she becomes, not in virtue of the benefits she experiences and the burdens she avoids. Against this position, David Velleman argues that each person has a right to be created with due consideration for the value of humanity, which requires the provision of more than a life worth living (Velleman 2008). Specifically, Velleman argues that prospective parents must give their children the best start in life. On Velleman's account, being born with a disability can violate the child's right, so it would be impermissible to conceive a disabled child out of a failure to give due consideration to the quality of the child's life, and there is something regrettable about having a disabled child more generally (Velleman 2008).

In addition to the possibility that having a disability does not necessarily make a person's life worse, we might also question Velleman's claim that people should avoid creating a life that is worse because of a disability. If parents must give their children the best start in life, then Velleman's conception of parental duty seems excessively demanding. In addition, though Velleman agrees that parents have reason to love their disabled children, his arguments against creating disabled children are in tension with other claims he makes about the nature of love and morality, where he argues that love is a moral emotion that consists in seeing the full value of humanity in a particular person, regardless of that person's physical characteristics or properties (Velleman 1999a). Since the moral emotions that we have in recognition of the value of humanity do not usually depend on whether a person has an abled or disabled body, it is unclear why accounting for the value of humanity would require people to avoid creating disabled children.

Another reason to reject Velleman's argument that conceiving a disabled child violates the child's rights is that it is unclear whose rights are violated at the moment of conception. If a child has a right to be born nondisabled and parents have a duty to not conceive disabled children, then parents who comply with such a duty would refrain from conceiving a disabled child for the sake of a child that does not, and in virtue of their decision, never will exist. People have duties to respect each other because they are required to recognize value of autonomy in themselves and others. But non-existent people have no such value, so no such claims can be made about their rights (Parfit 1986). At what point then would conceiving a disabled child violate his rights? It is default to locate the source of a duty to not have created a disabled child since satisfying that duty, by necessity, would consist in satisfying a duty to no one.

The same cannot be said, however, about causing an infant or very young child to become disabled or nondisabled. On one hand, parents and health professionals should make medical decisions on behalf of children because children do not have the standing in virtue of their autonomy to demand that others respect their choices (Dare 2009). It is then an open question which values should inform that decision-making. Many people argue that decisions should be made to promote a child's interests going forward, but leave open which interests merit consideration (Committee on Bioethics 1995). Others argue that parents and professionals should act in ways that children would subsequently consent to, though this proposal faces the obvious challenge of predicting what a person would subsequently consent to (Davis 2004). Barnes claims that it is not necessarily wrong to cause an infant to become disabled, but it is risky, just as it is risky to cause an infant to become nondisabled, suggesting that decision makers should maintain a child's ability status until he is capable of choosing for himself (Barnes 2014).

Kantians tend to approach children as people whose autonomy is temporarily deficient. In these circumstances, Tamar Schapiro argues that the conditions that usually give moral norms their force are incomplete because the child does not yet have the standing to demand that others respect her choices (Schapiro 2006). Respecting a child's rights is impossible because people have rights in virtue of their autonomy, but children are not yet entirely autonomous—over the course of childhood they develop their autonomy within limited domains until they are sufficiently autonomous to command our respect as members of the moral community. This doesn't mean that all bets are off when interacting with children, however, or that people should try to promote a child's well-being either in the moment or over the course of the child's life. Instead, Schapiro argues that people should respect children's choices in the domains where they are capable of making decisions, partly in recognition of their authority within that domain and partly in order to further develop their autonomous capacities and to bring them into a moral relationship with others (Schapiro 1999). Schapiro writes, "Our end as adults cannot be to control children, it must be to make them free to control themselves" (Schapiro 1999, p. 736).

A Kantian may return to the question of causing children to be nondisabled or disabled with this ideal in mind. A parent or medical professional acts wrongly to the extent that he changes a child's ability status in order to control him. If a parent or professional causes a child to be disabled or nondisabled in order to further his autonomous development, then intervention is permissible. For example, a physician may choose to amputate a pediatric cancer patient's leg in order to spare the child of high-dose radiation treatment, which could undermine his ability to reason going forward. Or a physician may recommend cochlear implants as a way of helping a deaf child who is struggling in school and socially.

This perspective is similar to Matthew Liao's argument that all human beings are right-holders because they all have the genetic basis for moral agency, which Kantians emphasize as well (Liao 2010). But perhaps unlike the Kantian perspective, Liao argues that even those who have genetic conditions that make it genuinely impossible to make autonomous decisions have the genetic basis for moral agency in virtue of their humanity. Patrick Kain argues that Kant would have favored respecting beings without the capacity to act autonomously at least for pragmatic reasons and because he thought that all members of the human species shared an essential disposition to be autonomous, which is sufficient for moral status (Kain 2009).

Alternatively, proponents of the Kantian approach might regard the possession of autonomous capacities (even if they are dormant or impaired) as a necessary condition for others to have duties to respect a being. According to such a view, people with severe cognitive disabilities would not have the moral status I described above and their choices would not command the same respect as autonomous people's choices. For example, paternalism toward people whose disabilities substantially inhibit their autonomy would be justifiable when paternalistic interference with autonomous people in similar circumstances would not.

Furthermore, insofar as parents and others have moral reasons to cultivate their children's autonomy, it would be impermissible to cause children to have cognitive disabilities that permanently impaired their autonomy (Schapiro 1999).[16] These considerations would not necessarily prohibit creating humans that are permanently non-autonomous in virtue of a genetic condition, just as creating beings with other disabilities does not harm or wrong those who are created. However, if parents had access to cognitive enhancements that could cause their non-autonomous disabled children to become autonomous, then the same considerations that support parental duties to promote the autonomy of their nondisabled children would also support parental duties to cognitively enhance their non-autonomous disabled children.

Even on this interpretation of the Kantian framework, there may still be reasons to care for non-autonomous humans who have severe cognitive disabilities. Consider for example Korsgaard's argument in favor of animal rights—she argues that each person is required to recognize not only the value of humanity but also the value of all beings who are the source of normative claim (Korsgaard 2004).[17] Animals generate different kinds of normative claims—they act for the sake of their natural good rather than in order to achieve their ends, but just as we must recognize the normative claims that other people make on us to respect their choices, we should also recognize animals' claims that their natural good be advanced. A similar justification may explain why intrinsically non-autonomous persons with severe cognitive disabilities still have a kind of moral status that would give us reason to refrain from mistreating them or using them as means, though such an argument would not support a duty to respect their choices.

6   TESTIMONY AND DEFERENCE

To this point I have argued in favor of a Kantian approach to disability. On this approach, questions about the relationship between well-being and ability are not relevant to questions about causing disability or about the treatment of disabled people, except in cases where a disability undermines a person's autonomous capacities in ways that make autonomous choice going forward impossible. But Kantian approaches to disability are also relevant to debates about disability and well-being. To close, I will discuss how a Kantian theory of value may inform debates about whether disability is a hardship or a mere difference.

According to Kant and Kantians, autonomy (aka "the good will") has intrinsic value. It is "like a jewel" that shines having full worth in itself, meaning that the value of autonomy doesn't depend on whether it is useful, or whether it serves any other value (Kant 2012, p. 10). The value of an autonomous person doesn't even depend on whether she values herself, since in order to act autonomously at all, she must presuppose that her will has a kind of value, even if she doesn't recognize it (Langton 2007). In contrast, happiness is only valuable in the presence of a good will. Though people may value happiness for its own sake, Kantians claim that it is only because people value happiness that happiness is valuable (Langton 2007). In other words, happiness is only subjectively valuable.

This Kantian understanding of the value of welfare reframes debates about whether disability is a mere difference or a hardship. The answer is that it depends on whether people (who are objectively and intrinsically valuable) subjectively value being disabled or nondisabled. Because the Kantian approach to welfare is informed by the subjective experiences of disabled people, policies that are informed by this approach are more likely to avoid practical problems of testimonial injustice—where disabled people's experiences are treated as less credible in virtue of ablest prejudices (Fricker 2009).

This way of thinking about value lends further support to disability rights advocates' calls for greater deference to the lived experiences of disabled people. Many disabled people do not experience their disabilities as hardships but do experience stigmatizing arguments that it is worse to be disabled as a hardship. Since the value of disability is determined by the subjective experience of people who are disabled, people should therefore defer to disabled people's value judgments about these topics and refrain from characterizing disability as an intrinsic hardship. On the other hand, people should also defer to the judgments of disabled people who report negative experiences and who would value becoming nondisabled. So, while Barnes rejects the language of "curing" disability on the grounds that it expresses the view that disabilities are negative physical conditions that should be avoided, for some people, this view and the language of curing disability is appropriate (Barnes 2014).

Those who hold an objective theory of well-being may object on the grounds that intuitively, disabled people's preferences are adaptive responses to unjust conditions and ought to be discounted.[18] Or, one may defend a conception of harm whereby being harmed is defined as being physically disabled, and thus, disability always involves a kind of moral loss.[19] To this point, disability advocates reply that those who characterize disability as a harm and disability pride as an adaptive preference face significant epistemic hurdles in establishing this claim since, even according to most objective theories of well-being, the first-person testimony of disabled people would be one of the best sources of evidence about whether a disability is bad for a person (Barnes 2009a). The Kantian approach lends further support to this argument by denying the claim that well-being is objectively valuable in the first place. Since physical disabilities do not impair a person's ability to confer value on her condition, disabled people who identify with the disability pride movement are correct when they claim that disability is a valuable form of difference, just as disabled people who seek "cures" are correct in claiming that disability is a misfortune.

7   CONCLUSION

Many debates about the ethics of disability and disability rights focus on the hardships associated with being disabled. In this chapter, I have argued that whether being disabled is a hardship or a mere difference should not change our judgments about causing disability or disability rights. Instead, I developed a Kantian framework for understanding disability. The Kantian approach can explain why it doesn't matter whether causing nondisability or disability is good or bad for a person; rather what matters is whether a person consents to become disabled or nondisabled. I also described ways that a Kantian framework can inform debates about disability discrimination, accommodation, creating disabled people, changing the ability status of children, and the treatment of people with cognitive disabilities. Finally, I defended a Kantian answer to the question of whether disability makes a person's life worse, and I argued that the value of being disabled or nondisabled depends on people's attitudes toward their ability status. Stepping back from these particular arguments, as a general rule, the Kantian approach supports a policy of respecting the choices of disabled and nondisabled people and deferring to people with disabilities about the value of their ability status.

NOTES

1. To get a sense of the descriptive account of disability, it may be helpful to see how it would function for different disabilities and different theories of well-being. For example, say that a desire-satisfaction theory of well-being is correct. If so, then whether deafness is bad for a person would depend on whether deafness made it more difficult for her to satisfy her present desires, her desires overall, her higher-order desires, or the desires she would have if she were fully informed and rational. When asking these questions, we should answer them with respect to the independent effect of deafness,

considered apart from anti-deaf discrimination and the difficulties of living in an oralist culture. Or, say that the correct theory of well-being is hedonism. If having mobility impairments due to an amputated foot causes a person to experience less pleasure, or if mobility impairments barred someone from experiencing higher-order pleasures, then the disability of having mobility impairments would make a person's life worse.

2. If the correct theory of well-being is an objective list theory, then it is unclear whether disability is defined in a welfarist way or not. One may have an objective list theory of well-being that includes normal species functioning or physical ability as necessary for human flourishing. If so, then even though one may have a descriptive definition of disability, it will be extensionally identical to a welfarist definition of disability, like Savulescu and Kahane's, because the set of conditions defined as disability would be coextensive with a set of conditions that reduced well-being. On the other hand, if an objective list theorist of well-being emphasizes conditions like autonomy and meaning, then conditions that are defined as disabilities according to descriptive definitions of disability may include some conditions that do not hinder well-being.

3. And similarly, proponents of the medical model of disability are likely to answer these questions with reference to a moral theory that values normal functioning or health promotion.

4. Kant called an action an imperative if it was way one should act, and he argued that imperatives could be either categorical, referring to the things one should do in any circumstances, or hypothetical, referring to the things one should do only in some circumstances. To illustrate this point, it may be helpful to consider an analogy to the norms governing belief. Some beliefs are hypothetical, such as "If I won the lottery, I would give 80 percent of my wealth to charity" and others are categorical, such as "$1+1 = 2$". But unlike hypothetical and categorical theoretical reasoning, imperatives in practical reasoning could not be avoided by merely suspending judgment because while a person may refrain from forming beliefs, she cannot refrain from acting.

5. Kant also concluded that people should not act on the basis of principles that would contradict other principles they held (The Formula of Universal Law) and that people should act in ways that are consistent with both the Formula of Humanity and of Universal Law. He called the hypothetical world where people obeyed these two formulas the Kingdom of Ends.

6. Another way of capturing this idea is by examining the distinction between will and interest theories of rights. Interest theorists argue that rights should function to promote a person's well-being, whereas will theorists argue that rights should function to protect people's authority to make decisions about

their lives. On this distinction, the function of rights that I am focusing on is in line with the will theory of rights. (Wenar 2015)

7. Some people appeal to Kantian principles in order to show that people have a duty to promote the autonomy of others too (Ebels-Duggan 2008). As long as promotion of people's autonomy is limited by people's duties to respect others' choices, this view is compatible with the Kantian principles I outlined in this section. In contrast, what Smith calls a "consequentialism of rights," where one holds that people have duties to minimize rights violations or promote the exercise of people's rights, would not be compatible with the Kantian principles I am defending (Smith 2009). For example, when philosophers, such as Denis Arnold and Norman Bowie, argue that Kantian principles require that managers promote the autonomy of workers, their interpretation of Kantianism departs from the principles I am defending (Arnold and Bowie 2003).

8. Where physical disabilities are defined as those that do not impair their ability to make autonomous decisions. These include disabilities that primarily affect non-cognitive abilities, such as mobility, hearing, or sight, as well as conditions that cause chronic pain.

9. For example, we might imagine people who develop heightened cognitive abilities through natural selection, cultural evolution, or human enhancement, and that their ability to make autonomous choices, such as the ability to follow through with long-term plans, might exceed most people's current capacities. But the presence of such trans-humans would not undermine Kantian justifications for individual rights, since on the Kantian account, one must possess only the ability to choose for her choices to merit respect (Buchanan 2009).

10. Against this position, David DeGrazia argues that that people's rights could plausibly vary with respect to their cognitive capacities, including the capacity to make autonomous choices (DeGrazia 2008).

11. On this point, Darwall distinguishes between recognition respect and appraisal respect (Darwall 1977). Though one may have more or less appraisal respect for a person in acknowledgment of whether he has achieved things or displayed properties that merit more or less respect of this sort, recognition respect refers to the way in which a person may be worthy of respect in virtue of his mere membership in the moral community, which does not vary with respect to a person's properties (Darwall 2009).

12. And on some accounts, such as Velleman's, the same can be said of suicide (Velleman 1999b).

13. Other philosophers have tied the wrongness of discrimination to the inappropriateness of assigning benefits or burdens to people who do not deserve them (Altman 2015; Goldman 2015). But unlike these accounts of why discrimination is wrong, the Kantian argument against discrimination does

not require that we accept particular standards of merit in industries or admissions criteria. Instead, the Kantian arguments only require that all people merit equal moral consideration and equal respect.

14. Whether it is objectionably perfectionistic to privilege health or ability in matters of distributive justice is controversial. According to the Kantian framework that I am developing, some health-related goods may reasonably be distinguished from other goods by their relation to autonomy. Norman Daniels develops an argument to this effect when he argues that officials should provide people foremost with the resources that are necessary for them to participate as equals in a fair society, and not simply with whatever resources would further their interests or promote their well-being (Daniels 1981). A similar argument may be made on behalf of privileging goods that would facilitate the development or exercise of a person's autonomous capacities.

15. In emergency situations where consent is impossible, the following discussion about causing disability and nondisability in children (who, like an unconscious patient, are temporarily non-autonomous) would apply to temporarily non-autonomous adults too.

16. I say "in most cases" because, in some cases, pregnant mothers may be entitled to cause prenatal injuries that prevent a child from developing his autonomous capacities (e.g. by using certain drugs or making a risky labor decision). And while she would have strong moral reasons not to cause such an injury, it would be permissible in the sense that she would not be liable to be interfered with or punished for her choice because causing prenatal injury would be a choice she was entitled to make in virtue of her bodily rights.

17. It is controversial to draw an analogy between cognitively disabled people and animals (Wasserman et al. 2013), and I have suggested that there may be other ways to distinguish between cognitively disabled humans and nonhuman animals. However, this analogy is appropriate as an example of one way that a Kantian framework may inform questions about how people with cognitive disabilities should be treated.

18. Philosophers sometimes make similar arguments regarding women's economic preferences or low wage workers' preferences to remain in harmful industries (Nussbaum 2001; Zimmerman 2003).

19. Seana Shiffrin defends a view like this with respect to causing disability, and elsewhere she links the harm of being disabled to an ideal of autonomy, which is undermined by disability (Shiffrin 1999, 2012). Elizabeth Harman also conceives of disability as pro tanto intrinsically harmful (Harman 2009).

REFERENCES

Altman, Andrew. 2015. Discrimination. In *The Stanford encyclopedia of philosophy*, ed. Edward N. Zalta. http://plato.stanford.edu/archives/fall2015/entries/disc rimination/

Arneson, Richard J. 2015. *Disability, discrimination and priority*. https://books.google.com/books?hl=en&lr=&id=I4FACwAAQBAJ&oi=fnd&pg=PT48&ots=ZE7WEbOgvt&sig=-ssJrFNOXETYH7tYj955ka6ajTk

Arnold, Denis G., and Norman E. Bowie. 2003. Sweatshops and respect for persons. *Business Ethics Quarterly* 13 (2): 221–242.

Asch, Adrienne, and David Wasserman. 2014. Reproductive testing for disability. In *The Routledge companion to bioethics*, ed. John D. Arras, Elizabeth Fenton, and Rebecca Kukla. New York/Oxon: Routledge.

Barnes, Elizabeth. 2009a. Disability and adaptive preference1. *Philosophical Perspectives* 23 (1): 1–22.

———. 2009b. Disability, minority, and difference. *Journal of Applied Philosophy* 26 (4): 337–355.

———. 2014. Valuing disability, causing disability. *Ethics* 125 (1): 88–113. doi:10.1086/677021

Bognar, Greg. 2015. Is disability mere difference? *Journal of Medical Ethics*, November, medethics – 2015-102911. doi:10.1136/medethics-2015-102911

Buchanan, Allen. 2009. Moral status and human enhancement. *Philosophy & Public Affairs* 37 (4): 346–381. doi:10.1111/j.1088-4963.2009.01166.x

Committee on Bioethics. 1995. Informed consent, parental permission, and assent in pediatric practice. *Pediatrics* 95 (2): 314–317.

Daniels, Norman. 1981. Health-care needs and distributive justice. *Philosophy & Public Affairs* 10 (2): 146–179.

Dare, Tim. 2009. Parental rights and medical decisions. *Pediatric Anesthesia* 19 (10): 947–952. doi:10.1111/j.1460-9592.2009.03094.x

Darwall, Stephen. 1977. Two kinds of respect. *Ethics* 88 (1): 36–49.

———. 2009. *The second-person standpoint: Morality, respect, and accountability*. Cambridge, MA: Harvard University Press.

Davis, John K. 2004. Precedent autonomy and subsequent consent. *Ethical Theory and Moral Practice: An International Forum* 7 (3): 267–291.

DeGrazia, David. 2008. Moral status as a matter of degree? *The Southern Journal of Philosophy* 46 (2): 181–198. doi:10.1111/j.2041-6962.2008.tb00075.x

Ebels-Duggan, Kyla. 2008. Against beneficence: A normative account of love. *Ethics* 119 (1): 142–170. doi:10.1086/592310

Fricker, Miranda. 2009. *Epistemic injustice: Power and the ethics of knowing*. 1st ed. Oxford/New York: Oxford University Press.

Goldman, Alan H. 2015. *Justice and reverse discrimination*. Princeton: Princeton University Press.

Harman, Elizabeth. 2009. Harming as causing harm. In *Harming future persons: Ethics, genetics and the nonidentity problem*, ed. Melinda A. Roberts and David T. Wasserman, 137–154. Springer. http://link.springer.com/cha pter/10.1007/978-1-4020-5697-0_7

Harris, John. 2001. One principle and three fallacies of disability studies. *Journal of Medical Ethics* 27 (6): 383–387.

Hellman, Deborah. 2008. *When is discrimination wrong?* Cambridge, MA: Harvard University Press.

Hill, E. Thomas, Jr. 2010. Moral responsibilities of bystanders. *Journal of Social Philosophy* 41 (1): 28–39.

Kahane, Guy. 2009. Non-identity, self-defeat, and attitudes to future children. *Philosophical Studies* 145 (2): 193–214.

Kain, Patrick. 2009. Kant's defense of human moral status. *Journal of the History of Philosophy* 47 (1): 59–101. doi:10.1353/hph.0.0083

Kant, Immanual. 2012. *Groundwork of the metaphysics of morals*. Cambridge: Cambridge University Press.

Korsgaard, Christine M. 1996. *Creating the kingdom of ends*. Cambridge: Cambridge University Press.

———. 2004. Fellow creatures: Kantian ethics and our duties to animals. *The Tanner Lectures on Human Values* 25: 26.

Langton, Rae. 1992. *Duty and desolation*. http://philpapers.org/rec/RAEDAD

———. 2007. Objective and unconditioned value. *The Philosophical Review* 116 (2): 157–185.

Liao, S. Matthew. 2010. The basis of human moral status. *Journal of Moral Philosophy* 7 (2): 159–179.

McMahan, Jeff. 2005. Causing disabled people to exist and causing people to be disabled*. *Ethics* 116 (1): 77–99.

Moller, Dan. 2011. Wealth, disability, and happiness. *Philosophy & Public Affairs* 39 (2): 177–206.

Moreau, Sophia. 2010. What is discrimination? *Philosophy & Public Affairs* 38 (2): 143–179.

Nussbaum, Martha C. 2001. Symposium on Amartya Sen's philosophy: 5 adaptive preferences and women's options. *Economics and Philosophy* 17 (01): 67–88.

Okin, Susan Moller. 1991. *Justice, gender, and the family*. 50843rd ed. New York: Basic Books.

Overall, Christine. 2007. Public toilets: Sex segregation revisited. *Ethics & The Environment* 12 (2): 71–91.

Parfit, Derek. 1986. *Reasons and persons*. Oxford: Oxford University Press.

Sandel, Michael. 2004. The case against perfection. *The Atlantic Monthly* 293 (3): 51–62.

Savulescu, J. 2001. Procreative beneficence: Why we should select the best children. *Bioethics* 15 (5–6): 413–426.

Savulescu, Julian, and Guy Kahane. 2011. Disability: A welfarist approach. *Clinical Ethics* 6 (1): 45–51. doi:10.1258/ce.2011.011010

Schapiro, Tamar. 1999. What is a child? *Ethics* 109 (4): 715–738. doi:10.1086/233943

———. 2006. Kantian rigorism and mitigating circumstances. *Ethics* 117 (1): 32–57. doi:10.1086/508036

Shiffrin, Seana Valentine. 1999. Wrongful life, procreative responsibility, and the significance of harm. *Legal Theory* 5 (02): 117–148.

———. 2012. Harm and its moral significance. *Legal Theory* 18 (Special Issue 03): 357–398. doi:10.1017/S1352325212000080

Singer, Peter. 2011. *Practical ethics*. 3rd ed. New York: Cambridge University Press.

Smith, Michael. 2009. Two kinds of consequentialism. *Philosophical Issues* 19 (1): 257–272. doi:10.1111/j.1533-6077.2009.00169.x

———. 2011. Deontological moral obligations and non-welfarist agent-relative values. *Ratio* 24 (4): 351–363. doi:10.1111/j.1467-9329.2011.00506.x

Valentini, Laura. 2012. Ideal vs. non-ideal theory: A conceptual map. *Philosophy Compass* 7 (9): 654–664. doi:10.1111/j.1747-9991.2012.00500.x

Velleman, J. David. 1999a. Love as a moral emotion. *Ethics* 109 (2): 338–374. doi:10.1086/233898

———. 1999b. A right of self-termination? *Ethics* 109 (3): 606–628. doi:10.1086/233924

———. 2008. Love and nonexistence. *Philosophy & Public Affairs* 36 (3): 266–288.

Wasserman, David. 2005. The nonidentity problem, disability, and the role morality of prospective parents*. *Ethics* 116 (1): 132–152.

Wasserman, David, Adrienne Asch, Jeffrey Blustein, and Daniel Putnam. 2013. Cognitive disability and moral status. In *The Stanford encyclopedia of philosophy*, ed. Edward N. Zalta. http://plato.stanford.edu/archives/fall2013/entries/cognitive-disability/

Wenar, Leif. 2015. Rights. In *The Stanford encyclopedia of philosophy*, ed. Edward N. Zalta. http://plato.stanford.edu/archives/fall2015/entries/rights/

Zimmerman, David. 2003. Sour grapes, self-abnegation and character building: Non-responsibility and responsibility for self-induced preferences. *The Monist* 86 (2): 220–241.

Zwolinski, Matt. 2006. Why not regulate private discrimination. *San Diego Law Review* 43: 1043.

PART III

Aging

CHAPTER 7

Dementia, Advance Directives, and the Problem of Temporal Selfishness

Ryan W. Davis

Every life contains intrapersonal distributive choices. We can often control whether to enjoy some good in the present at the expense of our future self, or whether to incur some cost in the present for the sake of our future self's good. Many such choices are mundane. Work today and take tomorrow off, or work tomorrow and take today off. Endure a painful dental procedure to be free of pain in the future. Part of what makes these choices mundane is that the considerations bearing on them are straight forward. It is some-times obviously better for me, overall, to experience some good in the present, and it is sometimes obviously better for me, overall, to allocate a good to my future self. Other intrapersonal distributive choices are less mundane. Is the future security bought by a high paying job worth its negative consequences for present quality of life? Will the costs of raising a young child now be repaid by gains enjoyed by a later self's fulfilling personal relationships?

Understanding the rational norms associated with intrapersonal distrib-utive choices—if in fact there are any—is an important philosophical topic in its own right.[1] Here, however, I aim to focus on one subclass within the larger category of such choices. Broadly put, I will be concerned with intrapersonal distributive choices in which the agent experiences some physical or psychological change between the time at which the choice is

R.W. Davis (✉)
Brigham Young University, Provo, UT, USA

© The Author(s) 2018
J. Flanigan, T.L. Price (eds.), *The Ethics of Ability and Enhancement*,
Jepson Studies in Leadership, DOI 10.1057/978-1-349-95303-5_7

made and the time when its effects transpire. Two examples will help render this issue more perspicuous. First, consider a case in which a person issues an advance directive requesting that in the event that she develops dementia, she not be given life-extending medical treatment. Suppose the agent develops dementia, and then contracts a life threatening (but treatable) illness. It is possible that the agent with dementia may enjoy a positive quality of life. Philosophers have debated, in cases like this, whether it is better for the agent that her earlier will be honored, or her current happiness be extended through treatment (Dworkin 2002; Jaworska 1999; McMahan 2002; Jennings 2009). Or, consider the case of physical disability. It is apparently common for nondisabled persons to steeply discount the well-being of an imagined future with a disability. However, persons with disabilities often do not discount their well-being at all.[2] For example, persons with disabilities will sometimes refuse any hypothetical offer of a shorter life in return for not having a disability (Nord et al. 2009).

In cases like these, persons make choices about whether experiencing some good in the present is worth giving up something in the future. What complicates these choices is that the future self's values—or, more fundamentally, the future self's way of valuing—are not continuous with the present self. Intrapersonal distributive choices must sometimes be made within a single life, but across significant evaluative fault lines. Philosophers usually take a third personal vantage point on these cases. Should we honor an advance directive or satisfy the patient's present interests? How should we think about disability and well-being from a public policy point of view?

My aim this essay will be to consider these questions from a first-personal perspective. How should we think about intrapersonal distributive cases in which our values or valuing capacities may shift significantly in the interim? For ease of exposition, I will focus first on the case of dementia. Following a recent paper by Jennifer Hawkins (2014), I will favor the hypothesis that there can be genuine conflicts of reasons about how to treat dementia patients like the one described above. An agent can face conflicting considerations about how to make plans for one's own life. Second, I describe one type of error in responding to these reasons, which I call the problem of temporal selfishness. Third, I will tentatively diagnose the problem of temporal selfishness as a failure of the norms of agency. My conclusion is that a failure to grant due weight to one's future values can constitute a fundamental failure of one's agency. Insisting now on how my future self ought to act, or ought to be treated by others, can count as an instance of temporal selfishness.

I realize this conclusion may sound unhelpfully abstract. In more practical terms, this essay can be understood as an effort to vindicate a kind of flexibility or modesty as an agential virtue. To put it simply, it is easy to demand too much consistency from one's own values. The cases of dementia and disability reveal the virtue of refraining from excessive commitment about how the story of one's own life should unfold. Or so I will try to show.

1   Self-Conflict and Reasons

This section will begin by looking in detail at the case of advance directives relating to dementia. Jennifer Hawkins presents the case of Rupina, who writes an advance directive stating that if she develops Alzheimer's, she will not receive treatments extending her life. Rupina is aware of the facts about Alzheimer's and knows that this directive could shorten significantly shorten her life. Rupina later develops Alzheimer's, but continues to have "certain cognitive capacities, as well as many things she cares about," and generally enjoys her life (Hawkins 2014, p. 508). Rupina develops pneumonia, which could be treated successfully by antibiotics. If untreated, it will likely be fatal.

Her advance directive notwithstanding, Hawkins argues that it is in Rupina's interest to be given antibiotics. Hawkins's article is rich and subtle, but I will here be interested in only one of her arguments. She contends that Rupina has no interest in having her advance directive honored, and she does have an interest in continuing to live. So, at least with respect to her well-being, the matter is straight forward. There is reason to give her the anti-biotics and no reason not to. In so arguing, Hawkins denies that Rupina has competing interests, notwithstanding her past desires. Why not think that Rupina's past desire to not receive the antibiotic gives at least some welfare-based reason not give her the antibiotic? After all, one could accept this while simply holding that the reason is defeated by present Rupina's interests. In order for weighing of competing considerations to make sense, one would have to accept a principle such as:

Self-Conflict An individual's well-being consists in the well-being of different temporal parts of the individual's life, and these interests can sometimes come into conflict.

However, Hawkins rejects *self-conflict*. Hawkins supposes that if Self-Conflict were true, then it would be common to see different parts of a person's life as yielding competing reasons about the person's overall well-being. Yet, this is not the case. To extend another of Hawkins's cases, imagine a person who—in her youth—wanted to be a poet. As part of this desire, she wanted to have a volume of her poetry published. She later abandons the desire to be a poet and decides instead to become a literary critic. Stipulate that it is bad for a literary critic to have a volume of poetry published. In this case, Hawkins suggests, there is no sense in which publishing the volume would be good for the agent's welfare (Hawkins 2014, p. 516). The fact that she previously had a desire for the volume to be published does nothing to make its publication good for her.

Cases like these show, at a minimum, that conflict in desire between one's present and past selves is not sufficient to establish Self-Conflict. Perhaps Rupina's earlier desire to not be given the antibiotic lacks any bearing on Rupina's well-being. However—as Hawkins also points out—it does not follow that Rupina's past desire lacks normative relevance altogether (pp. 509–510). Contrast the cases considered so far with:

Estate Ruby has a large estate, a part of which has been set aside to be given to charity upon her death. Her children, as executors of her will, must decide whether to donate to one of two possible organizations: AID and GIVE. Suppose that AID and GIVE are comparable in all the relevant ways: they are similarly effective in their use of resources to achieve morally desirable outcomes. However, they use different strategies and techniques to bring these ends about. As it happens, Ruby mistakenly believed that methods like those used by AID were morally reprehensible. In fact, she actively opposed the use of these methods, and took any opportunity to denounce them. GIVE, on the other hand, used methods and supported causes that Ruby deeply appreciated, and to which she felt personally connected. Unfortunately, however, later in life Ruby has developed dementia, and has largely forgotten her earlier beliefs, desires, and projects.

To which organization should Ruby's children donate her money? I suggest that they should donate to GIVE rather than to AID, as it would better cohere with Ruby's earlier beliefs, desires, and projects. In this way, it would represent a better continuation of Ruby's values, and of her participation in her own social world more generally.[3] Setting aside for now how these goods might be theorized, it seems like this is something there is reason to want.

If this is the right way of understanding Estate, then it is possible that a past self's desires can continue to have normative significance in the present, even if those desires have been forgotten. It may be misleading to put the point this way, since in Estate, it may not be the mere fact of past Ruby's desires that has this normative significance, but also further facts about how these desires fit into the broader narrative of her life. Nevertheless, the fact that she has forgotten them does not appear sufficient to cancel their reason-giving status. An objector could also point out that even if this is true, it does not yet show any conflict of reasons, and so could not be used to support Self-Conflict. However, we could amend the case to include also that Ruby has not only forgotten her earlier beliefs, desires, and projects—she has also acquired a weak preference that the money be given to AID rather than to GIVE. Importantly, the issue is not that she has had a change of heart or renounced her earlier values. She has merely forgotten them, and has formed a weak desire in the opposing direction. Suppose, for example, she finds AID's brochures to be appealingly packaged. In this case, it seems that there would be a conflict in the reasons Ruby's executors would have in dispersing her estate. Her current preference conflicts with her earlier values, which she never renounced or otherwise disowned.

In a case of this kind, it seems plausible that the Ruby's executors could decide that they had overall most reason to honor Ruby's past values, rather than her current preference. Imagine Ruby had spent her life working for— say—justice in prison reform. On the other hand, she had long been a skeptic about environmental protection groups—viewing them as a vehicle for "conspicuous conservation" by the affluent. She may have even told her children never to give to environmental groups. If later, demented Ruby nevertheless comes to prefer the environmental organization for irrelevant reasons, it seems reasonable for her executors to honor her earlier values. Even if they are otherwise indifferent between the two charities, they might think they have greater reason to use Ruby's estate in ways that furthers her life's central values. These values, I suggest, are better identified with her earlier core projects, beliefs, and desires than with her present preference.

If this is right, it still does not support Self-Conflict, since the reasons Ruby's executors have to honor her past self's values may not contribute to her well-being. Ruby's life may not go better if her executors honor her past values, even if it is distinctively her past self's values that provide them with these reasons.[4] After all—as Hawkins points out of similar cases—we would not expect Ruby to respond positively to such a choice, were she to become aware of it. And if some event does not (and could not, in the future) enter an agent's experience in a positive way, it is at least not obvious how that event could be in the agent's good.[5]

Whether events of this kind can contribute to a person's well-being in some way is a matter of ongoing philosophical controversy. This paper takes no final stand on the question. However, one might also wonder, if such events do not contribute to a person's well-being, how could there still be reasons specifically related to the person? In other words, how could there by reasons to honor Ruby's past self's values that are somehow grounded in facts about Ruby and her life, rather than independently of her life. To label this rough idea, we might ask how there could be Ruby-relative reasons to act in a given way, if the action does not affect her well-being?

One strategy for answering this question is that there are reasons of respect. Past Ruby's values were autonomously chosen, and so there might be reason to defer to her autonomous choice, even if such deference does not contribute to her well-being.[6] In this way, Ruby's situation is similar to Rupina's. (Hawkins underscores that there might be reasons to respect to honor Rupina's advance directive, even if doing so is not good for her now.) A second strategy draws on a significant difference between Ruby and Rupina. While past Rupina had certain desires about her future life, past Ruby not only had desires, but also projects, beliefs, and commitments organized in a particular way. These organizing features gave her life a certain shape or narrative arc, and this narrative might continue to be a source of reasons even after Ruby has forgotten her earlier attitudes. A number of philosophers have recently argued that a life's narrative can be a significant to understanding the life's overall prudential value (Rosati 2013; Dorsey 2015; Matthew and Kennett 2012; Mackenzie and Poltera 2010; Glasgow 2013). A life is better, according to these views, to the extent the events comprising it constitute a certain kind of meaningful narrative. To recite perhaps the most obvious case, a life beginning in hardship and ending in triumph is—all else equal—better than a life beginning in triumph and descending to hardship. Even though the total hedonic utility of both lives may be the same, the narrative of ascent and achievement from early failure is better than a narrative of slow decline and ultimate misery (Velleman 2000).

Narrative considerations might appear to reinstate exactly the issue of well-being about which I had just promised neutrality. And in fact, many theorists do interpret narrative value as a component of personal well-being. On this interpretation, the narrative considerations offered above would just amount to one way of supporting Self-Conflict, thereby objecting to

Hawkins's view. However, we might also interpret these narrative considerations as providing reasons of respect rather than well-being. Even if it does not make Ruby's life better to use her estate in a way that fulfills or realizes a broader narrative of her life, it might be seen as a fitting response to her status as the author of her own life. Attention to the narrative she had charted to this point could be a way of sharing in the effort to realize her ends, regardless of whether those ends are understood as advancing her well-being. Described in this way, it seems that narrative considerations bear more on respect than welfare.

One lesson may be that well-being and respect are not so easily divided. On some views, respectful treatment is regarded as instrumental to well-being.[7] On other views, what counts as in an individual's well-being is decided in part by their own aims and goals (Scanlon 1998; Ebels-Duggan 2008). Although the direction of fit between the two is reversed, these alternatives share the idea that respect and well-being are not altogether separate.[8]

A final possibility is that the reasons to act on Ruby's earlier values represent a way of responding to her value as a person that differs from those already considered. Perhaps it is not that she left an advance directive which respect requires we honor, and neither will our actions now benefit her in some way. Instead, her children might act on her values as a way of acknowledging her value as person, or perhaps a way of recognizing the ongoing value of their relationships with her. Following David Velleman, we might say that they act for her sake. Velleman emphasizes that such actions may not be taken so as to realize any state of affairs in particular:

> If an end is anything *for the sake of which* an action is to be done, then it shouldn't have to be something the action is done *in order to achieve*. Perhaps you ought to attend church or synagogue this weekend for the sake of your dear departed mother, or just for old times' sake. Old times aren't something that you act in order to achieve; neither is your mother. So 'for the sake of' and 'in order to' are not interchangeable constructions. (Velleman 2006, p. 89, emphases in original)

My suggestion here is that given certain facts about Ruby's life and commitments, it may be possible to act for her sake, but without any attendant suggestion that one is respecting a specific demand or request she made, and neither is one advancing her interests. As Velleman points out, acting "for the sake" of a departed parent is intelligible, but not equivalent to acting "for the sake of fulfilling their wishes." In so doing, Ruby would play the role of an "end" of action in the Kantian sense—not as something to be realized but as a kind of motive.[9]

For now, I will leave aside the details of how such considerations might be sourced. This section has merely sought to show that there can be conflicting reasons arising from different temporal parts of a person's life. Perhaps this is because, contra Hawkins, Self-Conflict is correct, although there may be other explanation for the cases like those described here. A weaker principle might be given as follows:

Reasons Conflict The reasons arising from an individual's distinctive value consist in reasons that follow from different temporal parts of the individual's life, and these reasons can sometimes conflict.

In this principle, the "individual's distinctive value" is meant to refer to whatever the final explanation for temporal conflict might be, whether it is in well-being, or a combination of well-being and respect, or in reasons that follow from an appreciative response to the person in some other way.

2   TEMPORAL SELFISHNESS

The last section considered conflicting reasons arising from different temporal parts of a person's life, where there those reasons are primarily the considerations that bear on third-party action. What are the reasons, for example, that bear on the actions of Ruby's executors? Analogous cases can also be generated in strictly first-personal situations. Suppose again Ruby had organized her life around working for a certain component of justice. She had gone to law school to acquire the skills and resources to meaningfully effect change, and had long held doing so as an overarching goal. However, just as she was about to gain a major legal victory for her cause, she falls into a period of doubt. She becomes indifferent between pursing her current life, and taking a lucrative job in an unrelated field. (For the sake of excluding other considerations, assume that if she took such a job, she would still give a large sum of money to support morally worthy causes, and so would bring about a comparable amount of good.) Again, I suggest that Ruby could reasonably decide to continue her former life, even if she is indifferent between the options, looking forward. Her past actions, commitments, and values could continue to provide her with reasons (Kelly 2004; Dorsey 2015). Nor would these reasons be canceled if she has developed a slight preference in favor of abandoning her past life trajectory. So, cases of Reasons Conflict can also occur in first-personal deliberation.

As mentioned in the introduction, this phenomenon is not uncommon. My aim in this section will be to characterize a rational error that can occur when deliberating in the face of Reasons Conflict. I will call it the problem of *temporal selfishness*. The issue I have in mind involves prioritizing a certain part of life in a way that is sub-optimal from the point of view of one's complete life. I might refuse to go to the dentist out of a fear of the pain of a cavity filling, only to suffer much greater pain later. Or I might refuse to enjoy the moment and keep working, even though my sacrifice never yields an equal return of value. To illustrate, consider two cases[10]:

Deathbed Regret A young woman dedicates her life to success in business. After gaining great wealth, she retires and lives out her days alone in her sprawling home. At the end of her life, she wishes she had dedicated more time to developing relationships with others earlier on.

Prodigal Son A young man inherits a large sum of money, but spends it all on a few years of whimsical living and adventure. Warned by his parents that he should plan for the future, he decides that they have simply lost their love of life.

Both of these cases describe agents who could be accused of sub-optimal intrapersonal distributive choices. The woman in Deathbed Regret comes to believe it would have been better for her, overall, to have taking greater concern for her late-life well-being. The man in Prodigal Son is accused of disregarding his future for the sake of his present. Let us suppose, for a moment, that these accusations are correct. A variety of explanations might be given for such choices. For example, the agents might have made good faith efforts to decide which temporal distributions were best, but simply made mistakes. Or, they might have acted without such deliberation at all, or acted akratically. I will not refer to any of these errors as instances of temporal selfishness. Instead, I will reserve that term for cases in which an agent forms a judgment about some intrapersonal distribution being best, but that judgment privileges the part of the agent's life from which it is issued.

To clarify the contrast, consider two different kinds of explanations for cases like those above. First, consider the woman in Deathbed Regret. One explanation for her regret is that she has gained wisdom over the course of her life, and has realized that—in fact—her earlier dedication to her business was a mistake. It would have been better, overall, for her to cultivate relationships while she was young that would continue to benefit her when she was old. Similarly, in the case of Prodigal Son, one might hold that his parents really were correct that he should plan more for the future, and his early life of whimsy and adventure is—from the point of view of his complete life—a mistake.

A second kind of explanation is also possible. This kind of explanation will not take for granted that agents' actions represent intertemporal mistakes. For example, it could be that the woman in Deathbed Regret wishes that her past self would have cultivated relationships precisely because doing so would benefit her older self. Her judgment that it would have been better for her younger self to plan more for the future is motivated by the fact that such an arrangement would have been better for her now. Her regret is not, on this view, a reflection of the wisdom of age, but just of the fact that she would prefer her current time-slice self to be enjoying a larger share of the benefits distributed across her life as a whole.[11] Likewise, it is possible that Prodigal Son's choices of adventure and whimsy represent a rationally permissible way of organizing one's life. If so, his parents' insistence on planning might be motivated by the fact that the benefits of adventure will be primarily realized by their son, while they might incur some of the risks associated with their son's choices.

Explanations of this latter sort are cases of what I want to call temporal selfishness. In these cases, an agent assigns special priority to one part of life at least partly because that it the life-stage the agent currently inhabits. The idea of such arbitrary priority is familiar from cases of interpersonal selfishness. If I insist that I, rather than you, should receive the final ice cream cone even though our claims on it are comparable, it seems that I am simply being selfish. If I insist that my claim is stronger due to some putative fact about me, observers might be suspicious that my asserted difference was motivated. If, for example, I insisted that my love of ice cream meant that I would get greater utility from it than you would, you might be forgiven for wondering whether my belief depended on my selfish desire for the ice cream, rather than the evidence. Likewise, although it is possible that judgments in cases like Deathbed Regret and Prodigal Son may really reflect the evidence, we might wonder whether they are motivated by a selfish desire favoring the present part of one's life.

Temporal selfishness involves an apparent privileging a certain part of one's life at the expense of other parts of one's life. However, such privileging alone is not sufficient. Suppose that the young woman in Death-bed Regret happened to agree at the end of her life that business success was the right thing for her to pursue, notwithstanding that it differentially imposed costs on her later self. If the agent has a unified view across time on the values of her life, then prioritizing one part of life does not seem potentially selfish. Rather, it simply seems like one way of ordering values. Some people might favor the youth and adventure of their early life, and others might favor the stability and relationships of later life.[12] But I will not suppose that there is any particular norm governing these choices. Even if prioritizing a certain life stage is prioritized arbitrarily, it still seems that doing so is not objectionably selfish if an agent is consistent in this prefer-ence across life stages.

At the heart of temporal selfishness, then, is a kind of disunity among one's own judgements across time about how intrapersonal distributive choices should be made. We might provide a rough description, as follows.

Temporal Selfishness An agent is temporally selfish if the agent has conflicting judgments about how some good should be distributed across their complete life, at least one of these judgements is not rationally justified, and the unjustified judgement is motivated in part by partiality to one's present time slice.

This principle gives at least an approximate sufficient condition for the errors in practical reasoning like those described earlier in this section. It is important to add that at least one of the judgments must be unjustified in order to separate cases of temporal selfishness from cases of simply revising one's view in response to new evidence.

The opposite of temporal selfishness is a kind of diachronic unity of the will; so it is not surprising that such unity is often praised by philosophers as a characteristic virtue of good agency (cf. Dannenberg 2015). Recall Parfit's famous case of the young Russian nobleman. In Parfit's story, the young nobleman believes he should distribute his inheritance—once he receives it— to the peasants. However, he fears that as he ages, he will abandon the socialism of his youth, and so will fail to follow through with his plan when the time comes. Accordingly, he makes a contract now—which can only be canceled with his wife's consent—to distribute the inheritance when he receives it. He asks his wife to promise that she will not allow the contract to be cancelled, even if his older self reverses course and asks her to cancel it (Parfit 1984, pp. 327–328).

The young Russian nobleman is convinced that if he should change is mind, the change would be unjustified. He supposes that only a betrayal of the moral truth would motivate his later self to switch position. His strategy is to deny his future self any say in the decision, and in that sense he will not entertain the possibility that any departure from his present view could be in response to reasons. In her treatment of the case, Christine Korsgaard describes the Russian nobleman as someone who "cannot make the decision together with himself" (2009, p. 187). On Korsgaard's reading, the Russian nobleman's problem is that he lacks a unified will. She supposes that he does not fear his future self will become irrational; rather, his future self will just adopt values which his present self disavows. His action is aimed at denying his future self the same standing that he arrogates to his present self in making the decision. On Korsgaard's view, his present action thereby fails to form and act on a unified set of intentions. And in that sense, he not only is in conflict with his future self, but is in conflict with his present self. As Korsgaard puts it, "his problem is not disrespect for his future self, but disrespect for himself here and now" (Korsgaard 2009, p. 204).

What lessons can be learned from these examples for cases like those of Ruby or Rupina? To recall: Rupina is an agent who issues an advance directive that she be allowed to die, but then it turns out that death is not in the interest of her later self (with dementia). As Hawkins points out, it advances her well-being to be given medication so as to continue to live, given that there are no cases of Self-Conflict. However, the last section then argued that there are possible cases of Reasons Conflict—it just happens that we don't know enough about Rupina's reasons for her advance directive to know if there are conflicting reasons in her case. In Ruby's case, her earlier self continues to provide reasons that may conflict with the preferences of her later self. To see this point, consider a revised version of the Rupina case, in which Rupina's life narrative might plausibly appear to give rise to a conflict in reasons.

Rupina* is similar to Rupina as described above. However, Rupina* has dedicated her life to the development of her personal autonomy, with which she identifies more than any other personal attribute. She regards the loss of her cognitive ability to reflect on her own attitudes as an event that would destroy what she cares about most in herself. Along with these values, she has prided herself on achieving a kind of independence from others. She has struggled to achieve the ability to provide for herself without depending on others for basic needs, and she cannot imagine relinquishing this independent status. In light of these personal values, she decides to issue an advance directive that she be allowed to die, should she develop dementia. Unfortunately, Rupina* develops dementia, but continues to have a relatively high quality of life. She contracts a potentially fatal disease, but one that could be cured with medication.

The case of Rupina* seems plausibly to be an instance of conflicting reasons. Although it would serve at least her later self's well-being to be given the medication, the narrative of her life appears to provide considerations against providing her with the medication. Suppose, for example, that if she receives the medication and continues to live, her life will end in a way that runs contrary to her value of personal autonomy, in both of its aspects. She will lose the cognitive capacity for reflection, and will also lose her ability to live independently of others. Her reasons for issuing the advance directive specifically included wanting to avoid such a conclusion to the story of her life. And this concern seems well-founded. If given the medication, the narrative arc of her life will conform less well to her avowed values than if she is not given the medication. Whether we understand this consideration to be tied to her well-being, to respect for her choice, or to some other value of her person, it appears to provide a reason that conflicts with the reasons given by her well-being later in life.

Does this conflict in reasons indicate that Rupina*'s earlier decision was temporally selfish? After all, Rupina* issues an advance directive that she intends to override the values of her future self, should her values change after she develops dementia. In this sense, she arrogates to her present self a standing to make the choice that she also denies to her future self. In this respect, Rupina* is similar to the young Russian nobleman. However, Rupina*'s advance directive does not seem intuitively self-disrespectful, at least not in the same way as his disregard for his future self. For one thing, she differs with the young Russian nobleman in that she assumes that the subject of her advance directive will be irrational, and so there is a basis for denying equal standing to that self for making the decision. However, whether this counts as a sufficient defense depends on exactly what is wrong with the diachronic disunity that characterizes cases of objectionable temporal selfishness. I will take this question up in the next section.

3   TEMPORAL SELFISHNESS AS A RATIONAL FAILING

So far, this essay has tried to show that that reasons from different parts of a person's life can conflict, and that some ways of responding to this conflict appear temporally selfish. Just as interpersonal selfishness appears to be some kind of vice, so also temporal selfishness is an apparent vice. The last section identified temporal selfishness with a kind of disorganization of the will, but it did little to explain exactly that kind of disunity should be understood as a rational failing. The aim of this section is to close that gap, and in particular to consider whether there is something rationally amiss with disregarding the reasons of your future self, if that self suffers from dementia.

To begin, I will briefly rehearse a standard (although not uncontroversial) explanation for the problem of diachronic disunity. This is the explanation given by a Kantian or constitutivist understanding of the norms of rational agency.[13] Constitutivists about agency believe that norms of assessment for agents can be derived from the features of agency. To put it differently, we can understand the norms of agency simply by understanding the concept of agency. If we understand the concept of an "agent," we can understand what makes an agent better or worse (Thomson 2008; Smith 2013). Given that agents have both beliefs and desires, a good agent is one whose beliefs are correct, and who succeeds at realizing their desires. Unfortunately, for any agent, these two dimensions of good agency can come into conflict. I might desire to believe some proposition, even though it is false. In this case, I must either fail to fully satisfy my desires, or else I must fail in adopting accurate beliefs.

Should such conflicts arise, how would an ideal agent resolve them? One could prioritize either the capacity to form true beliefs, at the expense of realizing desires. Alternatively, one could prioritize the capacity to realize desires, giving up the commitment to true beliefs. A third option is that one could try to maximize one's composite "score" of true beliefs and satisfied desires. Michael Smith has recently argued that none of these options provides a satisfactory account of ideal agency (2012). The first two arbitrarily privilege one agential capacity above another, and the third fails to combine norms into a single coherent account of good agency. Instead, Smith proposes that good agency must involve, in part, the presence of desires that prevent—as much as possible—such conflicts in the first place (Smith 2012, pp. 312–313). For example, agents should have "coherence inducing desires" against interfering with their belief forming capacities. So, it is constitutive of ideal agency that one follows a norm of non-interference with one's own rational capacities.

Just as there can be present conflicts in an agent's capacities, there can also be conflicts with respect to an agent's future exercise of their capacities. An agent might have a desire to hold some false belief in the future, or might desire now that their future desires not be realized. And as before, an ideal agent will minimize these tensions by following norms against interfering with their future exercise of belief-forming or desire-realizing capacities (Smith 2011). So we can infer that a constitutive norm of agency is that an agent ought not interfere with the satisfaction of their own future desire-fulfillment.

With this in mind, we are in position to review the case of Rupina*. Rupina* has strong reasons, given the narrative arc of her life, to want her life to not continue if she develops dementia. However, if she issues the advance directive, she will be interfering with the realization of her future self's desires. And according to the constitutivist argument about the norms of agency, that is something that any agent has reason not to do. If that is right, there isn't just a conflict between the reasons she has favoring the advance directive, and the reasons that her future self will have to continue living. There is also an issue of how Rupina*'s agency could be best organized, overall. And if the forgoing view is correct, then—ceteris paribus—it seems that respect for her own agency also tells against issuing the directive. So Rupina* and the young Russian nobleman do have something in common. They both fail to think of their future selves as agents whose capacities have the normative importance that they attribute to their present capacities. And, at least as a first approximation, this looks like a mistake.

One might protest that there is an important asymmetry between the agential incoherence of Rupina* and the young Russian nobleman. Although the nobleman has reason to believe that his future self will have all of the rational capacities that his present self enjoys, Rupina* will lack many of her present rational capacities if she develops dementia. At the extreme, one might even think that in some cases, the conditions of personal identity connecting Rupina* to her future self might not be preserved.[14] In that case, the objector could deny that Rupina* is diachronically disunified, and so also deny that her advance directive is temporally selfish.

To consider this objection, the foregoing constitutivist account of agency can be taken one step further. An important insight from the constitutivist strategy, recall, is that an agent is more ideal to the extent that the agent's psychology displays a higher level of coherent organization.[15] With this in mind, we can imagine a case in which an agent acts to realize some desire, but the process of acting to realize the desire brings it about that the agent who completes the action is not continuous with the agent who initiated the action. The conditions of personal identity are not preserved. Still, the constitutivist can hold that even then, the agent should not interfere with the future agent's exercise of capacities to realize her desires. There are at least two ways of arguing for this conclusion. Begin with the question of coherence. Consider two possible agents who desire to realize some goal, but will become different agents (personal identity will not be preserved) over the course of realizing the goal. Suppose that one of these agents, on learning that their identity would be altered, abandons the desire entirely. The other agent, even after learning of the change in identity, retains the desire. It seems plausible that the second agent is more coherent than the first.

In general terms, coherence can be understood in terms of inferential linkages. A more coherent psychology is one in which the elements of the psychology can be inferred from or explained by other elements in the psychology (Bartelborth 1999; Mackonis 2013). A psychology is incoherent if its elements cannot be used to jointly explain why it would make sense to hold one of its constituent attitudes. For example, if I feel contempt for someone, become angry every time I talk about them, but also aspire to be like them, it might seem that my attitudes are not coherent (cf. Velleman 2008). My aspiration to emulate a person cannot be inferentially linked to the other attitudes I hold toward them.

With this general conception of coherence, we can see why the agent who retains a desire even when personal identity is not preserved is more coherent than the agent who does not. Say that I desire to cure cancer, and am working on that project. If I discover that in the process, my personal identity will somehow be altered, it would be strange to think that this would have anything to do with the reasons for which I held the desire in the first place. So, given my other presumed attitudes, I should still hold the desire even if the agent who realizes it will not be the same as me. Abandoning the desire seems to require some further explanation, and this explanatory deficit can be understood as a kind of incoherence. Given the constitutivist case against incoherence, an agent would be better if they retain the desire. And so an ideal agent would not interfere with their realization of future desires even if the conditions of personal identity are not preserved.

Here is a second avenue to the same conclusion. It is a virtue of set of attitudes to exhibit systematic justifiability—or to be such that they are mutually supportive (Smith 1994; Markovits 2014). All else equal, a mutually supportive set of beliefs is better than a non-mutually supportive set of beliefs, and a mutually supportive set of desires is better than a non-mutually supportive set of desires. But what makes a set of desires mutually supportive? Julia Markovits suggests that a set of ends is more mutually supportive if the ends are regarded as acquiring worth from a common source (Markovits 2014, pp. 132–134). It would not be coherent to have some aim as an end, and at the same time to ascribe no worth to it at all. And it would also not be coherent for an agent to have a diversity of ends, all with differing final grounds. Better, one might think, if the grounds or diverse ends could somehow be unified. Following the Kantian tradition, Markovits suggests agents should see their agency as the source of worth to their ends (Markovits 2014, p. 136). But if this is true, then a different agent would also be the source of worth to their respective ends. And so the maximally coherent agent will not only see herself as having reason to not interfere with her realization of her own ends, but will also see herself as having reason to not interfere with the ends of other agents.

Both these strategies point to the conclusion that one should not interfere with another agent's fulfillment of their desires for the same reasons that one should not interfere with one's own future self. Perhaps cases of dementia occupy a kind of middle ground between a future agent being identical with oneself, and being a separate agent altogether. Cases of this sort form a bridge for the constitutivist between concern for one's own agency, and concern for others. If the constitutivist project succeeds (and I have not dealt with any of the controversy surrounding it here), then it provides resources for explaining what is wrong with interfering with one's future self. Deciding to interfere, on the view described in this section, is a way of failing to abide the fundamental rational norms that govern agency and are also constitutive of it.

4   REASONING ABOUT ADVANCE DIRECTIVES

We are now in position to assemble components from the previous sections into an argument that bears on the question that opened this essay: How should individuals make intrapersonal distributive choices in the face of prospective disability or dementia? The first sectioned argued, pace Hawkins, that there can sometimes be conflicting reasons arising from different parts of an individual's life. Agents can respond to these reasons either in ways that are diachronically unified, or else are temporally selfish. Diachronic disunity can be understood as a rational error, or a failure to conform to the constitutive norms of agency. This can provide a general explanation of what is wrong with temporal selfishness. Because agents at least have significant reasons to avoid interfering with their future selves (or, the future persons who psychologically connected to them), there are also significant reasons against issuing advance directives to facilitate one's death in the event of dementia.

The argument might be given as follows:

1. Practical reasons arising in different parts of an agent's life can come into conflict.
2. If there is a conflict in reasons from different parts of an agent's life, the agent can respond to these reasons in a way that is diachronically unified, or that (often) risks temporal selfishness.
3. Diachronic unity is required by constitutive norms of agency.
4. So, temporal selfishness is (often) opposed by constitutive norms of agency.
5. Advance directives can sometimes create risks of temporal selfishness.
6. So, advance directives can sometimes be opposed by constitutive norms of agency.

It's now important to add a series of qualifications to this argument. I do not intend to suggest that individuals should not have a right to issue advance directives, or that those advance directives should not be honored (including temporally selfish advance directives). Nor do I claim that if an advance directive is opposed by the constitutive norms of agency, that it follows that the advance directive is morally wrong. Indeed, the present case may call attention to a puzzle for constitutivist theories of agency. When constitutivist standards tell against an action that does not involve other agents, the error is usually regarded as one of practical rationality, but not morality.[16] On the other hand, when constitutivist standards tell against an action that does involve other agents, it is generally assumed that the standard in question is a moral one (Smith 2011, 2013). The case of advance directives complicates this division by introducing ambiguity about whether another agent is involved. What is needed, I suggest, is some principled constitutivist rationale for distinguishing moralized from non-moralized agential norms.

In cases like those described here, it is not obvious if personal identity is preserved, and neither is it obvious whether failures of diachronic unity should count as morally objectionable. As suggested in the last section, some cases of temporal selfishness look like morally relevant mistakes. Just as

I should not disregard others, or artificially suppose my interests to have exceptional properties, I should not disregard other parts of my life, or regard my present time-slice self has having exceptional properties. Such disregard seems like something I have moral reason to avoid. On the other hand, it is tempting to think that if a person has considered that their future interest may change, but still wants to issue an advance directive, then that should be within their prerogative—not just in the sense that they should have a right to do it, but also that it would be permissible.

For this essay, I will set aside questions about the nature of the reasons given by the constitutivist norms. I will proceed with the more general conclusion that constitutivist standards provide some reasons against issuing advance directives that can cause an agent to become diachronically disunified. Readers who see nothing amiss with any advance directive might take the argument here as a reason to reject constitutivism, which is independently controversial. However, I will suppose that there is something intuitively right about the suggestion that there are sometimes reasons against issuing advance directives.

To see what lessons might be drawn, I will return to the two cases of diachronic planning with which this essay opened. First, consider the case of Rupina*, whose life narrative provides her with reason to want to avoid leading a life of reduced autonomy and dependence on others. If reasons from different life parts can conflict (as affirmed by Reasons Conflict), then Rupina* faces a dilemma. Her commitment to her own autonomy gives her reasons to want to issue an advance directive about her death. However, if the forgoing is correct, then the constitutive standards of agency give her reason to avoid issuing such an advance directive. But the autonomy to which she is committed may be similar (or even identical) to the constitutive standards of agency in question (Korsgaard 2009; Smith 2011). How should she proceed?

Although I cannot offer a determinate answer to this question, I will offer two possible avenues for thinking about the problem. First, Rupina* could reimagine what kind of conclusion to her life would count as the appropriate fulfillment of her life's commitments and values. As I described the case before, her commitments to autonomy and independence led her to favor her future self's death, should she develop dementia. Better to die than to fail to live autonomously. However, she could perhaps frame her commitment to autonomy differently. She could judge that she should allow her future self's valuing activity to guide medical choices for that time slice of herself, and in that way she could honor the autonomy of the final part of her own life. She would also be allowing her future self a kind of independence from her present self. She would be adopting a kind of deference to her future self, but this deference might be seen as of a piece with her present self's valuing of autonomy. So even if her future self might lack some of the features of autonomy that she has valued, that end of life could still be seen as a way of honoring those values.

Of course, not all narratives will be so open to re-negotiation, and for some people, conflicts in reasons may be intractable. In these cases, perhaps all that can be said is that there are considerations of agential coherence that count against issuing advance directives that could potentially lead to diachronic disunity. Intrapersonal selfishness is, in this case, a kind of risk that an agent should at least be live to (cf. Lacy et al. 2006). The Prodigal should think about whether his current lifestyle is disregarding his future self's interests. (Likewise, the Prodigal's parents might do well to reflect on whether their opposition to his lifestyle is motivated by the part of life *they* now occupy.) In the same way, a person who thinks about issuing an advance directive should not only think about their present values, but should try to adopt a unified point of view with their future self. In short, they should entertain that self's values in a serious way.

The same might be said for cases of acquired disability more generally. The opening of this essay noted how persons without disabilities tend to discount the value of an imagined future with a disability, whereas people who acquire disabilities often do not regard them as a significant detriment to their well-being. One possible explanation for this difference can be given in terms of life narrative. If I have formed commitments and plans that a disability would prevent me from fulfilling, it is tempting to think of my life with a disability as one in which my commitments and values would be persistently frustrated. This thought is formed by holding constant my current plans and commitments, and imagining the counterfactual in which I could not realize them. This circumstance would make for an unsatisfying life narrative—one of frustration and defeat (cf. Moller 2011b). However, what this thought ignores is the likely endogenous effect of my disability on my plans and commitments. Were I to become disabled, I would likely modify my plans and goals in ways that rendered them realizable in my future state. So, although it is now tempting to believe that were I to become disabled, it would undermine my life's narrative, that temptation results from comparing the present to a relatively unlikely counterfactual.

The literature on narrative value can at times appear to encourage this temptation. We are told that what is axiologically significant to a life's narrative value is its "global or long-term" projects or goals, or the effective exercise of an agent's capacities in the pursuit of such goals (Dorsey 2015, p. 313; Kauppinen 2012, p. 368). Emphasis on successfully using one's capacities to reach long-term goals can raise disconcerting questions about the value of a life in which one's capacities are changed or impaired, or in which one loses the abilities to follow through with long held goals. The lesson here, I suggest, is that a life's narrative value is not as fixed as these locutions make it seem. As a matter of fact, cases of disability teach us that success in a life as a whole can involve manipulation of goals and alteration of the capacities used to reach them. But beyond that, agency itself tells in favor of modesty about what can be demanded of my future self. On pain of temporal selfishness, I should not commit myself now to act now for reasons that I may be unable to act on in the future. I should be deferential enough to my future self to acknowledge that my values might change in ways that are beyond my present control. And accordingly, I should relinquish the aspiration for my present self to have global control over my future self's values and commitments. If this is right, it tells in favor of a kind of flexibility with respect to one's future self. I should allow that my future self's values may differ from my present values, and so I should try to manage my present commitments in a way that will avoid unnecessary tensions among parts of my life.

5   Conclusion

It is a philosophical commonplace to identify resoluteness in living by one's own values as a kind of moral or agential virtue. To be unwilling to abandon one's own value commitments is the mark of personal integrity (Williams 1973). On the other hand, altering one's values can display a failure of self-respect. Nothing I have said here denies these thoughts. However, accepting them risks occluding another kind of agential virtue. If the constitutive norms of agency tell against intrapersonal conflicts across time, then I should not only hold to my present values, but I should do so in light of what I can anticipate my future self's values will be. And, if I am unsure what my future self's values would be, then I should hold my present values in a way that is open to a variety of possible developments—including undesired losses of my present capacities. At times, this flexibility may tell in favor of tempering my present commitments. This can be an uneasy thing to do. It seems like allowing for change in my present values betrays those values by failing to affirm them in a maximally robust way. And that, in turn, can feel like an affront to one's integrity. But if what I've said here is on the right track, then such choices are not only compatible with integrity, they can indicate an active responsiveness to my future self's valuing activity. Flexibility in my present values can be a way of respecting my future self. And respect for my future self is at least a part of self-respect for my own personhood.

Notes

1. Recent entries on related issues include Nebel (2015), who argues in favor of the rational permissibility of status quo bias, and Greene and Sullivan (2015), who argue against the rational permissibility of the conjunction of accepting future bias but denying near bias.
2. For discussion of the well-known "disability paradox," see Ubel et al. (2005); Dunn and Brody (2008).
3. For an insightful discussion of this phenomenon's normative significance, see Scheffler (2013).
4. On some theories of well-being, her life does go better. On others, it will not. One relevant issue is whether all well-being must be at one point in time, which Velleman's original entry (2000) denies, but subsequent philosophers have affirmed.
5. This is a gloss on NA, which Hawkins (2014, p. 527) thinks is a necessary condition for some occurrence to be part of a person's good.
6. Following Davis (2004), we could say that Ruby had a resolution preference in favor of her earlier values, where a resolution preference is a preference about how to resolve competing preferences held at different times in the agent's life.
7. See, for example, Pettit and Smith (2004).
8. Although Hawkins is at pains to emphasize that considerations of respect are being set aside, this may suppress sources of self-conflict in a somewhat artificial way. There may, however, still be good theoretical reasons to try, as Hawkins does, to isolate one kind of consideration.
9. Some actions are not aimed at bringing about a state of affairs. On the distinction between state-directed and act-directed motives, see Nye et al. (2015).
10. These are modeled on illuminating examples from Moller (2011a).
11. Moller (2011b) offers an insightful concluding discussion of these issues.
12. Street (2009) argues that arbitrary local time preferences can be rationally permissible.

13. For leading examples, see Katsafanas (2011), Korsgaard (2009), and Velleman (2009; 2006).
14. For discussion, Buchanan and Brock (1990).
15. This case is adapted from Smith (2012; 2015). I discuss the issue in more detail in Davis (2016).
16. Examples here include failures of instrumental reasoning, or failures to believe in ways that are constitutively require by the concept of belief.

REFERENCES

Bartelborth, Thomas. 1999. Coherence and explanations. *Erkenntnis* 50 (2–3): 209–224.
Buchanan, Allen E., and Dan Brock. 1990. *Deciding for others: The ethics of surrogate decision-making.* Cambridge: Cambridge University Press.
Dannenberg, Jorah. 2015. Promising ourselves, promising others. *The Journal of Ethics* 19: 159–183.
Davis, John K. 2004. Precedent autonomy and subsequent consent. *Ethical Theory and Moral Practice* 7: 267–291.
Davis, Ryan W. 2016. Which Moral Requirements Does Constitutivism Support? *Law, Ethics and Philosophy* 4: 8–31.
Dorsey, Dale. 2015. The significance of a life's shape. *Ethics* 125: 303–330.
Dunn, Dana S., and Clint Brody. 2008. Defining the good life following acquired disability. *Rehabilitation Psychology* 53 (4): 413–425.
Dworkin, Ronald. 2002. *Life's dominion.* New York: Vintage.
Ebels-Duggan, Kyla. 2008. Against beneficence: A normative account of love. *Ethics* 119 (1): 142–170.
Glasgow, Joshua. 2013. The shape of a life and the value of loss and gain. *Philosophical Studies* 162: 665–682.
Greene, Preston, and Meghan Sullivan. 2015. Against time bias. *Ethics* 125 (4): 947–970.
Hawkins, Jennifer. 2014. Well-being, time, and dementia. *Ethics* 124 (3): 507–542.
Jaworska, Agnieszka. 1999. Respecting the margins of agency: Alzheimer's patients and the capacity to value. *Philosophy & Public Affairs* 28: 105–138.
Jennings, Bruce. 2009. Agency and moral relationship in dementia. *Metaphilosophy* 40 (3–4): 425–437.
Katsafanas, Paul. 2011. Deriving ethics from action: A Nietzschean version of constitutivism. *Philosophy and Phenomenological Research* 83: 620–660.
Kauppinen, Antti. 2012. Meaningfulness and time. *Philosophy and Phenomenological Research* 84 (2): 345–377.
Kelly, Thomas. 2004. Sunk costs, rationality, and acting for the sake of the past. *Nous* 38 (1): 60–85.

Korsgaard, Christine. 2009. *Self-constitution: Agency, identity, and integrity.* Oxford: Oxford University Press.

Lacy, Heather P., Dylan M. Smith, and Peter A. Ubel. 2006. Hope I die before I get old: Mispredicting happiness across the adult life span. *Journal of Happiness Studies* 7 (2): 167–182.

Mackenzie, Catriona, and Jacqui Poltera. 2010. Narrative integration, fragmented lives, and autonomy. *Hypatia* 25 (1): 31–54.

Mackonis, Adolfas. 2013. Inference to the best explanation, coherence, and other explanatory virtues. *Synthese* 190 (6): 975–995.

Markovits, Julia. 2014. *Moral reason.* Oxford: Oxford University Press.

Matthew, Steve M., and Jeanette Kennett. 2012. Truth, lies, and the narrative self. *American Philosophical Quarterly* 49 (4): 303–315.

McMahan, Jeff. 2002. *The ethics of killing: Problems at the margins of life.* New York: Oxford University Press.

Moller, Dan. 2011a. Anticipated emotions and emotional valence. *Philosopher's Imprint* 11 (9): 1–16.

———. 2011b. Wealth, disability, and happiness. *Philosophy & Public Affairs* 39 (2): 177–206.

Nebel, Jacob M. 2015. Status quo bias, rationality, and conservatism about value. *Ethics* 125 (2): 449–476.

Nord, Erik, Norman Daniels, and Mark Kamlet. 2009. QALYs: Some Challenges. *Value in Health* 12: S10–S15.

Nye, Howard, David Plunkett, and Ku. John. 2015. Non-consequentialism demystified. *Philosopher's Imprint* 15 (4): 1–28.

Parfit, Derek. 1984. *Reasons and persons.* Oxford: Oxford University Press.

Pettit, Philip, and Michael Smith. 2004. The truth in deontology. In *Reason and value: Themes from the moral philosophy of Joseph Raz,* ed. R. Jay Wallace, Philip Pettit, Samuel Scheffler, and Michael Smith. Oxford: Oxford University Press.

Rosati, Connie S. 2013. The story of a life. *Social Philosophy & Policy* 30 (1–2): 21–50.

Scanlon, T.M. 1998. *What we owe to each other.* Cambridge: Harvard University Press.

Scheffler, Samuel. 2013. *Death and the afterlife.* New York: Oxford University Press.

Smith, Michael. 1994. *The moral problem.* Oxford: Wiley-Blackwell.

———. 2011. Deontological moral obligations and non-welfarist agent-relative values. *Ratio* XXIV: 351–363.

———. 2012. Agents and patients, or: What we learn about reasons for action by reflecting on our choices in process-of-thought cases. *Proceedings of the Aristotelian Society* CXII: 309–330.

———. 2013. A constitutivist theory of reasons: Its promise and parts. *Law, Ethics and Philosophy* 1: 9–30.

————. 2015. The magic of constitutivism. *American Philosophical Quarterly* 52: 187–200.
Street, Sharon. 2009. In defense of future Tuesday indifference: Ideally coherent eccentrics and the contingency of what matters. *Philosophical Issues* 19 (1): 273–298.
Thomson, Judith Jarvis. 2008. *Normativity*. Chicago: Open Court.
Ubel, Peter A., George Loewenstein, Norbert Schwarz, and Dylan Smith. 2005. Misimagining the unimaginable: The disability paradox and health care decision making. *Health Psychology* 24 (supplement): S57–S62.
Velleman, David. 2000. Well-being and time. In *The possibility of practical reason*, ed. David Velleman. Oxford: Oxford University Press.
————. 2006. *Self to self*. Cambridge: Cambridge University Press.
————. 2008. A theory of value. *Ethics* 118: 410–436.
————. 2009. *How we get along*. Cambridge: Cambridge University Press.
Williams, Bernard. 1973. A critique of utilitarianism. In *Consequentialism: For and against*, ed. J.J.C. Smart and Bernard Williams. Cambridge: Cambridge University Press.

CHAPTER 8

How Old Is Old? Changing Conceptions of Old Age

Christine Overall

Every person is old compared to another individual or by reference to a particular standard. For example, you might be too old to qualify for the girls' soccer team, or just old enough to be legally eligible to vote. At 20 you are probably already too old to become a concert violinist or a world-class baseball player (Mothersill 1999, p. 19). Even a cryopreserved embryo can be "old" if, for example, it is created in the lab and then frozen for 10 years.

But the archetypal use of "old" is in application to human beings near the end of their lives. "How old is old?" is fundamentally a philosophical question. It invites us to consider what we mean by the word "old" in its application to human beings and human aging, and how that meaning (or meanings) may be similar to or different from the meaning of "old" with respect to non-human beings. Is there a viable objective sense of "old," independent of social perceptions and expectations? Or is aging—becoming old—an entirely relative concept, so that a human being is old only by reference to some cultural perspective or criterion?

This chapter was originally printed in *The Palgrave Handbook of the Philosophy of Aging*.

C. Overall (✉)
Department of Philosophy, Queen's University, Kingston, ON, Canada

© The Author(s) 2018
J. Flanigan, T.L. Price (eds.), *The Ethics of Ability and Enhancement*,
Jepson Studies in Leadership, DOI 10.1057/978-1-349-95303-5_8

My aim in this chapter is not primarily to give a definitive answer to the question in the title, but, rather more modestly, to reveal how complex the concept of oldness is, and the kinds of factors that might influence how one determines how old is old. I am interested in exploring not only changing conceptions of old age, but also, and even more, whether and to what extent conceptions of old age *should* change. It is arguable that the concept of "old" needs revision, both because of recent empirical changes in human lives, and for normative reasons, having to do with justice and human well-being. I will therefore offer a response to the "How old is old?" question that is both political and philosophical in content.

1   THE CONNOTATIONS OF "OLD"

In order to answer the titular question, a few comments about the connotations of "old" are necessary. The word "old" in the title of this chapter is an adjective. In the sense that is relevant to this discussion, "old" applies primarily to persons, and means something like "aged" or "elderly." But "old" is also multiply ambiguous. My Internet thesaurus suggests that it may mean "deep-rooted" or "longstanding." Yet, it is noteworthy that many of the synonyms for "old" have pejorative connotations: "worn out," "used," "outmoded," "hoary," "timeworn," "archaic," "dated," "outdated," "out of date," "antiquated," "old-fashioned," "outmoded," "past its prime," "over the hill," and "on its last legs."[1] It might be objected that the words in this latter group principally apply to objects, possessions, time periods, buildings, monuments, styles, ideas, and art forms. But it is hardly controversial to suggest that in a culture obsessed with what is new, novel, up-to-date, current, fresh, innovative, and futuristic, being old might be perceived as a shortcoming not just of things and themes but also of human beings.[2]

Being old is generally stigmatized in youth-oriented cultures. As Lillian Rubin observes,

> [W]e live in a society that worships youth, that pitches it, packages it, and sells it so relentlessly that the anti-aging industry is the hottest growth ticket in town: the plastic surgeons who exist to serve our illusion that if we don't look old, we won't be or feel old; the multibillion-dollar cosmetics industry whose creams and potions promise to wipe out our wrinkles and massage away our cellulite; the fashion designers who have turned yesterday's size 10 into today's size 6 so that 50-year-old women can delude themselves into believing they still wear the same size they wore in college—all in the vain hope that we can fool ourselves, our bodies and the clock. (Rubin 2011)

When a word denotes an entity or a concept that is regarded as unpleasant, frightening, or vulgar, the threat borne by the denotation may be reduced via the substitution of a euphemism in place of the more direct word. As Margaret Morganroth Gullette remarks, "'Old age' is so unsayable it needs a euphemism; 'aging' was and still is used in its place, so 'aging' too has come implicitly to signify decline" (Gullette 2004, p. 181).

As a result, contemporary English-language usage offers many euphemisms to avoid the use of the word "old" in application to human beings. For example, old people are conventionally referred to as "senior citizens" or merely "seniors"—terms that are odd not least because no one refers to young people as "junior citizens" or "juniors" (the latter being used only, if ever, in the context of sports teams or schools). The concept of seniority can suggest the possession of greater experience, and it often references authority. While old people almost certainly have more experience than younger ones, whether they have (or are recognized or allowed) to have authority is a separate issue. Indeed, although lip service is often paid to the greater experience and supposed wisdom of old people, in a youth-oriented culture it is unlikely that most old people—and especially old people who are not white, and old women of any race—are perceived as having authority. Hence, the terms "senior citizens" and "seniors" not only are euphemistic in their function but also possess a covert irony, given the reality of the social position of many old people.

In addition, my Internet thesaurus (bizarrely) offers "mature" as a synonym for "old." That meaning is at least questionable, since one can easily be mature (both physically and psychologically) long before becoming elderly. Ben Yagoda points out the frequent and growing use of the term "*older* people" rather than "old people," whose function is to soften the negative value burden of oldness (Yagoda 2015). Presumably the covert assumption is that one can be older (than another person or persons) without being elderly, so "older" is a euphemism that attempts to disguise the reality of being old.

Given that "old" has many negative connotations, and that "young" is a term of approbation, it is likely that the meaning of "old" in contemporary Western society is closely related to, perhaps a product of, ageism. I define "ageism" as prejudice, stigmatization, negative discrimination, and even oppression aimed at a particular person or group of people because of their age. Ageism can and does target young people, including children, at times—witness the existence of sometimes kneejerk distrust of and condescension toward adolescents. But ageism's target is more likely to be old people (however "old" is construed), who may be described as burdens, as failing to contribute, as being greedy, forgetful, preoccupied, dependent, helpless, and even senile (Kingston 2014).[3] Oldness is thought to subsume an individual's entire being (Gadow 1991, p. 117), dominating and defining the person regardless of her other characteristics and abilities. Thus, ageism exacerbates the challenges of old age, by contributing to the negative values associated with aging and inducing the internalization of horror about being old.[4]

As Rubin puts it, old age is

> a time of loss, decline and stigma.
>   Yes, I said *stigma*. A harsh word, I know, but one that speaks to a truth that's affirmed by social researchers who have consistently found that racial and ethnic stereotypes are likely to give way over time and with contact, but not those about age. And where there are stereotypes, there are prejudice and discrimination—feelings and behavior that are deeply rooted in our social world and, consequently, make themselves felt in our inner psychological world as well. (Rubin 2011, her emphasis)

In addition, ableism plays a role in the stigmatization of oldness. Ableism is prejudice, stigmatization, negative discrimination, and even oppression aimed at a particular person or group of people because of their impairment (s) or perceived impairments. Persons who have lived a very long time are likely to be dealing with a greater incidence of disease and impairments. But, unsurprisingly, societies valorize being able-bodied and free of disease and impairment. Hence, to be old is to be doubly devalued.[5] Thus, as this discussion of the connotations of "old" indicates, being old is seen as having a variety of characteristics that are at least considered undesirable, or even the object of public avoidance, rejection, or revulsion. Frits de Lange puts it plainly: "The idea of old age as horrific, disgusting, and tainted by mortality has a long history. Nonetheless, today the attitude of many young people toward growing old can be summed up in the three Rs of 'Repudiation,' 'Repugnance,' and 'Repulsion'" (de Lange 2013, p. 176).[6]

For these reasons, "How old is old?" is partly a question about when an individual is likely to become a target of ageism and ableism, and vulnerable to the stigma of being treated as old. While ageism and stigma are not the whole story of being old, they are features that cannot be ignored, even when a more objective response to the question is sought.

2   An Objective Answer to the Question

At least prima facie, the question in the title, "How old is old?" is linguistically and conceptually odd. If one were to *assert* that "Old is old," the statement would appear to be an obvious tautology. But of course, it would be a tautology only if "old" is used in the same sense in each of its two occurrences. In order for the question "How old is old?" to have content and to be worth asking, it is necessary to reinterpret the two occurrences of "old" as having different meanings. What might these two meanings be?

In English, the word "old" has at least one objective sense, a sense that is not always imbued with negative connotations. When we ask of someone, "How old are you?" we are simply inquiring about the number of years the individual has lived. Custom and etiquette tend to dictate that one be cautious about asking this question of individuals—and women especially—past their third decade (presumably on the grounds that no longer being a youth is a liability or even something of which to be ashamed). Yet "How old are you?" is a question that can logically be asked of anyone, at any age. So, I suggest that the question "How old is old?" is best interpreted with the first occurrence of "old" being about chronological age, the number of years lived.

But oldness is not just about chronological age. It is appropriate to be skeptical of the idea that "age is just a number," especially since this cliché is most frequently used not in regard to children, adolescents, or 20- or 30-somethings, but in regard to those who are at least considered middle-aged or, more often, old. Horace Kallen points out that "Aging is another word for living on, from conception to death, which prevailing usage today applies to a *late stage* of this process. ... Our culture reserves 'aging' for the lives we live some time *after* we have 'come of age'" (Kallen 1972, p. 4, my emphasis). Age is not just a number, but rather something that becomes the special focus of individual and social concern late in life.

What is the meaning of the second occurrence of "old"? One possibility is that it refers to biological conditions: (1) the material and bodily conditions that often accompany aging, or (2) the proximity to death. Simone de Beauvoir points out that "chronological and biological ages do not always coincide" (de Beauvoir 1972, p. 30), and the World Health Organization observes, "Although there are commonly used definitions of old age, there is no general agreement on the age at which a person becomes old. The common use of a calendar age to mark the threshold of old age assumes equivalence with biological age, yet at the same time, it is generally accepted that these two are not necessarily synonymous" (WHO). Nonetheless, "How old is old?" could be a question about the ways in which chronological age and biological age are *related*. I will consider (1) and (2) separately.

Aging itself is not a disease or collection of diseases (Hayflick 2002, p. 419), but oldness is often accompanied by deterioration, diseases, and losses of function. Microbiologist and gerontologist Leonard Hayflick says that "aging processes by definition are losses in function or physiological capacity" (Hayflick 2002, p. 420)[7] and "the aging process is the leading risk factor for all age-associated diseases" (Hayflick 2002, p. 421). Philosopher Helen Small *defines* "old age" as "the later years of a long life, when there is an inevitable and irreversible *deterioration in the organism* as a consequence of its age" (Small 2007, p. 3, my emphasis). Philosopher Anita Silvers defines "old age" as "a stage of life when individuals are at higher than species-typical risk of encountering *impediments to their usual modes of functioning*" (Silvers 2012, p. 11, my emphasis). Thus, "How old is old?" could mean, "What is the chronological age of deterioration and loss of function?"

Of course, it cannot be assumed that all persons who have lived many decades are naturally infirm and debilitated. Despite the fairly homogeneous negativity with which oldness is perceived, it is striking just how heterogeneous people who have lived a long time are. Silvers points out, "In regard to other biological changes associated with old age, not every individual undergoes these changes at the same time in life. Nor is every biological decrement associated with aging equally debilitating for everyone. . . . [And] modern medicine may place retrieval of youthful functional capacity within the reach of the old, if the price for such restorative medical services can be paid" (Silvers 2012, p. 9). Moreover, cultural conditions may contribute to the creation of problems that are supposedly only "natural." Gullette suggests that people learn to blame their bodies for their problems, rather than "the forces that structure feelings of decline and that link 'age' to the body in knotted chains of signifiers. Your pain, the *same* pain, once it is considered 'age-related,' may entail *more* suffering" (Gullette 2004, p. 133, her emphasis). The decline that is associated with old age is simultaneously seen as very personal and individual, yet at the same time "a *universal* biological process (an effect that erases economics, other group vulnerabilities, and one's latent power to describe one's own age identities differently)" (Gullette 2004, p. 134, her emphasis).

Oldness may also be understood, conventionally, in terms of proximity to death. Yet people who have lived only a few decades do die, while people who have lived a long time are not necessarily and inevitably on the verge of death. Hence, it is precarious to assume that all who have a high chronological age are about to die. Nonetheless, as Mary Mothersill observes, it may be that the only "*distinctive* feature of old age is that, for the subject it presages death" (Mothersill 1999, p. 20, her emphasis). Geoffrey Scarre writes, "I remember once reading about an old man, well past his hundredth year, who woke up each morning with the thought, 'Still here?' When one reaches extreme old age, it is obviously foolish to bank on having many more days of life" (Scarre 2007, p. 27).

Thus, one strong motivation for the question, "How old is old?" is a concern about the onset of age-related infirmities, the shrinking of one's future, and the closeness of death. Interpreted this way, "How old is old?" would be concerned with empirically objective facts about the likely onset of physical deterioration and diseases and the probable age of death.

In this objective and empirical sense, the answers to "How old is old?" will of course vary depending on the species to which individuals belong. For example, a 19-year-old cat is likely to be infirm and debilitated, and is probably close to death, but a human being who is 19 is still a youth. Thus, the oldness of an individual in this objective and empirical sense is not just a function of number of years lived, but is also at least partly a function of the number of years lived in comparison to the number of years an individual of that species can be *expected* to live.

The maximum life span for members of a particular species is the greatest number of years that a member of that species has lived (Hayflick 2002, p. 417). For human beings, the maximum life span was famously set by Frenchwoman Jeanne Calment, who—based on verified dates of her birth and death—is known to have lived to 122 (Whitney 1997).

More important for our purposes than maximum life span is life expectancy, the average amount of time a person is predicted to live. Whereas maximum life span is defined as the number of years lived by the longest-lived person (and has remained constant since Calment's death in 1997—no one has outlived her), life expectancy is highly variable. First, it varies by nation. Life expectancy has been increasing steadily over the last century, especially in developed nations. In 2012, life expectancy at birth was 79 in the United States and 81 in Canada. It is highest in Japan, where it was 83 years in 2012, but much lower in impoverished, disadvantaged, or war-ravaged nations dealing with endemic diseases and weak and inadequate health care systems. For example, in the Democratic Republic of Congo, life expectancy at birth in 2012 was 50, while in Swaziland it was only 49 (World Bank 2015c).

Within nations, life expectancy also varies by factors such as sex/gender and race. For example, life expectancy for females in the United States was 81 in 2012 (World Bank 2015a), whereas for males it was only 76 (World Bank 2015b). Life expectancy is also higher in the United States for whites than for non-Hispanic blacks, but it is still higher for members of the Hispanic population (Arias 2014).

Information about life expectancy and maximum life span provides a way to answer the question, how old is old? First, it is surely uncontroversial to say that Jeanne Calment—and other outliers who live past 100—are objectively very old by human standards. In addition, it seems reasonable to say that persons who are at or approaching the typical life expectancy for their nation and their particular demographic category are objectively old. Thus, it is plausible to say that in North America, 80 is old.

Basing oldness on life expectancy has an interesting implication. If average life expectancy for one's nation and demographic is the criterion, then being old will vary from one nation to another and even from one group to another. By this criterion, 83 is old in Japan, but in Swaziland one may be old at 49. What constitutes old age, then, is not just a function of years lived, but is dependent on one's geographical and demographic location. Public perceptions of old age may in fact contribute, via social policy, to how well or how badly individuals age. They may, for example, influence what kinds of health care are provided to elderly people, what kinds of living arrangements are available to them, how accessible the transit system is, what kinds of work (paid or unpaid) they are allowed or expected to do, and how they are treated by younger people, in public or in private. Being old is, therefore, not a condition that one can easily alter or postpone *simply* by making judicious and virtuous choices about one's nutrition, exercise, drinking, smoking, and drug habits. Instead, being old is determined largely by social forces that may or may not make good food available, healthy work possible, adequate medical care accessible, and "lifestyle" habits a matter of real choice.[8] Oldness is, in part, an expression of social policies, both intranational and international, as well as the social status, privileges, and oppression of different groups of people within a given society.

For these reasons, "How old is old?" cannot be answered merely by an appeal to subjective feelings. Because of the valorization of youth, those who are old are encouraged and even expected to be, feel, and act "young at heart;" they are required to strive to "age well;" they are told (contrary to fact) that they are only as old as they feel. But as de Beauvoir observes, it is "a complete misunderstanding of the complex truth of old age" to say that provided you feel young, you are young (de Beauvoir 1972, p. 284). Contrary to the cheery Pollyanna-ish rhetoric of developed societies, according to which you are "only as old as you feel," being elderly is mainly a product of social and material conditions over which individuals have little or no control. Oldness, defined in terms of morbidity and proximity to death, is not individually defined or subjectively chosen; it is largely imposed, by objective material and social conditions.

Of course, life expectancy is, by definition, an *average*, a sum of all the various ages of people who die within a particular jurisdiction or group divided by the total number of deaths. There will be plenty of people who outlive it. Moreover, historically in developed nations, and still within poorer nations, the figures for life expectancy are heavily influenced by maternal, infant, and child mortality. High rates of any or all of them (and they usually vary together) will lower life expectancy, because if large numbers of children die in infancy and large numbers of women die during their childbearing years, a substantial chunk of the population has no chance of living for many decades. Such deaths may pull down the average life expectancy without necessarily reducing the chronological point at which old age (defined in terms either of deterioration and loss of function, or of proximity to age-related death) arrives. In nations with rates of high child and maternal mortality, individuals who survive childhood (and in the case of women, survive childbearing) might very well live well past the standard life expectancy for their society.[9] In a nation where the life expectancy is 49, although persons over the age of 50 will be far rarer than they are in societies with higher life expectancies, individuals might not be old by biological standards until they reach their 60s or 70s. Thus, life expectancy is at best an imperfect measure of oldness.

3   NOT AN AGE BUT A STAGE?

Oldness may also be defined relative to one's proximity to events and life landmarks that are considered to be significant. In Western nations, life stages are changing and how they are conceptualized is becoming ever more complex. As Andreas Göttlich notes, "[D]ifferences can be found concerning the number of phases into which life is partitioned, the strictness of the borderlines between them, the features and traits a typical representative of an age group is supposed to have, his/her rights and duties, the rites that mark the passage between phases of life, and also the question of when one switches over to the next age group" (Göttlich 2013, p. 231).

De Beauvoir remarks that there are no "initiation ceremonies" that mark the entering of old age; an old person still has the same political rights and duties, and the liability for upholding the law, as a person half his age (de Beauvoir 1972, pp. 20–23). Nonetheless, becoming old can mean the shedding of some roles and entitlements (by choice or not) and perhaps the acquisition of others (by choice or not). These roles and entitlements may be related to familial relationships (whether, for example, one becomes a grandparent, or is expected to take on the care of young members of the family); social and civic rights (such as whether one is eligible to retire from paid work, or entitled to a pension or state support); responsibilities and burdens (whether, for example, one is expected to give up authority, or defer to one's adult children); and eligibility for membership in groups or institutions (such as special groups for "senior citizens," pensioners, or retired persons).

According to the World Health Organization, ideas about the end of paid work and the start of pension payments support dominate Western understandings of oldness: "Most developed world countries have accepted the chronological age of 65 years as a definition of 'elderly' or older person.... While this definition is somewhat arbitrary, it is many times associated with the age at which one can begin to receive pension benefits" (WHO 2015). If pension eligibility is taken to be the standard for oldness then it is not surprising that, according to Jan Baars, the lowering of the retirement age in Europe has redefined 55 as "aged," and people over 40 may be spoken of as "older workers" (Baars 2007, p. 18).[10] Baars refers to this phenomenon as "the paradoxical acceleration of ascribed aging in a situation of rising life expectancies" (Baars 2007, p. 19).

Some people conceptualize oldness more generally in terms of its relationship to the narrative of individuals' lives (Velleman 1993)[11] and its place in giving life its meaning. According to one common line of thought, one is old when life's main events and accomplishments either have already been achieved or are no longer attainable. To be old is to experience events that no longer contribute as much value to one's life because they are near the end of it, and so they have less effect on one's life as a whole. In old age, Göttlich writes,

> The future, understood as the undisclosed open horizon of the present, shrinks bit by bit, and the implementation of certain projects is no longer realistic. In other words, the idealizations of "And so on" and "I can do it again" are called into question. This consequence is intensified by the decline of the human body.... [T]his means that the domain of our free motivational relevances—of our *in order-to-motives* ...—is constricted. (Göttlich 2013, p. 226, my emphasis)

From this point of view, one is old when one's perspective is, legitimately and inevitably, less and less on the future, and rests more and more on what has already happened.

But this view of oldness is not the only possible narrative account of old age. There is, in fact, a potential problem with seeing old age as a stage at which an individual has lived long enough to have had a complete and full life. For, on the one hand, some people may manage to live long and fully and yet not be old by any chronological or biological measure. And on the other hand, some people may live a very long time yet not have had sufficient education, opportunities, or social support to be able to live a complete and full life (Overall 2003, pp. 47–51).

Moreover, the idea of oldness as the culmination and endpoint of a long and full life may rest on a particular notion of personhood. James Lindemann Nelson points to a distinction between two ways of being a person: the *career self* (an idea introduced by Margaret Urban Walker) and the *seriatim self* (an idea introduced by Hilde Lindemann). The career self sees his life as a "unified field," organized by a life plan, a quest, or a project (Nelson 1999, p. 122). Walker speaks of the concept of career self as "the idea of an individual's life as a self-consciously controlled career." This, she says, is a form of "horizontal integration": the "achievement of continuity in which the individual's unidirectional stream of life is seen as adding up to 'a life career'" (Walker 1999, p. 106). By contrast, "[t]he seriatim self may see her life as made up of many jobs, lots of them quite big enough, thank you, but none necessarily life-defining, nor especially valued for the particular role they play in contributing to the achievement of a 'rational plan' for the whole" (Nelson 1999, p. 123). The seriatim self "may live a life both more shaped by contingencies than by the expression of personal agency and more involved in relationships prized intrinsically, not because they are instrumental to achieving the agent's quest. ... Seriatim selves may, then, place a greater importance on the goods of relationship, rather than the goods of agency and experience" (Nelson 1999, pp. 123–124). From Walker's point of view, the seriatim self leads a life of "vertical integration," which "stresses 'timeless transcendent recognition' that endures and does not pass away, what has been called at different times: epiphany, moments of being, revelation, satori, transcendence" (Walker 1999, p. 106).

For the career self, then, life stages depend on achievements accomplished and landmarks reached, and old age is the point where one's life plan or quest or "career" is almost complete. But for those who live as a seriatim self, old age may not be so very different from other stages of life, all of them being devoted to in-the-present activities and relationships. For the seriatim self, being old is not a dénouement or a point where nothing more lies ahead; it is simply another opportunity to experience the benefits and challenges of living one's life.

4   THE NORMATIVE QUESTION

Many of my observations in the last two sections were about *empirical* issues, and concerned both the ways in which material circumstances affect aging and the varieties of perceptions of old age. But the question "How old is old?" can also be interpreted *normatively*, as a question about *when it is appropriate, fair, or justified to regard someone as old*. "How old is old?" then becomes the question at what chronological age individuals are justifiably classed as belonging to the category of old people. At what point in a person's life *should* we apply the term "old"?

People disagree about how to answer the question. Unsurprisingly, perceptions of oldness may be relative to one's chronological placement vis-à-vis other human beings. Consider how old 20 looks when one is 10, and how old 40 looks when one is 20. It's likely that people's implicit ideas of what is old change as they live longer, and that our perceptions of oldness are related to what we anticipate and understand to happen at each chronological age. For example, in a 2009 survey, the average response of 3000 Americans to the question when old age begins was 68. But survey respondents over 65 said that old age begins at 75, whereas those who were under 30 said that it begins at 60 (Arnquist 2009).

The immediacy of asking when it is justified to classify a person as old can be experienced viscerally if you ask yourself when you would find it appropriate to call a colleague, a friend, or a beloved family member old. Or even more directly, when, if ever, would you consider *yourself* to be old?

Although life expectancy provides an objective answer to the question whether someone is old, labeling a person "old" is not likely to be free of value judgment. As the discussion in this chapter has shown, the connotations of "old" are often negative: "worn out," "used," "outmoded," "hoary," "timeworn," "archaic," "dated," "outdated," "out of date," "antiquated," "old-fashioned," "outmoded," "past its prime," "over the hill," and "on its last legs." Moreover, the condition and experience of oldness are exacerbated by ageism and ableism. And using a life-stage approach to oldness also invokes implications about the value of old age and the significance of the time left.

Perhaps, given the negative connotations of "old" and the social stigma that ageism attaches to being an old person, calling a colleague, a friend, or family member—let alone oneself—"old" is too demeaning and insulting ever to be justified. Perhaps there is no point when we should be willing to consign someone else—or ourselves, for that matter—to the social abjection that is being treated as old. It might therefore be contended that no one should be called "old" no matter what their age. Sympathetic to this approach, Ros Altmann argues,

> It's time to shed the labels. Describing someone by their age should be as unacceptable as describing them by their gender, race, religion or skin colour. These characteristics do not necessarily signify fitness for work, recruitment for a particular position, or training for certain skills. (Altmann 2015)

According to this view, a person's age—the number of years she has lived—should make no difference to what opportunities or responsibilities she is accorded, how she is treated, or whether she is respected. What matters is not her age—it's "just a number"—but her physical, psychological, and cognitive abilities, her social situation, and her personal needs.

The intention behind this proposal is commendable. It is true that one's age—whatever it might be—does not necessarily represent one's abilities or one's fitness for work. But if "age" simply means years lived, then it is an objective fact about individuals, and surely nothing to be ashamed of, no matter what ageism and ableism might suggest. Liberation is not won by denying or obscuring facets of one's reality. And refusing to call anyone "old" may simply be a concession to the very ageist stereotypes that anti-ageists hope to avoid. It might also contribute to the fiction that one can still be youthful in one's late 70s or 80s, or that the last years of life require no particular social or medical support.

Instead, I want to call for a more thoughtful approach to the use of the concept of oldness. There is a need, among the not-yet-old, for solidarity with respect to old people. One form that solidarity could take is claiming the use of the word "old" for oneself. Instead of distancing themselves from old age, people could welcome it. Since second-wave feminism, some feminists have already initiated this process by reclaiming terms like "crone" and "hag," which have become words of disapprobation for old women.[12] I am therefore advocating that all of us who are getting old or are near old chronologically should consider claiming to *be* old.

Doing so might be too much to expect from people who are in their 30s. But it would be legitimate to expect from people in their 70s, 60s, and even 50s. Making this claim would not require engaging in stereotyped behavior. Indeed, the value and effectiveness of the claim would be enhanced through its use by people who engage in a wide variety of activities and forms of life, thus creating a strong mode of resistance to stereotyping and stigma: "This is what being old looks like." Claiming the label "old" would then be based, not on a subjective feeling, not on acquiescence to ageism, but on political convictions and moral values.

Calling oneself "old" even before society pastes the label on oneself is a way of reclaiming the term. It is a pre-emptive move against ageism, in which one defies the relegation of old people to the margins by proclaiming loudly and proudly, "I am old." Oldness will begin to have different and better meanings when being old is regarded as an identity worth asserting rather than a characteristic to be denied, repressed, or concealed.

5   CONCLUSION

How old is old? It is plausible to understand oldness in terms of its relationship to maximum life span and to life expectancy, the latter of which varies from nation to nation and from group to group. We can say that people who have reached their society's life expectancy are old in the sense of being likely to experience declining health and function, and to be close to death (though not inevitably so).

Conceptions of old age may be in the process of changing, at least because people in the West are living so much longer. And these conceptions *should* change, because ageism and ableism make the lives of aging people harder than they otherwise need to be. On the one hand, to be old is not necessarily to be feeble and debilitated; on the other hand, many of the social and medical problems associated with oldness itself are affected by social perspectives on aging and the socio-economic deprivation and oppression they produce.[13] As Anne Kingston remarks, "How we perceive aging and the old has profound consequences in terms of how we actually age, the medical care we will and won't get, and how financially and emotionally prepared we will be for what can be a long chapter in life" (Kingston 2014).

In reaction to the negative connotations of oldness, it is sometimes asserted that old people have special qualities, abilities, and virtues that are less commonly found among young people. I have not made that claim here. While it is indubitable that old people have lived longer than younger ones, and hence are likely to have had a greater variety of experiences, old people are just as diverse as those of any other age. The way to encourage greater respect for oldness, along with fairness to and better treatment of old people, is not by making claims about old people's supposed special qualities, but by asserting their humanity and their entitlement not to be marginalized.

I am not arguing that oldness is merely a function of perception, or that it is unanchored in material realities. To be old is not just whatever we want to make it or whatever we happen to "feel." There are good pragmatic and moral reasons to recognize an objective reality to oldness. First, most people's health and capacities really do change and usually decline near the end of life. Second, in terms of social justice, it is significant that people's needs for services and support tend to be greater when they are chronologically old than at any time other than, perhaps, infancy and childhood. It is important to continue to recognize that old age is a significant stage of life, even if it is arriving later, within some societies at least.

Oldness is a universal possibility, and if we are fortunate, we will all get old. There is therefore all the more reason not to stigmatize it, but instead to (re)claim oldness as a valued identity and stage of life.

Acknowledgements I am very grateful to Geoffrey Scarre for his comments on an earlier version of this chapter.

NOTES

1. Sometimes "old" carries positive connotations, for example when we speak of old wine, old masters, or old institutions. But the positive connotations are more usual in application to things than to people, and there are fewer of these than of cases where "old" has a negative connotation.
2. It's significant that there are at least two main classes of antonyms of "old": An entity that is not old either may be young or it may be new. Some of the negative connotations in Western culture of "old" as applied to people may come from the fact that the word is also the antonym of "new."
3. I will not argue here for the existence of ageism and its manifestations, but ample evidence of ageism is presented by Margaret Morganroth Gullette (2004, 2011).

4. Deborah Gale points out that, in response to ageism, aging Baby Boomers often strive for "agelessness" via technological and medical enhancements (Gale 2012, pp. 55–56). As Susan Wendell says, "expectations of decline and ideals of graceful aging occur together" (Wendell 1999, p. 136).

5. Even though to be old is not necessarily to be ill, impaired, feeble, or debilitated. One has only to consider the case of Olga Kotelko, who in her 90s was setting track records (Grierson 2014).

6. This observation may seem exaggerated, perhaps even grotesquely so. And it might be objected that, while youth often regards oldness with revulsion, old persons sometimes regard young ones with disdain. The difference, however, is that Western culture is devoted to preserving and enhancing youthfulness for as long as possible, with entire industries dedicated to approaching that goal. But no aspect of western culture encourages aspirations to oldness; being old is a condition to be postponed or avoided, and hence to be dreaded.

7. Indeed, the *American Heritage* Dictionary says that "old" 'suggests at least a degree of *physical infirmity and age-related restrictions*' (quoted in Yagoda 2015, my emphasis).

8. As Gullette notes, "Many people are systematically disadvantaged throughout their lives. Their midlife wage-peak is low. Old age—if by that ugly shorthand we mean, as so many do, income declines and physical ailments—for them starts young" (Gullette 2011, p. 74).

9. Gullette goes so far as to say that before the decline in infant mortality in the USA around 1900, old people seemed the healthiest group precisely "because they had survived so much. Death occurred so frequently to newborns and children under five that *they* seemed heavy with it, heavier perhaps than all other categories but the enfeebled" (Gullette 2004, p. 108, her emphasis).

10. Silvers remarks, "feeling old or being treated as old seems to happen when people age out of productive social roles. … Where work roles demand youthful capacity for great physical exertion and stamina, people are likely to be considered old at an earlier age. Also, and especially for women, being viewed as no longer executing a reproductive role often prompts being designated as old" (Silvers 2012, p. 9).

11. "[A]n event's contribution to the value of one's life depends on its narrative relation to other events" (Velleman 1993, p. 344).

12. Concepts of oldness can be highly gendered. For discussion of this theme, see the papers in Pearsall 1997.

13. Perhaps if Western society valued oldness as much as it values youth—or better yet, valued *all* stages of life as significant for the human project—at least some of the problems associated with old age would be diminished.

REFERENCES

Altmann, Ros. 2015. Who are you calling old? Let's ditch ageist stereotypes. *The Guardian.* http://www.theguardian.com/society/2015/feb/04/old-ditch-ageist-stereotypes. Accessed 8 Mar 2015.

Arias, Elizabeth. 2014. United States life tables, 2010. *National Vital Statistics Reports.* http://www.cdc.gov/nchs/data/nvsr/nvsr63/nvsr63_07.pdf. Accessed 18 Mar 2015.

Arnquist, Sarah. 2009. How old do you feel? It depends on your age. *The New York Times.* http://www.nytimes.com/2009/06/30/health/30aging.html?ref=heal th&_r=0. Accessed 11 Mar 2015.

Baars, Jan. 2007. A triple temporality of aging: Chronological measurement, personal experience, and narrative articulation. In *Aging and time: Multidisciplinary perspectives,* ed. Jan Baars and Henk Visser, 1–42. Amityville: Baywood Publishing.

De Beauvoir, Simone. 1972. *The coming of age.* New York: Putnam's.

De Lange, Frits. 2013. Loving later life: Aging and the love imperative. *Journal of the Society of Christian Ethics* 33 (2): 169–184.

Gadow, Sally. 1991. Recovering the body in aging. In *Aging and ethics: Philosophical problems in gerontology,* ed. Nancy S. Jecker, 113–120. Clifton: Humana Press.

Gale, Deborah. 2012. Longevity in the 21st century: Re-evaluating the aging baby boomers' role. *The New Bioethics* 18 (1): 50–67.

Göttlich, Andreas. 2013. When I was young: The idealization of the interchangeability of phases of life. *Human Studies* 36: 217–233.

Grierson, Bruce. 2014. *What makes Olga run? The mystery of the 90-something track star and what she can teach us about living longer, happier lives.* New York: Henry Holt.

Gullette, Margaret Morganroth. 2004. *Aged by culture.* Chicago: University of Chicago Press.

———. 2011. *Agewise: Fighting the new ageism in America.* Chicago: University of Chicago Press.

Hayflick, Leonard. 2002. Anarchy in gerontological terminology. *The Gerontologist* 42 (3): 416–421.

Kallen, Horace M. 1972. Philosophy, aging and the aged. *Journal of Value Inquiry* 6: 1–21.

Kingston, Anne. 2014. Why it's time to face up to old age. *Maclean's.* http://www.macleans.ca/society/health/an-age-old-problem/. Accessed 22 Feb 2015.

Mothersill, Mary. 1999. Old age. *Proceedings and Addresses of the American Philosophical Association* 73 (2): 9–23.

Nelson, James Lindemann. 1999. Death's gender. In *Mother time: Women, aging, and ethics,* ed. Margaret Urban Walker, 113–129. Lanham: Rowman & Littlefield.

Overall, Christine. 2003. *Aging, death, and human longevity: A philosophical inquiry.* Cambridge: MIT Press.

Pearsall, Marilyn, ed. 1997. *The other within us: Feminist explorations of women and aging.* Boulder: Westview Press.

Rubin, Lillian B. 2011. The hard truth about getting old. *Salon.* http://www.salon.com/2011/08/04/lillian_rubin_on_ageism/. Accessed 22 Feb 2015.

Scarre, Geoffrey. 2007. *Death.* Montreal: McGill-Queen's University Press.

Silvers, Anita. 2012. Too old for the good of health? *American Philosophical Association Newsletter on Philosophy and Medicine* 22 (2): 6–12.

Small, Helen. 2007. *The long life.* Oxford: Oxford University Press.

Velleman, J. David. 1993. Well-being and time. In *The metaphysics of death*, ed. John Martin Fischer, 329–355. Stanford: Stanford University Press.

Walker, Margaret Urban. 1999. Getting out of line: alternatives to life as a career. In *Mother time: Women, aging, and ethics*, ed. Margaret Urban Walker, 97–111. Lanham: Rowman & Littlefield.

Wendell, Susan. 1999. Old women out of control: Some thoughts on aging, ethics, and psychosomatic medicine. In *Mother time: Women, aging, and ethics*, ed. Margaret Urban Walker, 133–149. Lanham: Rowman & Littlefield.

Whitney, Craig R. 1997. Jeanne Calment, world's elder, dies at 122. *The New York Times.* http://www.nytimes.com/1997/08/05/world/jeanne-calment-world-s-elder-dies-at-122.html. Accessed 21 Mar 2015.

World Bank. 2015a. Life expectancy at birth, female (years). http://data.worldbank.org/indicator/SP.DYN.LE00.FE.IN/countries. Accessed 18 Mar 2015.

———. 2015b. Life expectancy at birth, male (years). http://data.worldbank.org/indicator/SP.DYN.LE00.MA.IN/countries. Accessed 18 Mar 2015.

———. 2015c. Life expectancy at birth, total (years). http://data.worldbank.org/indicator/SP.DYN.LE00.IN. Accessed 22 Feb 2015.

World Health Organization. 2015. Definition of an older or elderly person. http://www.who.int/healthinfo/survey/agingdefnolder/en/. Accessed 18 Mar 2015.

Yagoda, Ben. 2015. The older man and the dea. *Lingua Franca.* http://chronicle.com/blogs/linguafranca/2015/01/09/the-older-man-and-the-sea/. Accessed 3 Feb 2015.

PART IV

Enhancement

CHAPTER 9

Why Parents Should Enhance Their Children

Christopher Freiman

Imagine a father named "Homer." Homer feeds his eight-year old daughter Lisa a steady diet of Cap'n Crunch and Dr. Pepper. Most days, Homer plops Lisa in front of the television instead of taking her to the playground to get some exercise and sunshine. He skips Lisa's vaccinations and dentist appointments. Homer forgets Lisa's birthday every year and never reads her bedtime stories. He homeschools her, but he's an incompetent and uninterested teacher, so Lisa ends up with no shot at attending college or getting a good job. Homer's parenting leaves Lisa unhealthy, unhappy, and unequipped for long-term success.

Homer is incontrovertibly a bad parent. He isn't meeting his parental obligations. Homer owes it to Lisa to do what he can to help her be healthy, happy, and successful. But he isn't creating an environment that's conducive to those ends.

My argument is simple: all else equal, if parents don't pursue biotechnological enhancements for their children that would help them be healthier, happier, and more successful, then they're failing to meet their parental obligations. In short, if parents don't enhance their children, they're doing something *wrong*. There's no principled difference between failing to

C. Freiman (✉)
College of William & Mary, Williamsburg, VA, USA

© The Author(s) 2018
J. Flanigan, T.L. Price (eds.), *The Ethics of Ability and Enhancement*,
Jepson Studies in Leadership, DOI 10.1057/978-1-349-95303-5_9

enhance your children's environment and failing to enhance your children's genetic makeup, for example.

I start by arguing that parents have a defeasible obligation to do the best they can for their children, an obligation that implies that parents have a defeasible obligation to use biotechnological enhancements as they become safe and accessible (1). Since the burden of justification rests with those who oppose biotechnological enhancements, I then consider defeaters for the parental obligation to enhance. Some argue that we should only use bio-technology to cure diseases rather than enhance beyond some norm (2). Others allege that enhancing children will corrupt their relationship with their parents (3). Then I address worries about the social costs of wide-spread enhancement (4). I conclude that the case for enhancement ulti-mately stands (5).

1   PARENTAL OBLIGATIONS

All else equal, parents are obligated to do what they can to help their children live happier, healthier, and more successful lives. I won't spend much time defending this claim because I doubt it's controversial. To be clear: I'm not claiming that parents must maximize their children's long-term welfare all-things-considered. Parental obligations are defeasible. Par-ents may spend a night at the movies even if their children would be marginally happier with them at home. They may also donate money to charity overseas that could be spent upgrading their children's bikes. And there are familiar deontic constraints: for instance, don't injure a stranger's child to ensure that your daughter wins a spot on the basketball team.

So why think that parents have a defeasible obligation to improve their children's welfare? Let's look at some cases. Imagine you can send your child to one of two schools. They are equal in all respects, except that school A will better prepare your child for college and the job market than school B. Or, you can take your child to one of two pediatricians. They are equal in all respects except that, under the care of Dr. Adler, your child will experi-ence fewer colds and broken bones than she would under the care of Dr. Brooks. Lastly, suppose you can move to one of two towns. The towns are equal in all respects except that your child will be happier in town A than town B.

In these three cases, a parent would be doing something wrong (nothing else considered) if they chose the worse school, doctor, or home for their child. These cases suggest that parents have an obligation to make their children happier, healthier, and more prepared for long-term economic success. I take this judgment to be as uncontroversial as any starting point we can expect in philosophy.

But if parents owe it to their children to increase their odds of health, happiness, and success, then it seems as if they ought to pursue biotechnological enhancements for their children when doing so increases their children's odds of health, happiness, and success. The reason that counts in favor of, for example, sending your child to a better doctor—optimizing her health—also counts in favor of pharmaceutical or genetic interventions.

A few initial clarifications are in order. First, by "enhancement" I mean pharmaceutical or genetic modifications of existing embryos or children.[1] Second, my argument takes a conditional form: *if* enhancement technology that would make children happier and healthier is accessible and safe, then parents ought to use it (ceteris paribus). The reason I focus on the conditional is because I'm interested in the principle of the thing, not the practice. So I set aside feasibility and safety concerns. Think of it like this. If your child has to swim across a crocodile-infested river to get to soccer practice, then you shouldn't send her to soccer practice. This consideration doesn't show that it's intrinsically bad to sign up your child for soccer—it's just too risky given the circumstances.

2   CURING CHILDREN VERSUS ENHANCING CHILDREN

As noted, the obligation to enhance your children can be defeated. One popular objection presses the moral difference between "cures" and "enhancements."[2] To cure a child is to raise them to the norm. To enhance a child is to raise them above the norm. (Specifying what counts as the "norm" is tricky; more in a minute.) Some ethicists argue that cures, but not enhancements, are morally acceptable. So parents may rightfully use genetic engineering to fight their children's cancer but not to endow them with superhuman speed.

In support of this distinction, consider the difference between placing your daughter's broken arm in a cast and giving her elective Tommy John surgery (replacing her arm's ligament with a tendon from her leg) to accelerate her fastball. No one objects to the former, but I'd wager that most object to the latter. One plausible explanation for our different attitudes toward the two procedures is that the first cures but the second enhances. That is, fixing a broken bone raises your daughter to the norm but elective Tommy John surgery raises her above it.

Despite its intuitive appeal, the moral distinction between cure and enhancement doesn't survive scrutiny. Let's start with a problem at the heart of the distinction: what counts as the norm that we ought not surpass? We could take *normal* to denote something like "statistically average." Most people have unbroken bones, so repairing your daughter's broken arm is acceptable. On the other hand, most people don't have leg tendons in place of their arm's ligament, so elective Tommy John surgery is off the table.

This statistical specification of *normal* doesn't work. Imagine propaganda alleging that fluoridation is a Communist conspiracy sways every parent in the world—except you. In this case, brushing your son's teeth with fluoridated toothpaste would make him statistically anomalous. Still, you should brush your son's teeth with fluoridated toothpaste. Why? Because it's good for him. This case suggests that what's relevant to parental decision making is whether something hurts or helps your children, not whether it's typical or atypical.

An alternative way to specify what counts as the norm is to appeal to some notion of what's natural for human beings. To help us fix ideas, consider a rough formulation: X is natural just in case human beings evolved to X.

The trouble is, we do plenty of things that are unnatural according to this formulation. Nick Bostrom elaborates:

> Our current extended phenotypes (and the lives that we lead) are markedly different from those of our hunter-gatherer ancestors. We read and write, we wear clothes, we live in cities, we earn money and buy food from the super-market, we call people on the telephone, watch television, read newspapers, drive cars, file taxes, vote in national elections, women give birth in hospitals, and life-expectancy is three times longer than in the Pleistocene [...] In the eyes of a hunter-gatherer, we might already appear 'posthuman'. Yet these radical extensions of human capabilities – some of them biological, others external – have not divested us of moral status or dehumanized us in the sense of making us generally unworthy and base. Similarly, should we or our descendants one day succeed in becoming what relative to current standards we may refer to as posthuman, this need not entail a loss of dignity either. (Bostrom 2005, p. 213)

We have already artificially enhanced human nature in countless ways. Driving a car, for instance, takes us beyond our natural capacities—it doesn't cure a disease—but there's nothing morally wrong with it. Indeed, we've become so accustomed to our existing enhancements that we tend to forget that they really are artificial enhancements over and above the natural human state. The polio vaccine enhances our immunity beyond what is natural, but there is no moral problem with using the polio vaccine.[3] To the contrary, as a parent, you're doing something morally *wrong* if you don't vaccinate your kids. More generally, it's hard to see why some traits being statistically average or conducive to your great-great-(etc.) grandparents' producing more offspring and eating more venison is reasons-implicating.

Leon Kass fields a subtler version of the worry that enhancements take us beyond the natural in an objectionable way: "To the extent that an achievement is the result of some extraneous intervention, it is detachable from the agent whose achievement it purports to be [..] If human flourishing means not just the accumulation of external achievements and a full curriculum vitae but a life-long *being-at-work* exercising one's *human* powers *well* and without great impediment, our genuine happiness requires that there be little gap, if any, between the dancer and the dance" (Kass 2003, p. 23, italics in the original). Kass's concern is not so much with what's natural and what's not, but rather with no longer being able to see our accomplishments as our own instead of the products of external enhancements.

One difficulty with Kass's position is figuring out when an "extraneous intervention" cheapens our achievements. Let's flash back thousands of years into the past and consider the first human to strap shoes on her feet. With this enhancement, she is able to hunt deer more effectively and comfortably. Still, it doesn't seem like the shoes detach the achiever from the achievement. They *assisted* the achievement to be sure, but not in a way that obviated the use of her human powers. (We don't think that the accomplishments of contemporary marathoners are cheapened because they get to wear shoes.) Similar remarks apply to, for instance, enhancements that enable runners to strengthen their leg muscles beyond their natural endowments. As John Harris notes, "If I take a pill which improves my memory or powers of concentration, I will still have to study, and use that study to draw conclusions, formulate ideas, or write books for which I may take appropriate credit or blame: credit for the work and ideas but not the powers of concentration or memory that helped me to those achievements" (Harris 2010, p. 133).

Kass's related objection that "biotechnological shortcuts" will undermine "disciplined and dedicated striving" falls short as well (Kass 2003, p. 21). To see why, think of the natural variation in talents. LeBron James faces fewer obstacles to playing basketball well than I do. I must undertake far more disciplined and dedicated striving than LeBron to even graze the rim of a basketball hoop. Still, I don't think that LeBron's achievements on the basketball court are thereby diminished. (I'm reminded of a poster on the wall of my high school math class that featured a quotation from Einstein: "Do not worry about your difficulties in mathematics. I can assure you mine are still greater.")

To bring this discussion back to the context of enhancing one's children, consider a case. Suppose I discover that my child, thanks to a one-in-a-million result in the genetic lottery, has the physical makeup of a young LeBron James. Surely it would be bad parenting on my part to deprive him of calcium and exercise—thereby hampering him Harrison Bergeron-style—to increase the amount of disciplined and dedicated striving he'll need to undertake to play basketball well.

Along these lines, Nick Bostrom and Toby Ord propose that we subject arguments in the enhancement debate to what they call the "reversal test":

> When a proposal to change a certain parameter is thought to have bad overall consequences, consider a change to the same parameter in the opposite direction. If this is also thought to have bad overall consequences, then the onus is on those who reach these conclusions to explain why our position cannot be improved through changes to this parameter. If they are unable to do so, then we have reason to suspect that they suffer from status quo bias. (Bostrom and Ord 2006, p. 665)

Let's apply the reversal test to the case at hand. If you think that increasing your child's natural musculature would be bad, ask yourself if you think *decreasing* your child's natural musculature would also be bad. If so, that means you are committed to the claim that your child's natural musculature is perfect—there's no room for improvement. That the status quo is perfect is of course *possible*, but as Bostrom and Ord stress, improbable. So Bostrom and Ord argue that the burden of justification rests with those endorse the optimality of the status quo. If Kass wants to claim that I should not improve *or* impair my child's natural musculature, then he must meet the challenge of explaining why my child's natural musculature is perfect.

Interestingly, it's not entirely clear what Kass's stance on my thought experiment would be. He says,

Drugs to steady the hand of a neurosurgeon or to prevent sweaty palms in a concert pianist cannot be regarded as "cheating," for they are not the source of the excellent activity or achievement. And, for people dealt a meager hand in the dispensing of nature's gifts, it should not be called cheating or cheap if biotechnology could assist them in becoming better equipped—whether in body or in mind. Even steroids for the proverbial 97-pound weakling help him to get to the point where, through his own effort and training, he can go head-to-head with the naturally better endowed. (Kass 2003, p. 22)

I agree with Kass here, but I think he concedes too much if he wants to maintain his anti-enhancement position. As discussed above, enhancing one's athletic ability or intelligence doesn't obviate effort—naturally athletic and intelligent people still exert effort. Maybe Kass is suggesting that the use of biotechnology is permissible if it helps someone reach the status quo—if, for instance, it helps the "proverbial 97-pound weakling [. . .] go head-to-head with the naturally better endowed" (Kass 2003, p. 22, italics in the original). But this move simply takes us back to the problematic cure-enhancement distinction. It implies that uses of biotechnology that take us beyond the status quo are impermissible. As we've seen, though, this result is implausible: it's permissible to give your child the polio vaccine or use fluoridated toothpaste even if no one else is doing it. (You might be thinking that the problem concerns enhancements that give your children competitive advantages, so vaccines and fluoride are fine. I'll address this objection in Sect. 4.)

Kass also worries that biotechnological enhancements will encourage a kind of passivity that's at odds with our flourishing:

Biomedical interventions act directly on the human body and mind to bring about their effects on a subject who is not merely passive but who plays no role at all. He can at best *feel* their effects *without understanding their meaning in human terms* [. . .] A drug that brightened our mood would alter us without our understanding how and why it did so—whereas a mood brightened as a fitting response to the arrival of a loved one or an achievement in one's work is perfectly, because humanly, intelligible. (Kass 2003, p. 22)

First things first—even if this argument provides adults with good reason to not use biotechnological enhancement, I don't think it carries over to the case of children. Generally speaking, children don't understand "how and why" interventions work to enhance their body and mind. The polio vaccine and fluoridated toothpaste, to take my two old standbys, act directly on children's bodies and only bad parents would deprive their kids of these treatments.

Consider also environmental modifications to "grease the wheels" of learning. No one thinks that using *Hooked on Phonics* to make it easier for children to learn how to read is morally dubious. And toddler meditation, which is increasingly trendy, apparently brightens children's moods without (I'm assuming) the children understanding "how and why" it does so. (Indeed, I'm skeptical that worries about passivity succeed in building a persuasive case against enhancement for adults. After all, I use fluoridated toothpaste and get flu vaccinations—treatments that act directly on my body—and I don't think my flourishing has been set back as a result.)

A final problem for the by-your-own-efforts objection is that it applies to cures as well as enhancements. Suppose your daughter is suffering from knee pain and dysfunction. Your doctor presents you with two equally safe and effective treatment options. The first is months of weight training and targeted stretching; the second is a knee replacement surgery that will have her up and running in a week. The surgery seems like a "biotechnological shortcut" that obviates "disciplined and dedicated striving." Still, I think most parents would opt for the surgery and rightly so.

3   THE PARENT–CHILD RELATIONSHIP

Maybe enhancing children would corrupt their relationship with their parents. We can cash out this objection in different ways.

Perhaps enhancements compromise children's autonomy. Sandel (2004) wonders whether "genetic enhancements for musical talent, say, or athletic prowess, would point children toward particular choices, and so designer children would never be fully free." But Sandel himself rejects this argument: children aren't in control of their genes with or without genetic modification. Whether the natural lottery or parents distribute genes, children themselves have no say.

An argument that Sandel *does* endorse claims that parents should value their children as gifts to be appreciated rather than products to be designed. Here's Sandel (2004):

> To appreciate children as gifts is to accept them as they come, not as objects of our design or products of our will or instruments of our ambition. Parental love is not contingent on the talents and attributes a child happens to have. We choose our friends and spouses at least partly on the basis of qualities we

find attractive. But we do not choose our children. Their qualities are unpredictable, and even the most conscientious parents cannot be held wholly responsible for the kind of children they have.

Handpicking the qualities possessed by our children would corrupt the attitude we have toward them. Consider the difference between shopping for a refrigerator and conceiving a child. When you shop for a refrigerator, you want to make sure it's the right size, made of the right materials, energy efficient, and so on. But it seems like this is the wrong attitude to have toward your child—that is, to try your best to ensure that she has the "right" height, weight, IQ, and so on. To think of your child in the same terms as your refrigerator degrades both you and your child. To reiterate Sandel's (2004) point, "Parental love is not contingent on the talents and attributes a child happens to have." Your attachment to your refrigerator is conditional on its possession of your desired attributes; by contrast, your attachment to your child should be *un*conditional.

To further support this idea, Sandel (2004) analogizes genetically enhancing children to hyperparenting. Just as micromanaging your children's environment is unhealthy, so too is micromanaging their genes. To see the dangers of such micromanagement, consider the case of Todd Marinovich. Marinovich's father, Marv, tried to optimize Todd's chances of excelling at football. A *Sports Illustrated* article titled "Bred to be a Superstar" described Todd as "America's first test-tube athlete":

> He has never eaten a Big Mac or an Oreo or a Ding Dong. When he went to birthday parties as a kid, he would take his own cake and ice cream to avoid sugar and refined white flour. He would eat homemade catsup, prepared with honey. He did consume beef but not the kind injected with hormones. He ate only unprocessed dairy products. He teethed on frozen kidney. When Todd was one month old, Marv was already working on his son's physical conditioning. He stretched his hamstrings. Pushups were next. Marv invented a game in which Todd would try to lift a medicine ball onto a kitchen counter. Marv also put him on a balance beam. Both activities grew easier when Todd learned to walk. There was a football in Todd's crib from day one. "Not a real NFL ball," says Marv. "That would be sick; it was a stuffed ball." (Looney 1988)

Tragically (although perhaps not unexpectedly), Todd has struggled with drug addiction (Streeter 2014).

Marv is a case of hyperparenting run amok. If ever there were a child who seemed designed by rather than gifted to their parents, it would be Todd. Certainly, Marv's approach to parenting Todd represents, in Sandel's words, "the one-sided triumph of willfulness over giftedness, of dominion over reverence, of molding over beholding" (Sandel 2004). It treats children as projects rather than gifts. Since it's wrong for Marv to micromanage Todd's environment to maximize his chances of becoming a professional football player, wouldn't it be wrong to micromanage a child's genes for the same purpose?

In reply, I'd like to emphasize the distinction between management and *micro*management. Just because Marv erred in giving his son excessive exercise doesn't mean that giving your child the opportunity to exercise is bad. You can have too much of a good thing. That you shouldn't give your child an *over*dose of Tylenol doesn't imply that you shouldn't give your child the *correct* dose of Tylenol when she runs a fever. Similarly, micromanaging your child's environment is bad parenting, but *wisely* managing your child's environment is good parenting. There is nothing wrong with inclining your children in certain directions and not others. This is precisely what good parents do. Good parents design environmental conditions that incline their children toward empathy, education, self-discipline, and good health. My children's natural inclinations involve eating lots of sugar. And yet, I don't stock my pantry with chocolate chip cookies. Does this mean I'm not accepting my children "as they come," as gifts, because I'm trying to shape them in certain ways? Not at all. It's true that I'm trying to manage their environmental conditions, but I'm doing so to enable them to live happier and healthier lives over the long run. (If, like Marv, I never let my children eat a blueberry muffin, I'd be going overboard.) Similarly, micromanaging your children's genetic makeup—trying to design them into football players, for instance—is bad parenting, but managing your child's genetic makeup so that they live happier and healthier lives over the long run is good parenting.

Drawing a distinction between the use and misuse of biotechnology also enables me to address Sandel's objection that genetic enhancement would explode parental responsibility in undesirable ways. According to Sandel (2004), genetic enhancement wouldn't destroy responsibility, it would actually make us responsible for *too much*: "Parents become responsible for choosing, or failing to choose, the right traits for their children." Parents might become crushed by the burden of being responsible for pretty much everything about their children rather than being able to chalk certain things up to luck. As things stand, children might wish that their parents had raised them differently but they also realize that there are certain things parents have no control over, like the looks they passed on. But imagine how resentful future generations will be if they know that their parents picked out the nose they hate from a catalog.

Here again, I think the reply to Sandel's objection centers on the distinction between a wise use and a misuse of the opportunities afforded by enhancement. Consider that medicine today offers more diagnoses and possible treatments for children than it did in decades past. As a result, parents are responsible for their children's health in more ways than they were in 1916. Whether this expansion of responsibility turns out to be good or bad depends on the parent. A parent can obsessively scan WebMD every time their child has a cough and take them to the pediatrician twice a month, or they can make judicious use of medical tests and treatment. If it's the latter, the expansion of medical technology is good for parents and children because it enables better health.

The same analysis applies to biotechnological enhancement. If parents go overboard and obsessively micromanage all aspects of their children's body and personality a la Marv Marinovich, that's a bad decision. But that enhancement can be misused is no more an indictment of enhancement than the fact that glue can be huffed is an indictment of glue. Enhancement is a tool that, when used wisely, can help children flourish.

Finally, I'm not sure that Sandel is able to make his distinction between cures and enhancement stick. He says, "To appreciate children as gifts or blessings is not, of course, to be passive in the face of illness or disease. Medical intervention to cure or prevent illness or restore the injured to health does not desecrate nature but honors it" (Sandel 2004). It seems to me that if the giftedness argument works against enhancement, it also works against medical intervention to cure illness. Both involve deliberately altering your child's given nature. Here's Harris:

> The claim that attempts to alter our nature through biotechnology are different from both medicine and education or child-rearing seems wholly implausible. Medicine uses technology and biotechnology; indeed, much of medicine is a part of technology, it is a technological genre. For the rest, what matters surely is the ethics of altering our nature, not the means that we adopt. (Harris 2010, p. 125)

Organ transplants look like an attempt to actively control nature even though they merely restore the patient to health. By analogy, when a mechanic repairs a car it seems as though she is exercising a kind of mastery over the car no less than when she enhances the car by replacing the old engine with a newer and more powerful one.

4   SOCIAL COSTS

Here's another natural objection to biotechnological enhancement: rich parents are more likely to buy enhancements for their children, a result that would compound existing inequalities. It's already unfair that rich parents have a leg up on securing their child's spot at Yale; they shouldn't pile on by purchasing genetic advantages too.

Even if this objection works, it wins the battle at the cost of the war. After all, if your objection to enhancement is that too few people will receive it, you're implicitly acknowledging that enhancement itself is a good thing. That's why we want everyone to have it. (Sandel (2004) and Kass (2003) notice this too.)

Still, the unequal distribution of enhancement is a problem worth addressing. But there are a number of reasons to be optimistic that we can solve the problem. For one, access will probably expand over time. As Harris points out, technology tends to get cheaper: today's staple was yesterday's luxury (Harris 2010, p. 31). When I was in college, the iPod was reserved for a select and wealthy few. Today you can buy an MP3 player at Walgreens for an hour's wages. Rich first movers subsidize the research and development that makes products cheaper down the line.

Even if you're pessimistic about the market-driven democratization of enhancement, the inequality objection still isn't decisive: we can simply subsidize enhancement (Harris 2010). Many argue that, for example, widespread access to a college education is a sufficiently important social goal to justify the subsidization of a college education. I see little reason to treat biotechnological enhancement differently.

But suppose for argument's sake that inequalities in people's access to enhancement cannot be lessened via technological progress or subsidization. Even so, parents have reason to enhance their own children. To see why, consider two ways of specifying the inequality objection. The first objects to inequality in itself. On this view, enhancing your own child is wrong even if no one else is made worse off in absolute terms.

Consider a counterexample to this view. Suppose both your child and your neighbor's child have headaches. You only have one dose of children's Tylenol. If you use the pill to alleviate your own child's headache, you create an inequality between your own child and your neighbor's child. But I doubt anyone would blame you for helping your child.[4]

A second version of the inequality objection spotlights the ways in which inequality can worsen people's welfare in absolute terms. The clearest examples tend to concern competitions: the higher your child's SAT score relative to other college applicants, the worse the other applicants' chances of securing a spot at that college.

Plausibly, your special parental obligation to your own children trumps social costs, at least in some cases. Suppose that buying your child a college education puts those who cannot afford college at a labor market disadvantage. Even so, I don't think you're obligated to keep your child out of college. The same can be said for feeding your kid a healthy diet even if it puts her competitors for a spot on the basketball team at a disadvantage.

What's more, I'm not sold on the claim that enhancing your own child—be it environmentally, pharmaceutically, or genetically—typically creates social costs. Enhancing your children's education is apt to enrich their human capital, which can create positive externalities. It's good for society to have better educated teachers, doctors, and engineers. A similar point applies to biotechnological enhancement. It's good for society to have more talented teachers, doctors, and engineers. Elon Musk is more talented than I am—there's a (large) gap between us—but his talents help rather than hurt me. In a Rawlsian spirit, we should welcome inequalities that benefit us all, particularly the least advantaged. (And let's not overlook other kinds of biological enhancements, such as increasing empathy, that are clearly good for society on the whole.)[5]

We can also redeploy the reversal test to challenge the claim that unequal increases in intelligence (for instance) ought to be resisted. Suppose we reduced the intelligence of all Ivy League graduates by 10 percent. It seems as though this outcome would be bad for society even though it reduces inequalities in intelligence. But the social cost objection to enhancement alleges that *increasing* inequalities in intelligence is bad too. The implication, then, is that we just happen to be at the socially optimal distribution of intelligence. Given that this coincidence is highly unlikely, the burden rests with the opponent of enhancement to argue for this conclusion.

Lastly, consider the objection that giving parents the option to enhance their children will produce an arms race. If biotechnological enhancements become the norm, then parents must use them (even if they'd otherwise prefer not to) to ensure that their children keep pace with their peers.[6]

In reply to this objection, let me note that the availability of certain environmental advantages can produce arms races too. If most job applicants have gone to college, failure to send your child to college is a serious parenting mistake. But if college attendance is beneficial (or at least harmless), then the lesson should be to expand access to college rather than to stop sending your children college. Similarly, since it's good for children to be happy or healthy, we should expand access to biotechnology that encourages these traits rather eschew them entirely.

Maybe the argument is that an enhancement arms race is socially wasteful—everyone is spending resources to enhance their children, but in the end no one gets ahead. However, this assumes that the proper use of enhancements is to confer competitive advantages on your children, and I don't think that's the case.[7] It would still be wise for me to increase my children's health, happiness, and intelligence in absolute terms even if it left their relative position in the distribution of these traits unchanged. These are good things for my children to have regardless of how much others have.

5   CONCLUSION

Harris (2010) suggests that disgust (he calls it the "yuck factor") explains the difference between our visceral reaction to artificial enhancements like binoculars on the one hand and to genetic modification on the other. Genetic modification involves invasive manipulation of our given natures—and that's disturbing.

I suspect that Harris is right here, but we'd need to undertake empirical inquiry to confirm this suspicion. That said, there's some suggestive evidence for Harris's claim. Psychologist Jonathan Haidt argues that concern for bodily "purity" or "sanctity" pervades commonsense moral judgment on both sides of the aisle. Haidt says, "Conservatives—particularly religious conservatives—are more likely to view the body as a temple [. . .] rather than as a machine to be optimized, or as a playground to be used for fun" (Haidt 2013, p. 175). Harvesting stem cells from embryos and having causal sex, for instance, are both conservative no-nos. Haidt suggests that sanctity intuitions may also play a role in left-leaning antipathy for the products of industrial capitalism—antipathy "not just for the physical pollution they create but also for a more symbolic kind of pollution—a degradation of nature, and of humanity's original nature" (Haidt 2013, p. 176). The intuition that there's something special about our original nature that shouldn't be corrupted by intervention seems to transcend political affiliation.

Suppose, then, that something like disgust is at least partly responsible for opposition to biotechnological enhancement. What's the *normative* upshot? At a minimum, we shouldn't take queasiness about tinkering with what's natural to settle any philosophical arguments. Our gut-level aversion to the "unnatural" has a bad track record. Anesthesia, for instance, was initially taken to be morally suspect (Jay 2009). Pain was seen as "an irreducible part of the human condition [...] 'the voice of nature'" and so something to endure rather than eliminate (Jay 2009). But today we think this attitude gets things backwards: no ethical twenty-first-century dentist extracts wisdom teeth without a painkiller. And this is just one example among many of disgust leading our moral judgment astray.[8]

Of course, our gut *might* be on target. But we shouldn't trust it without the backing of arguments. So I disagree with Kass's famous endorsement of the "wisdom of repugnance":

> Repugnance, here as elsewhere, revolts against the excesses of human willfulness, warning us not to transgress what is unspeakably profound. Indeed, in this age in which everything is held to be permissible so long as it is freely done, in which our given human nature no longer commands respect, in which our bodies are regarded as mere instruments of our autonomous rational wills, repugnance may be the only voice left that speaks up to defend the central core of our humanity. (Kass 1998, p. 687)

Even if Kass turns out to be right that "our given human nature" represents a boundary that we shouldn't transgress, he is wrong that this boundary is *unspeakably* profound. We can and should talk about it. And if, in the course of the conversation, we find that we have good reason to transgress the boundary of our given nature, then we should transgress it.

NOTES

1. So I am not making an argument about whether parents ought to *select* embryos for certain genetic traits. For an argument to this effect, see Savulescu (2001). The selection issue is wrapped up in the nonidentity problem in a way that the modification of existing children is not.
2. See Sandel (2004), Kass (2003).

3. For a good discussion of the vaccine case, see Harris (2010, chap. 3).
4. As Harris puts the point, it is "doubtful ethics to deny a benefit to any until it can be delivered to all" (Harris 2010, p. 28).
5. For discussion, see Persson and Savulescu (2012).
6. See Kass (2003, p. 16).
7. For a similar point, see Harris (2010, p. 22ff.).
8. See, for instance, Nussbaum (2004), Freiman and Lerner (2015), Harris (2010, chap. 2).

REFERENCES

Bostrom, Nick. 2005. In defense of posthuman dignity. *Bioethics* 19 (3): 202–214.
Bostrom, Nick, and Toby Ord. 2006. The reversal test: Eliminating status quo bias in applied ethics. *Ethics* 116 (4): 656–679.
Freiman, Christopher, and Adam Lerner. 2015. Self-ownership and disgust: Why compulsory body part redistribution gets under our skin. *Philosophical Studies* 172 (12): 3167–3190.
Haidt, Jonathan. 2013. *The righteous mind: Why good people are divided by politics and religion.* New York: Vintage Books.
Harris, John. 2010. *Enhancing evolution: The ethical case for making better people.* Princeton: Princeton University Press.
Jay, Mike. 2009. The day pain died: What really happened during the most famous moment in Boston medicine. *Boston Globe.* http://archive.boston.com/bostonglobe/ideas/articles/2009/06/07/the_day_pain_died_what_really_happened_during_the_most_famous_moment_in_boston_medicine/. Accessed 1 Dec 2016.
Kass, L.R. 1998. The wisdom of repugnance: Why we should ban the cloning of humans. *Valparaiso University Law Review. Valparaiso University. School of Law* 32 (2): 679–705.
Kass, Leon. 2003. Ageless bodies, happy souls. *The New Atlantis* 1: 9–28.
Looney, Douglas. 1988. Bred to be a superstar. *Sports Illustrated.* http://www.si.com/vault/1988/02/22/117185/bred-to-be-a-superstar-todd-marinovich-was-groomed-from-infancy-to-be-a-top-notch-quarterback. Accessed 1 Dec 2016.
Nussbaum, Martha Craven. 2004. *Hiding from humanity: Disgust, shame, and the law.* Princeton: Princeton University Press.
Persson, Ingmar, and Julian Savulescu. 2012. *Unfit for the future: The need for moral enhancement.* Oxford: Oxford University Press.
Sandel, Michael. 2004. The case against perfection. *The Atlantic.* https://www.theatlantic.com/magazine/archive/2004/04/the-case-against-perfection/302927/. Accessed 1 Dec 2016.

Savulescu, J. 2001. Procreative beneficence: Why we should select the best children. *Bioethics* 15 (5–6): 413–426.

Streeter, Kurt. 2014. On road to recovery, Todd Marinovich discovers painting. *Los Angeles Times.* http://www.latimes.com/local/la-me-marinovich-20141013-story.html. Accessed 1 Dec 2016.

CHAPTER 10

Cosmopolitan Moral Enhancement

Javier Hidalgo

1   INTRODUCTION

Cosmopolitanism holds that we have demanding duties to other people irrespective of their group affiliations. According to cosmopolitans, we have general duties to aid other people and duties to refrain from harming them simply in virtue of their humanity. Some cosmopolitans deny that ethnic, national, or other social groups have fundamental moral significance and that membership in these groups justifies special obligations. Other cosmopolitans argue that, even if we do have special obligations to our co-ethnics or compatriots, our general duties to other people trump these special obligations. Cosmopolitans oppose nationalism and other forms of in-group partiality, and advocate in favor of policies that aim to protect universal human rights.

Critics have long claimed that cosmopolitanism is unrealistic. These critics allege that people lack the motivation to make sacrifices for humanity at large. We care more about our local communities and nations than we care about humanity. Humans are ethnocentric. We are biased against out-groups and biased in favor of in-groups. We often believe that in-groups are trustworthy, friendly, and cooperative, while out-groups are

J. Hidalgo (✉)
Jepson School of Leadership Studies, University of Richmond, Richmond, VA, USA

© The Author(s) 2018   173
J. Flanigan, T.L. Price (eds.), *The Ethics of Ability and Enhancement*, Jepson Studies in Leadership, DOI 10.1057/978-1-349-95303-5_10

dangerous, unfriendly, and threatening. As a result, we are inclined to benefit the members of our groups when they need assistance and more disposed to harm out-groups if this is necessary to benefit in-groups. Critics contend that cosmopolitan moral demands are infeasible because we predictably refuse to comply with them.[1]

The critics might be right that cosmopolitanism is unrealistic. But this fails to show that we should reject cosmopolitanism. The problem lies with human nature, not cosmopolitanism. So, if possible, we should change our nature. In this chapter, I will consider the desirability of one way of modifying our dispositions in more cosmopolitan directions: cosmopolitan moral enhancements. I will use the phrase "moral enhancements" broadly to include biomedical interventions that alter people in ways that make their behavior more likely to be morally justified. Cosmopolitan moral enhancements are enhancements that make people more likely to comply with cosmopolitan moral requirements. It is unclear whether cosmopolitan moral enhancements will be viable in the near future. Thus, my argument is conditional: if cosmopolitan moral enhancements one day become viable, then we have strong moral reasons to use them.[2]

I have organized this chapter as follows. In Sect. 2, I will clarify and motivate cosmopolitanism. In Sect. 3, I will argue that ethnocentrism, xenophobia, a desire for social dominance, and other groupish aspects of human psychology explain why many people violate cosmopolitan moral requirements. In Sect. 4, I will make the case for cosmopolitan moral enhancements as a way of increasing compliance with cosmopolitan obligations. In Sect. 5, I will respond to objections. Section 6 concludes.

2   COSMOPOLITANISM

Cosmopolitans hold that we have general negative and positive duties to other people regardless of their group affiliations (by "general" duties, I mean duties that we owe to other people simply in virtue of their humanity). Most cosmopolitans believe general duties defeat special duties to members of our social groups when these duties come into conflict. I will now explain cosmopolitan commitments and the motivations for them in greater detail.

Let's start with negative duties. We should refrain from harming or coercing other people, and moreover, it is generally wrong to harm and coerce other people even if this benefits members of our in-groups. Consider a famous case. Imagine that a runaway trolley is about to hit and kill five people who are tied down on the track. You are standing on the overpass above the tracks. A large man stands next to you. If you push this man off the overpass, the trolley will hit him and his weight will stop the trolley before it hits the five people on the track (stipulate that you are unable to stop the trolley by sacrificing yourself). It seems wrong for you to kill the bystander in order to save the five victims on the track. But suppose that the bystander is Canadian, you are a citizen of the United States, and the people on the track are Americans. Nonetheless, it still appears impermissible to kill the bystander, even though he is a foreigner. In other words, it seems wrong to harm other people to benefit the members of your group. Cosmopolitans think that this judgment applies generally. They claim that it is wrong violate the rights of out-groups in order to benefit in-groups.

Cosmopolitans also think that we have demanding positive duties to the distant needy. To illustrate, consider a version of Peter Singer's famous thought experiment. Imagine that you are walking along one day and you notice a small child drowning in a shallow pond. To save the child, you must jump in the pond immediately, but this will ruin your clothes, which cost $500. It seems that you are morally required to save the child despite the cost to yourself. But imagine that you discover afterward that the boy is actually a foreigner. Suppose that the child is from Haiti, and you are a citizen of the United States. This fact makes no difference. You are obligated to aid the child even though he is a foreigner.

But now imagine that you could donate $500 to an effective charity and save the life of a child in Haiti. It seems that, if you ought to save the drowning child, then you ought to donate the $500 to charity. Singer uses this basic insight to argue that the citizens of affluent states are required to give a large fraction of their incomes to charities that benefit the global poor (Singer 2010). Many people disagree with Singer. People disagree about how demanding our positive duties are and about the best way to discharge these duties. But almost all cosmopolitans conclude that we are obligated to aid the distant needy if we can do so are reasonable cost to ourselves.

Cosmopolitans acknowledge that partiality is sometimes justified. Most cosmopolitans concede that we have special obligations to our intimate associates, such as our friends, spouses, and children. Yet cosmopolitans typically deny that we have special obligations to the members of larger and more impersonal groups, such as the members of our ethnic, racial, or national groups. Uwe Steinhoff describes cosmopolitanism as the view that "state borders and national or ethnic boundaries have no fundamental moral significance, that is, it is the view that there are no ethnic groups, nations or states such that membership in them would confer any moral rights, duties, liberties or responsibilities on responsible adult persons"

(Steinhoff 2013, p. 12). Richard Arneson says that cosmopolitanism is the view that "national communities and nation states lack fundamental (noninstrumental) moral significance. People do not incur moral duties toward the members of their own national community or nation state simply by virtue of membership in such groups" (Arneson 2016).

Radical cosmopolitans claim that our racial, ethnic, and national identities are morally arbitrary. Consider an analogy. We lack duties to other people simply in virtue of the fact that we may share the same eye or skin colors. Radical cosmopolitans say that we lack duties to other people just because they are members of the ethnic or national groups to which we belong. In contrast, more moderate cosmopolitans do allow for some group-based partiality. They claim that we can have special duties to our compatriots, say. Yet all cosmopolitans contend that our obligations to in-groups are delimited by stringent duties to out-groups. Thomas Pogge writes along these lines:

> Holding circumstances fixed, it is perfectly acceptable to be far more willing to help a family member than a neighbour, a neighbour than a compatriot stranger, a compatriot stranger than a stranger abroad. But it is not acceptable to have such a sliding scale in one's concern not to violate human rights. It is not acceptable, for example, to take greater drink-driving risks abroad on the ground that those one is endangering there are only foreigners. In seeking to avoid violating human rights, any agent must give exactly the same high weight to the human rights of every human being. (Pogge 2012, p. 328)

On this view, we can have special duties to in-groups, but duties to respect human rights trump or silence these duties if they come into conflict.

To sum up, I will refer to cosmopolitanism as the view that (1) we have negative and positive duties to other people irrespective of their group affiliations, and (2) it is generally wrong to violate general positive and negative duties to other people in order to benefit the members of one's own ethnic, racial, or national group. I will refrain from arguing in favor of cosmopolitanism here. I will instead assume cosmopolitanism in this paper and explore some of its implications.

3   ETHNOCENTRISM AND HUMAN NATURE

Many people fail to comply with cosmopolitan moral demands. We tend to support harming and coercing out-groups, and we neglect to aid them as much as we should. A cursory knowledge of history suggests that humans have long engaged in aggressive wars, ethnic violence, and discrimination against out-groups. The political scientist R.J. Rummel estimates that governments murdered about 169 million people during twentieth century and a large fraction of these victims were ethnic, racial, or religious minorities (Rummel 1997).

Aggression against out-groups is hardly a relic of the past. It is easy to find contemporary examples in which people harm outsiders or violate their rights. Discrimination against ethnic and racial minorities remains pervasive in many parts of the world. Many people also endorse harming or coercing foreigners. Here is an example. Most states enforce immigration restrictions. They use coercion to prevent foreigners from immigrating, and they deport unauthorized migrants and failed asylum-seekers. Most cosmopolitans endorse broadly open borders.[3] On their view, immigration restrictions violate negative duties because these policies coercively prevent millions of foreigners from escaping poverty, violence, and oppression. Cosmopolitans also argue that immigration restrictions reinforce global inequality. Economists argue that affluent states could reduce global inequality by allowing more immigration (Clemens 2011). Even small relaxations in global labor mobility might significantly benefit people in poor countries. However, immigration restrictions are popular (Pritchett 2006, p. 74). Most citizens of rich states approve of immigration restrictions. Public opinion helps explain why these states enforce restrictive immigration laws that frustrate the basic interests of foreigners.

Many of us fail to satisfy our positive duties to out-groups as well. Again, I will focus on foreigners although a similar point applies to ethnic and racial out-groups. Hundreds of millions of people continue to live in conditions of extreme deprivation. The citizens of affluent states are capable of aiding the global poor at reasonable cost. Some researchers estimate that it is possible to save a life by donating a few thousand dollars to the right charities, particularly charities that implement public health interventions in poor countries.[4] Moreover, the average citizens of high-income states are richer than the vast majority of humanity. Even the poorest citizens of rich states tend to be better off than most people in the world. But the citizens of rich states do little to help destitute foreigners. For instance, the governments of rich states only spend a tiny fraction of their budgets on foreign aid. In contrast, governments spend relatively large sums on reducing domestic poverty.

Private citizens often fail to discharge their duties to aid the global poor as well. When the citizens of rich states do give to charity, they tend to give to charities that benefit their relatively well-off compatriots. In 2009, United States citizens gave just $12 billion to organizations working in the developing world (Global Impact 2013). To put this number in perspective, Americans gave $300 billion to charity, and the gross domestic product of the United States was over $14 trillion in that year. Cosmopolitans maintain that the citizens of the United States are unjustly prioritizing the interests of their own citizens over the interests of more needy foreigners.

So, we routinely fail to conform to the demands of cosmopolitan morality. Why? Part of the answer is that we are tribal and ethnocentric. Evidence from psychology suggests that we have a tendency to trust and cooperate with our in-groups, while we distrust and dislike out-groups. We tend to excuse bad behavior if it is committed by members of in-groups, we attribute more positive attributes to in-groups, and we judge ambiguous behavior more favorably when it is performed by an in-group member. Ethnocentrism leads us to interpret bad behavior on the part of in-group members situationally, but we attribute bad behavior on the part of out-groups to their underlying natures or essences. People also derogate out-groups, especially when their group is under threat.[5]

Take nationalist ethnocentrism as an example. Nationalist ethnocentrism is the tendency to trust and be willing to cooperate with co-nationals, and a disposition to distrust and dislike foreigners. Nationalist ethnocentrism causes people to mistreat foreigners. Psychologists find that people with nationalist dispositions are willing to harm foreigners if this benefits their compatriots (Pratto and Glasford 2008) and that people who are more xenophobic and patriotic are also less disposed to give to international charities (Straume and Odeen 2010). Political psychologists argue that nationalist ethnocentrism helps explain opposition to foreign aid and support for policies that potentially set back the interests of foreigners, such as immigration restrictions, trade protections, and war.

Ethnocentrism is a deep and enduring feature of our psychologies. It is remarkably easy to induce people to form group attachments and to discriminate against out-groups. In an influential series of experiments, the psychologist Henri Tajfel showed that putting people into arbitrary groups generates ethnocentric responses (Tajfel et al. 1971). For example, one experiment placed people into different groups based on whether they preferred the paintings of Klee to those of Kandinsky. Another experiment put subjects into different groups on the basis of a coin toss. The experimenters asked the subjects to allocate rewards anonymously between the other subjects. The subjects favored members of their own groups at the expense of out-groups. In Tajfel's original experiment, over 70 percent of participants allocated rewards in a way that benefited their own group. Klee-lovers vigorously discriminated against admirers of Kandinsky. This evidence indicates that we are disposed to favor our own groups even if these groups are entirely arbitrary.

So, we favor in-groups over out-groups. This is true of racial groups, ethnic groups, national groups, and other groups as well. We sometimes favor in-groups even when this is individually costly. In addition, discrimination against out-groups is often rapid and unconscious. For example, implicit and unconscious biases help explain racial and ethnic discrimination in employment and in criminal justice procedures (Bertrand et al. 2005). People don't always display ethnocentric preferences. But most of the time they do (Bowles and Gintis 2011, pp. 34–35). Psychologists Mina Cikara and Jay Van Bavel note: "the propensity to prefer one's in-group has been observed in every culture on earth" (Citkara and Van Bavel 2014, p. 245).

Where does ethnocentrism come from? While social forces shape ethnocentrism, ethnocentrism appears to be ingrained in our natures. Here is one piece of evidence: young children exhibit ethnocentric tendencies. Children divide the world into social groups and believe that each group has an underlying essence that determines how the members of this group behave. Donald Kinder and Cindy Kam conclude: "Children come to these beliefs on their own. They do not need to be taught that race and sex and ethnicity are natural kinds; they know these things themselves. Children are ready, one might say, for ethnocentrism" (Kinder and Kam 2009, p. 33).

Ethnocentrism has an evolutionary origin. We are a tribal species. Our ancestral environment facilitated the evolution of ethnocentric tendencies although researchers disagree about how this happened. But many think that a predilection toward ethnocentrism may have evolved as a response to out-group threats. Here is one specific version of this theory: we may have evolved ethnocentric and xenophobic tendencies in response to the threat of infection. There is evidence that out-group antipathy is partly an evolved mechanism for disease avoidance (Faulkner et al. 2004). In ancestral environments, out-groups were sources of infectious disease. Hostility toward out-groups functioned to prevent contact with these groups and thereby stopped the spread of infection. As a result, humans evolved psychologies that are acutely sensitive to the threat that outsiders pose. This may also be why people associate out-groups with pests. Xenophobes throughout history have compared foreigners to non-human vectors of disease, such as cockroaches, maggots, rats, and lice.

Ethnocentrism is not the only disposition that leads us to harm outsiders and fail to adequately aid them. Other psychological dispositions, such as social dominance orientation, play a role as well. Social dominance orientation is a preference for inequality between groups. More precisely, a social dominance orientation refers to the desire that groups be organized in a hierarchy with high-status groups at the top of the hierarchy. People who score high in measures of social dominance orientation often view the relationship between groups as a zero-sum, competitive struggle for resources and status. Social dominance orientations inform our values and beliefs about a wide variety of subjects. Pinker writes:

> A social dominance orientation...inclines people to a sweeping array of opinions and values, including patriotism, racism, fate, karma, caste, national destiny, militarism, toughness on crime, and defensiveness of existing arrangements of authority and inequality. An orientation away from social dominance, in contrast, inclines people to humanism, socialism, feminism, universal rights, political progressivism, and the egalitarian and pacifists themes in the Christian Bible. (Pinker 2011, p. 523)

I would add: an orientation away from social dominance also leads people to cosmopolitanism more generally. One group of psychologists claim that social dominance orientation is "a potent predictor of generalized prejudice against, and persecution of, a wide array of denigrated groups, such as poor people, ethnic minorities, foreigners, gay people, women, immigrants, and refugees" (Ho et al. 2015, p. 1004).

Ethnocentrism, xenophobia, social dominance orientations, and other "groupish" elements of human nature explain why cosmopolitan morality seems infeasible to many observers. We tend to lack strong motivations to help out-group members and to refrain from discriminating against them. These elements of human psychology only partly explain why we violate cosmopolitan moral demands. Other factors matter too, such as institutions. For example, some cosmopolitans argue that the structure of the global order helps explain why states neglect the interests of foreigners.[6] The world is divided into states and states are mostly accountable to their own citizens (if that). Foreigners generally lack a voice in the political decision-making of other states. States thus have few incentives to care about the interests of foreigners. The predictable consequence is that states are prone to neglect the interests of foreigners and violate their rights. Yet, while institutional factors help explain why we violate obligations to outsiders, human psychology is, of course, also part of the explanation. Tribalism is mediated through institutions, but tribalism nonetheless affects the structure and output of institutions. Our tribal psychologies lead us to neglect the interests of outsiders and treat out-groups with indifference, contempt, and hatred.

4   THE CASE FOR COSMOPOLITAN MORAL ENHANCEMENT

It is easy to conclude that cosmopolitanism is a utopian moral standard. If humans are invariably tribal, then it seems unlikely that most of us will conform to cosmopolitan moral requirements. So, we face no choice but to learn to live with our tribal natures. The philosopher Jonathan Glover is sympathetic to cosmopolitan commitments, but says that because "tribalism runs so deeply in us, it may be impossible to eliminate. . . . For now, the only realistic option is to accept our tribal psychology as a fact of life" (Glover 2012, p. 149). Glover is right that we must accept tribal psychology as a fact of life—for now. But it is possible to envisage change. In the future, we might be able to alter people's dispositions through biomedical enhancements. We could conceivably enhance people so that they have more cosmopolitan dispositions. By "cosmopolitan dispositions," I mean psychological or behavior traits that dispose people to benefit the members of out-groups and refrain from harming them, and psychological or behavior dispositions that incline people away from ethnocentrism, xenophobia, and social dominance.

One way that we can promote cosmopolitan dispositions is through cognitive enhancements. Cognitive ability is associated with reduced ethnocentrism. People with higher cognitive abilities are also less prejudiced against out-groups (Hodson and Busseri 2012). Children with higher IQs are less likely to vote for nationalist parties when they are adults (Deary et al. 2008). In one longitudinal study, researchers found that people with low verbal intelligence are more likely to have a social dominance orientation (Heaven et al. 2011). In addition, people who score higher on tests of cognitive ability have more favorable views about foreign trade and immigration (Caplan and Miller 2010). People with lower cognitive ability are less open to change, less willing to cooperate with strangers, and exhibit greater anxiety about out-group threats (Hodson and Busseri 2012; Dhont and Hodson 2014).

Cognitive ability may be associated with more cosmopolitan attitudes because cognitive ability helps people take up the perspectives of other people. If you take the perspective of other people, you are less likely to be prejudiced against them and more likely to believe that their interests matter (Hodson et al. 2009). But perspective-taking is cognitively demanding. Perspective-taking requires the ability to abstract from your own circumstances and comprehend and interpret novel information. Cognitive ability enhances the capacity to see things from the perspective of out-groups and thereby reduces ethnocentrism and increases generosity toward these groups. This mechanism suggests that cognitive ability causally facilitates cosmopolitan beliefs and dispositions. Stephen Pinker powerfully argues that the Flynn effect (the observed rise in IQ over time) has driven moral progress, including better treatment of foreigners, by encouraging perspective-taking and greater consistency in our moral beliefs (Pinker 2011, pp. 650–670). If Pinker is right, then increased cognitive ability facilitates cosmopolitan orientations.

Biomedical techniques can increase cognitive ability. Certain drugs, such as Ritalin, Aderall, and Provigil, may enhance working memory, concentration, and executive function. Transcranial electrical stimulation and transcranial magnetic stimulations might improve cognitive ability and control. One suggestive study found that transcranial electrical stimulation reduced the implicit biases of subjects (Sellaro et al. 2015). Researchers hypothesized that transcranial stimulation improved cognitive control, which allowed subjects to override their negative biases against out-groups. We will likely discover new ways of increasing our cognitive abilities in the future as well.

Fear and anxiety helps motivate hostility toward out-groups, such as immigrants. Certain drugs could help people overcome these anxieties. There is some evidence that the blood pressure medication propranolol reduces implicit racial biases (Terbeck et al. 2012). One possible explanation for this effect is that propranolol dampens unconscious anxieties or fears about out-groups. In one study, consumption of hallucinogen psilocybin was associated with long-term increases in "openness," which is a personality construct that includes measures of tolerance toward different viewpoints and lifestyles (Maclean et al. 2011). Openness is positively associated with favorable attitudes toward immigrants and other out-groups (Dinesen et al. 2016). Oxytocin has intriguing effects on behavior toward out-groups. Oxytocin appears to increase in-group loyalty (De Dreu et al. 2011). But oxytocin may sometimes increase empathy for out-groups (Shamay-Tsorry et al. 2013) and the willingness to cooperate with them in non-competitive contexts (Israel et al. 2012).

Another cosmopolitan moral enhancement is sex selection. Men have been the main participants in violent conflicts throughout history and selective pressures may have pushed men to be more tribal and violent toward outsiders. Consequently, men are more likely than women to discriminate and commit aggression against out-groups if they perceive them as threats (Van Vugt 2009). Some social psychologists argue that men tend to score higher on measures of social dominance orientation.[7] We can observe these tendencies in the composition of nationalist political parties: the majority of the voters for right-wing nationalist parties are men (Givens 2004). So, it may be that women are, in general, more cosmopolitan than men.

Parents sometimes have the capacity to select for girls through fertility treatments and pre-implantation genetic diagnosis. If women are generally more cosmopolitan than men, then sex selection in favor of girls is a kind of cosmopolitan moral enhancement. As I will argue below, we have moral reasons to use cosmopolitan moral enhancements. Of course, these reasons may be outweighed. Perhaps sex selection is objectionably discriminatory. Alternatively, skewing a society's sex ratio in favor of women might bring about bad outcomes by encouraging polygamy and male dominance (Casal 2013) although it is worth noting that some societies already have more men than women because parents select for males in these societies—female selection might help equalize sex ratios in these circumstances. On my view, we have reasons in favor of selecting for girls on grounds of moral enhancement, but I will refrain from giving an all-things-considered judgment on the desirability of female selection here.

It may be possible to use genetic engineering to reduce ethnocentrism and increases empathy for out-groups. Genetics helps explain variation in ethnocentrism. Twin studies suggest that genetic differences may account for 18 percent of the variation in ethnocentrism (Orey and Park 2012).[8] Twin studies also find that social dominance orientation is partially heritable, which indicates that genetics play a role in this disposition (Orey and Park 2012). As ethnocentrism and social dominance have genetic determinants, we might be able to lower these dispositions through gene therapy or via the genetic screening and pre-implantation of embryos. It is presently beyond our ability to engage in genetic engineering with this kind of precision. But it may one day become possible to genetically modify ourselves or our children to be less disposed toward ethnocentrism and social dominance.

The above evidence suggests that we can modify our dispositions in cosmopolitan ways. Safe and cost-effective cosmopolitan moral enhancements are likely infeasible at the present. But they may one day become feasible. Let's assume that cosmopolitan moral enhancements will one day become viable, and that some of them will be safe and effective. I will now argue that, if these kinds of enhancements become feasible, then we should use them. Here is my argument. We have good reason to take steps to ensure that our conduct is permissible. By hypothesis, cosmopolitanism is true and cosmopolitan moral enhancements would make it more likely that we comply with cosmopolitan requirements when everything else is equal. So, we have good reason to use cognitive moral enhancements. To be clear, these are pro tanto reasons. There are significant reasons that speak in favor of using cognitive moral enhancements, but I acknowledge that other considerations can outweigh these reasons.

The first step in my argument is the claim that we should take steps to ensure that we act permissibly. Consider the following case:

> *Alcohol* John is normally a morally decent person. John is kind and respectful to his family and friends. But John changes when he consumes a large amount of alcohol. When he drinks, John sometimes becomes violent and abusive, and he neglects his children. Unfortunately, John is prone to alcoholism and he finds it difficult to refrain from drinking. So, John decides to take medication that reduces the pleasure he receives from drinking and his cravings for alcohol.[9] With the help of this medication, John stops drinking.

Here is my claim about this case: John has good reason to take this medication. John acts in impermissible ways when he consumes too much alcohol. He violates his obligations to his friends and family members. John should take precautions to stop himself from acting wrongly in the future. By taking medication, John prevents himself from acting wrongly.

Consider another case to illustrate the same point:

> *Disorder* Ben is a person who suffers from Intermittent Explosive Disorder, a behavioral disorder that is characterized by sudden and unprovoked outbursts of violence and aggression. During these episodes, Ben attacks and harms other people around him, such as his family members. However, if Ben takes the appropriate medication, this will substantially reduce the probability that he will experience any future outbursts.

It seems obvious that Ben should take medication for his disorder. Why? Well, this will likely prevent him from causing unjustified harm to other people. In other words, Ben should take the medication to reduce the chances that he will engage in serious wrongdoing. This again suggests that people should take the appropriate steps to prevent themselves from performing wrongful actions.

The same basic considerations that require John and Ben to take medication in these examples also imply that we should use moral enhancements. Consider the following thought experiment:

> *Self-Enhancement* Sam has racist and xenophobic tendencies. Sam discriminates against the members of other races, engages in political advocacy in favor of nationalist and racist politicians, and even desires to commit violent acts against immigrants and ethnic minorities. Sam is very well-off, but he declines to aid poor people in other countries at all. On some level, Sam realizes that his character and actions are morally defective, but he finds it difficult to change. However, a new medical technology has become available. If Sam uses this technology, he will become less ethnocentric and xenophobic. He will be more willing to aid the members of out-groups and less willing to harm them. Perhaps this intervention would enhance his sense of sympathy for out-groups, dampen unconscious anxieties or fears about these groups, or increase his cognitive abilities, which would allow Sam to more effectively see things from the perspectives of people that are different from him. Suppose also that this intervention is reasonably safe and effective.

It seems to me that Sam should use this technology.

Why though? As in the case of Alcohol and Disorder, Sam should take steps to ensure that he acts permissibly in the future. I am assuming cosmopolitanism in this paper. Let's assume that Sam will be more likely to violate cosmopolitan moral requirements if Sam declines to use the new technology in the above scenario. Sam will be less likely to support or contribute to harming the members of out-groups, and more likely to support or contribute to aiding them. If Sam should comply with cosmopolitan requirements, then he should also ensure that he has the right capacities and motivations to comply with these demands. This new technology will help Sam to acquire the right capacities and motivations. So, Sam should use this technology to enhance himself.

You might worry that, if Sam is unmotivated to change his behavior and actions on his own, then it is unlikely that Sam will voluntarily choose to use cosmopolitan moral enhancements. Maybe. But there are reasons why Sam might decide to enhance himself despite the fact that he is unmotivated to change on his own. First, Sam may want to change his attitudes and behavior on some level, but Sam could suffer from weakness of will. Moral enhancements might make it easier for Sam to reform his attitudes and behavior. Second, this technology could have other benefits that Sam wants. Sam might want cognitive enhancements for other reasons, such as the economic benefits of increased cognitive ability, and these enhancements generate moral improvements as side effects. Regardless, my aim here is only to establish that Sam has strong moral reasons to consume cosmopolitan moral enhancements. And this claim remains plausible even if Sam refuses to use these enhancements.

I have defended the claim that we have moral reasons to improve our own behavior. But things may be different when it comes to enhancing other people. Consider:

> *Other-Enhancement* A new medical technology is available. This technology allows parents to alter the behavioral and psychological dispositions of their children before birth (say, through genetic modifications). Parents can modify their children so that they have better cognitive control, greater empathy, and other qualities are associated with reduced ethnocentrism and social dominance orientation. Suppose that this intervention is reasonably safe and effective.

My view is that parents have strong reasons to use this enhancement. Most parents want their children to be good people. We want our children to act permissibly. To achieve this aim, we socialize and acculturate our children in ways that lead them to act correctly from a moral standpoint. This is moral education. But it is hard to see any fundamental difference between moral education and moral enhancements. If we aim to give our children the capacities that they need to act permissibly or admirably, then we have reason to enhance them in ways that improve their moral capacities.

Let's now turn to public policy. Most people accept that states and other large-scale organizations should encourage moral education and civic virtue. For instance, states promote civic education, which aims to improve the character of citizens. If states have good reason to promote civic education, then perhaps states should promote moral improvement in other ways, such as through cosmopolitan moral enhancements. The main justification for encouraging cosmopolitan moral enhancements through public policy is that the widespread use of these enhancements could have good effects. If people developed more cosmopolitan dispositions, then they would be less likely to harm outsiders and endorse policies that violate their rights. Support for policies that harm the members of out-groups may decline and this means that states are more likely to repeal these policies, at least in countries where governments are responsive to public opinion. Fewer people would be willing to participate in activities that facilitate harm to outsiders. People with cosmopolitan dispositions would be more inclined to satisfy their positive duties to protect the rights and basic interests of out-groups.

To clarify, I reject the view that states should compel people to use moral enhancements, just like I reject the view that states can permissibly force people (or, at least, adults) to attend mandatory civic education classes. But I have no principled objection to incentivizing moral enhancements. Perhaps states could subsidize cosmopolitan moral enhancements for citizens in order to encourage their use. Nonetheless, you might worry that, if states get involved in moral enhancement, then there will be a slippery slope to coercion. Maybe states will eventually force people to use moral enhancements. It is hard to know whether this is a reasonable worry without more evidence and experience with moral enhancements. Suppose though that it is ultimately a bad idea to get governments involved in promoting moral enhancements. If that's the case, then civil society could still have a role to play. Private civic organizations could subsidize cosmopolitan moral enhancements or try to persuade citizens to use them voluntarily.

Here is a summary of my argument for cosmopolitan moral enhancements:

1. We have strong reasons to prevent ourselves from engaging in future wrongdoing, and reasons to encourage other people to act permissibly as well.
2. Cosmopolitanism is true: we have demanding duties to aid and refrain from harming the members of out-groups.
3. Ethnocentrism, xenophobia, a desire for social dominance, and other tribal aspects of our psychologies lead us to violate cosmopolitan duties.
4. Cosmopolitan moral enhancements would make us less likely to violate cosmopolitan duties.
5. If tribal elements of our psychologies cause us to violate moral requirements and we have strong reasons to prevent ourselves from engaging in future wrongdoing, then we have strong reasons to use cosmopolitan moral enhancements if they become available.

6. Thus, we have strong reasons to use cosmopolitan moral enhancements.

As I have noted throughout, cosmopolitan moral enhancements are speculative. But one corollary of my argument is that we should expend effort and resources now in investigating cosmopolitan enhancements. If the means to improve our conduct are currently unavailable, then we should take steps to make them available. States and private organizations should begin to embark on research to discover effective and safe moral enhancements that promote cosmopolitan dispositions. We should try to find new ways to make ourselves less tribal and more cosmopolitan.

5   OBJECTIONS

In this section, I will respond to objections to moral enhancements in general and cosmopolitan moral enhancements in particular. I will refrain from trying to rebut all possible objections to human enhancements—others have also done so in detail elsewhere.[10] So, I will bracket general objections to human enhancement and instead focus on criticisms of moral enhancements.

One prominent objection is that moral enhancements somehow undermine freedom. John Harris articulates this worry. Harris says: "the sorts of traits or dispositions that seem to lead to wickedness or immortality are also the very same ones required not only for virtue but for any sort of moral life at all" (Harris 2011, p. 104). Harris worries that moral enhancement makes "the freedom to do immoral things impossible" and that this degrades our moral freedom (Harris 2011, p. 105). The suggestion here seems to be that moral enhancements would remove temptation and the desire to do morally bad things. But moral freedom is a valuable capacity. The worth of our choices and actions would diminish if we always lacked desires to act in impermissible ways. So, moral enhancement would impair a valuable capacity. Harris's argument seems to go like this:

1. Moral enhancement would undermine our capacity to make choices between morally good or bad options.
2. It is valuable to have the capacity to make choices between good and bad options.
3. So, moral enhancement threatens something valuable—our freedom to make moral choices.

Let's grant premise 2 for the sake of argument. But premise 1 seems false. Consider an example that I gave in Sect. 4. In Alcohol, John is prone to alcoholism and finds it hard to resist his desire to drink, even though this causes him to mistreat his friends and family members. But John's medication weakens his cravings for alcohol. As a result, John can more easily control his desire to drink. It would be absurd to object to John's use of medication on the grounds that it removes his capacity to make a moral choice. John still has the capacity to make moral choices. He must still exert control over his desire to consume alcohol and John must still decide to continue taking the medication. These are moral choices. But notice that John's medication is, in effect, a moral enhancement. It is a biomedical intervention that improves the likelihood that John will act in a morally justified manner.

Here is another way of seeing what's wrong with premise 1 of Harris's argument. Some people find it easier to be good than others. Take altruism. Altruism is heritable. Some people are more disposed to be altruistic than others, and genetics play a role in explaining this variation (Reuter et al. 2011). The same goes for morally bad traits. For instance, twin studies indicate that psychopathy is partially heritable as well (Blonigen et al. 2005). But it would be strange to say that people who are more disposed to behave permissibly are less free or less capable of exercising moral agency. Rather, they just find it easier to make the right choices. Moral enhancements also assist people in making better moral choices. In this way, they help correct for natural inequalities in our ability to act permissibly. Yet moral enhancements don't remove our capacity for moral choice.

One worry about cosmopolitan moral enhancements is that they could have unintended bad effects. For example, cosmopolitan moral enhancements would make people less ethnocentric. But perhaps ethnocentric dispositions are instrumentally valuable. Consider nationalism. Nationalism might facilitate stability, political participation, and support for redistributive welfare programs.[11] If people identify with their nations, they are more willing to cooperate with other citizens, contribute to public goods, and behave in morally desirable ways. If cosmopolitan moral enhancements diminish nationalist sentiments, then enhancements might frustrate these valuable ends.

It is possible that ethnocentrism does have good effects in certain contexts and I have refrained from arguing that we should eradicate ethnocentrism. I have instead argued that we should explore ways of *reducing* the influence that ethnocentrism and the desire for social dominance exert on our psychologies. So, my argument is compatible with the view that in-group favoritism is sometimes valuable. But we should be skeptical that the current distribution and intensity of ethnocentrism is morally optimal. Our ethnocentric dispositions are in part a product of evolution. Evolutionary forces favored in-group loyalty and hostility toward out-groups. But our present circumstances are extremely different from the environments of our evolutionary ancestors. It would be a remarkable if evolution endowed us with psychologies that are morally optimal in light of our present circumstances.

Nicholas Bostrom and Toby Ord write: "if a continuous parameter admits of a wide range of possible values, only a tiny subset of which can be local optima, then it is prima facie implausible that the actual value of that parameter should just happen to be at one of these rare local optima" (Bostrom and Ord 2006, p. 665). To illustrate, consider ethnocentrism again. Ethnocentrism has genetic determinants. Humans could be more or less disposed toward ethnocentrism. Why think that our current distribution of ethnocentric sentiments is the optimal one? As I noted in Sect. 3, out-group antipathy may be an evolved mechanism for disease avoidance. In ancestral environments, out-groups were sources of infectious disease and hostility toward out-groups functioned to prevent infection. Yet it is unlikely that hostility toward foreigners is useful as a mean of disease avoidance in modern societies. Many of our fellow citizens are more likely to infect us with disease than are foreigners. Furthermore, ethnocentrism and xenophobia are often destructive under modern conditions because they lead us to commit injustices toward out-groups. There is little reason to believe that ethnocentric dispositions that were adaptive in ancestral environments are morally justified today.

Bostrom and Ord argue that status quo bias infects our attitudes toward human enhancement. People unreasonably prefer the status quo even though reform would be preferable on reflection. Bostrom and Order propose a heuristic called "the reversal test" to mitigate status quo bias in debate about human enhancement. It goes like this:

> When a proposal to change a certain parameter is thought to have bad overall consequences, consider a change to the same parameter in the opposite direction. If this is also thought to have bad overall consequences, then the onus is on those who reach these conclusions to explain why our position cannot be improved through changes to this parameter. If they are unable to do so, then we have reason to suspect that they suffer from status quo bias. (Bostrom and Ord 2006, pp. 664–665)

The justification for the reversal test is that it is unlikely that we live in the best of all possible worlds. We need a good reason to believe that we live in an optimal situation. So, the burden of proof is on defenders of the status quo to show that unenhanced human nature is morally acceptable.

Let's apply the reversal test to our tribal dispositions. Let's imagine that humans were significantly more ethnocentric and xenophobic than they currently are. Suppose that we distrusted and disliked the members of out-groups even more, and were more indifferent to their interests. Or consider social dominance orientation. Envisage a world in which people had stronger desires for inequality between groups and had more intense preferences for low-status groups to be dominated by high-status groups. It is hard to believe that these changes would be for the best. In these possible worlds, there would likely be more group conflict and more injustice toward out-groups. But, if more tribalism would be worse, then it is difficult to deny that less tribalism would be better.

You may object at this point that we can coherently maintain that (a) it would be better if people had more cosmopolitan dispositions and (b) cosmopolitan moral enhancements are a bad idea. For example, an objector might argue that cosmopolitan moral enhancements are too risky. Nicholas Agar has this concern. Agar writes:

> Moral bioenhancers will fail to morally enhance when they strengthen to too great a degree one or some among the diverse influences on moral judgment. Unbalanced excesses in influences on moral thinking are likely results of attempts at moral enhancement by biomedical means. These resemble insufficiencies in cognitive, emotional and motivational inputs in making us less morally good. Both excesses and insufficiencies throw out the proper balance of psychological and emotional influences that informs sound moral judgment. (Agar 2015, p. 343)

Agar worries that moral enhancements will ultimately be counterproductive. Maybe these enhancements might make us too altruistic, too self-sacrificing, or too impartial. By boosting certain moral motives relative to others, we will become more unbalanced and less sensitive to a range of moral considerations. So, while enhancements might make us more cosmopolitan, they might make us morally worse in other ways.

It is possible that moral enhancements would backfire. Yet this is speculation. We can't know whether cosmopolitan moral enhancements would make us morally worse or better without evidence. That is, we are unable to determine how risky moral enhancements are in the absence of experimentation. Furthermore, we need to appropriately balance the risks of enhancement against the risks of forgoing enhancements. Cosmopolitan moral enhancements might be risky. But so is the status quo. Ethnocentrism and social dominance risk inducing us to commit injustices toward out-groups. Cosmopolitans think that this is a grave risk and we have excellent evidence that it is real. We must weigh this clear risk against the yet-unknown risks of moral enhancements. So, while Agar's concerns might justify caution, they fail to rule out investigating or using cosmopolitan moral enhancements.

Another objection to my position is that, if cosmopolitan moral enhancements potentially have undesirable effects, then we should instead rely on moral education in order to promote cosmopolitan dispositions. Cosmopolitans argue in favor of moral education that trains people to be empathetic and respectful of people of different ethnic or national backgrounds. For instance, Martha Nussbaum has influentially argued that universities and other educational institutions should aim to promote cosmopolitan dispositions (Nussbaum 1996). Skeptics of moral enhancement might contend that, instead of pursuing speculative and risky enhancements, individuals and large-scale organizations, such as universities, should focus on instilling cosmopolitan values and ideals in people through education. Critics of moral enhancement often argue that moral education can better achieve the aims that moral enhancements seek to promote. Why isn't cosmopolitan moral education enough?

Like other cosmopolitans, I endorse moral education that seeks to cultivate cosmopolitan dispositions. But it is unclear to me why this should rule out cosmopolitan moral enhancement. We can endorse both cosmopolitan moral education and enhancement. Consider an analogy with other kinds of enhancements. Proponents of enhancements that increase cognitive abilities reject the view that, if cognitive enhancements are effective, then we should stop promoting education. These proponents acknowledge that education and cognitive enhancements are not entirely substitutable and that cognitive enhancements may even raise the value of education by increasing people's ability to learn. The same goes with moral enhancements. If moral education and enhancements facilitate cosmopolitan dispositions, then this is surely a good thing from a cosmopolitan perspective. Moral enhancements may be complementary with education if enhancements increase people's interests in and receptiveness to cosmopolitan values and ideas. As long as enhancement makes people more cosmopolitan than education would on its own, then cosmopolitans should endorse both education and enhancement as means of promoting cosmopolitan dispositions.

6   CONCLUSION

Realists frequently dismiss cosmopolitanism as a utopian ideal. They say that human nature is tribal and that cosmopolitanism is incompatible with our psychologies. These critics conclude that cosmopolitanism should therefore be rejected.

We can challenge this objection to cosmopolitanism at several points. We might reject the view human nature constrains what justice requires. Perhaps we can be morally required to act in certain ways, even though it is unlikely that we will be motivated to do so. Alternatively, some cosmopolitans deny that cosmopolitanism is actually incompatible with human psychology. They think that cosmopolitanism is still realistic, even though humans are tribal and ethnocentric.

My strategy in this paper is different. I find it plausible that human psychology stands in tension with cosmopolitan moral demands. But I have argued that there is still an option left for cosmopolitans: change human nature. I have argued that cosmopolitans have good reason to endorse cosmopolitan moral enhancements that make us less ethnocentric and xenophobic. Cosmopolitans shouldn't take people as they are. Instead, we should enhance human nature so that it is more cosmopolitan.

NOTES

1. For examples of this critique, see: Barber (1996) and McConnell (1996). Versions of this critique can also be found in Miller (1995).
2. For a general defense of moral enhancement, see: Persson and Savulescu (2012).
3. For instance, see: Huemer (2010).
4. See: MacAskill (2015).
5. For evidence for these claims, see the overview from: Kinder and Kam (2009, chap. 1 and 2).
6. For his suggestion, see: Cabrera (2010).
7. Although this claim remains controversial. For discussion, see: Sidanius et al. (2006).
8. See also: Kandler et al. (2015).
9. This example is not science fiction. Some existing medications, such as Naltrexone, have these effects.
10. For instance, see: Buchanan (2013).
11. For a defense of these claims, see: Miller (1995).

REFERENCES

Agar, Nicholas. 2015. Moral bioenhancement is dangerous. *Journal of Medical Ethics* 41: 343–345.

Arneson, Richard. 2016. Extreme cosmopolitanism defended. *Critical Review of Social and Political Philosophy* 19 (5): 555–573.

Barber, Benjamin. 1996. Constitutional faith. In *For love of country: Debating the limits of patriotism*, ed. Joshua Cohen, 30–36. Boston: Beacon Press.

Bertrand, Marianne, Dolly Chugh, and Sendhil Mullainathan. 2005. Implicit discrimination. *American Economic Review* 95 (2): 94–98.

Blonigen, Daniel, Brian Hicks, Robert Krueger, et al. 2005. Psychopathic personality traits. *Psychological Medicine* 5: 637–648.

Bostrom, Nicholas, and Toby Ord. 2006. The reversal test: Eliminating status quo bias in applied ethics. *Ethics* 116: 656–679.

Bowles, Samuel, and Herbert Gintis. 2011. *A cooperative species*. Princeton: Princeton University Press.

Bryan, Caplan, and Steven Miller. 2010. Intelligence makes people think like economists: Evidence from the general social survey. *Intelligence* 38: 636–647.

Buchanan, Allen. 2013. *Beyond humanity? The ethics of biomedical enhancement.* New York: Oxford University Press.

Cabrera, Luis. 2010. *The practice of global citizenship*. New York: Cambridge University Press.

Casal, Paula. 2013. Sexual dimorphism and human enhancement. *Journal of Medical Ethics* 39 (12): 722–728.

Citkara, Mina, and Jay Van Bavel. 2014. The neuroscience of intergroup relations. *Perspectives on Psychological Science* 9 (3): 245–274.

Clemens, Michael. 2011. The economics of emigration. *Journal of Economic Perspectives* 25 (3): 83–106.

De Dreu, Carsten, Lindred Leura Greer, Gerben A. Van Kleef, et al. 2011. Oxytocin promotes human ethnocentrism. *PNAS* 108 (4): 1262–1266.

Deary, Ian, G. David Batty, and Catherine Gale. 2008. Childhood intelligence predicts voter turnout, voting preferences, and political involvement in adulthood. *Intelligence* 36: 548–555.

Dhont, Kristof, and Gordon Hodson. 2014. Does lower cognitive ability predict greater prejudice? *Current Directions in Psychological Science* 23 (6): 454–549.

Dinesen, Peter, Robert Klemensen, and Asbjørn Sonne Nørgaard. 2016. Attitudes toward immigration: The role of personal predispositions. *Political Psychology* 37 (1): 55–72.

Faulkner, Jason, Mark Schaller, Justin Park, and Lesley Duncan. 2004. Evolved disease avoidance and contemporary xenophobic attitudes. *Group Processes and Intergroup Relations* 7 (4): 333–353.

Givens, Terrance. 2004. The radical right gender gap. *Comparative Political Studies* 37 (1): 30–54.

Global Impact. 2013. *Assessment of U.S. giving to international causes.* http://chari ty.org/sites/default/files/userfiles/pdfs/Assessment%20of%20US%20Giving %20to%20International%20Causes%20FINAL.pdf. Accessed 15 Aug 2015.

Glover, Jonathan. 2012. *Humanity: A moral history of the 20th century.* New Haven: Yale University Press.

Gordon, Hodson, and Michael Busseri. 2012. Bright minds & dark attitudes: Lower cognitive ability predicts greater prejudice through right-wing ideology and low intergroup contact. *Psychological Science* 23 (2): 187–195.

Harris, John. 2011. Moral enhancement and freedom. *Bioethics* 25 (2): 102–111.

Heaven, Patrick, Joseph Ciarrochi, and Peter Leeson. 2011. Cognitive ability, right-wing authoritarianism, and social dominance orientation: A five-year longitudinal study amongst adolescents. *Intelligence* 39: 15–21.

Ho, Arnold, Nour Kteily, Felicia Pratto, et al. 2015. The nature of social dominance orientation: Theorizing and measuring preferences for intergroup inequality using the new SDO₇ scale. *Journal of Personality and Social Psychology* 109 (6): 1003–1028.

Hodson, Gordon, Becky Choma, and Kimberly Costello. 2009. Experiencing alien-nation: Effects of a simulation intervention on attitudes toward homosexuals. *Journal of Experimental Social Psychology* 45: 974–978.

Huemer, Michael. 2010. Is there a right to immigrate? *Social Theory and Practice* 36 (3): 428–461.

Israel, Salomon, Ori Weisel, Richard Ebstein, et al. 2012. Oxytocin, but not vaso-pressin, increases both parochial and universal altruism. *Psychoneuroendocrinology* 37 (8): 1341–1344.

Kandler, Christian, Gary Lewis, Lea Feldhaus, et al. 2015. The genetic and envi-ronmental roots of variance in negativity toward foreign nationals. *Behavior Genetics* 45: 181–199.

Kinder, Donald, and Cindy Kam. 2009. *Us against them: Ethnocentric foundations of american opinion.* Chicago: University of Chicago Press.

MacAskill, William. 2015. *Doing good better: How effective altruism can help you make a difference.* New York: Random House.

Maclean, Katherine, Matthew Johnson, and Roland Griffith. 2011. Mystical expe-riences occasioned by the hallucinogen psilocybin lead to increases in the per-sonality domain of openness. *Journal of Psychopharmacology* 25 (11): 1453–1461.

McConnell, Michael. 1996. Don't neglect the little platoons. In *For love of country: Debating the limits of patriotism,* ed. Joshua Cohen, 78–84. Boston: Beacon Press.

Miller, David. 1995. *On nationality.* New York: Oxford University Press.

Nussbaum, Martha. 1996. Patriotism and cosmopolitanism. In *For love of country?* ed. Joshua Cohen, 3–17. Boston: Beacon Press.

Orey, Byron, and Hyung Park. 2012. Nature, nurture, and ethnocentrism in the Minnesota twin study. *Twin Research and Human Genetics* 15 (1): 71–73.

Persson, Ingmar, and Julian Savulescu. 2012. *Unfit for the future the need for moral enhancement.* New York: Oxford University Press.

Pinker, Steven. 2011. *The better angels of our nature.* New York: Penguin Books.

Pogge, Thomas. 2012. Cosmopolitanism. In *A companion to contemporary political philosophy,* ed. Robert Goodin and Philip Pettit, 312–331. Malden: Blackwell Press.

Pratto, Felicia, and Demis Glasford. 2008. Ethnocentrism and the value of a human life. *Journal of Personality and Social Psychology* 95 (6): 1411–1428.

Pritchett, Lant. 2006. *Let their people come.* Baltimore: Brookings Institution Press.

Reuter, Martin, Clemens Frenzel, Nora Walter, et al. 2011. Investigating the genetic basis of altruism. *Social Cognitive & Affective Neuroscience* 6 (5): 662–668.

Rummel, R.J. 1997. *Death by government.* New Brunswick: Transaction Publishers.

Sellaro, Robert, Belle Derks, Michael Nitsche, et al. 2015. Reducing prejudice through brain stimulation. *Brain Stimulation* 8 (5): 891–897.

Shamay-Tsorry, Simone, Ahmad Abu-Akel, Sharon Palgi, et al. 2013. Giving peace a chance: Oxytocin increases empathy to pain in the context of the Israeli–Palestinian conflict. *Psychoneuroendocrinology* 38 (12): 3139–3144.

Sidanius, Jim, Stacey Sinclair, and Felicia Fratto. 2006. Social dominance orientation, gender, and increasing educational exposure. *Journal of Applied Social Psychology* 36 (7): 1640–1653.

Singer, Peter. 2010. *The life you can save.* New York: Random House.

Steinhoff, Uwe. 2013. Against Pogge's cosmopolitanism. *Ratio* 26 (3): 329–341.

Straume, Sivert, and Magnus Odéen. 2010. International and domestic altruism. *Journal of Applied Social Psychology* 40 (3): 618–635.

Tajfel, Henri, Michael Billig, Robert Bundy, and Claude Flament. 1971. Social categorization and intergroup behavior. *European Journal of Social Psychology* 1 (2): 149–178.

Terbeck, Syvia, Guy Kahane, Sarah McTavish, et al. 2012. Propranolol reduces implicit negative racial bias. *Psychopharmacology* 222 (3): 419–424.

Van Vugt, Mark. 2009. Sex differences in intergroup competition, aggression, and warfare: The male warrior hypothesis. *Annals of the New York Academy of Sciences* 1167: 124–134.

INDEX

Note: Page numbers followed by "n" refers to notes.

© The Author(s) 2018
J. Flanigan, T.L. Price (eds.), *The Ethics of Ability and Enhancement*,
Jepson Studies in Leadership, DOI 10.1057/978-1-349-95303-5

Printed by Printforce, the Netherlands